Contemporary Issues in High

The latest text in the *Core Concepts in Higher Education* series, this volume speaks to the complex dimensions that higher education scholars and educators need to understand about the shifting role of postsecondary education in the United States. Chapter authors clarify current issues affecting the field, and offer fresh perspectives articulating how policy, demographic, and institutional changes influence the everyday practices of those who work in higher education. This book explores macro perspectives affecting institutional decision-making and processes as well as students' perspectives on campus—from colleges' credentialing procedures to the current demographic changes in students' enrollments, to students' social identities. Guiding questions at the end of each chapter offer readers an opportunity to frame discussions in which they can engage and invite readers to consider avenues for future research and exploration. This is a valuable resource for graduate students, administrators, and researchers who seek to understand and improve the policies and contexts of higher education today.

Marybeth Gasman is the Judy and Howard Berkowitz Professor of Education and the Director of the Penn Center for Minority Serving Institutions at the University of Pennsylvania, USA.

Andrés Castro Samayoa is Assistant Professor of Educational Leadership and Higher Education at the Lynch School of Education at Boston College, USA.

The History of U.S. Higher Education: Methods for Understanding the Past
Edited by Marybeth Gasman

Understanding Community Colleges
Edited by John S. Levin and Susan T. Kater

Public Policy and Higher Education: Reframing Strategies for Preparation, Access, and College Success
By Edward P. St. John, Nathan Daun-Barnett, and Karen M. Moronski-Chapman

Organizational Theory in Higher Education
By Kathleen Manning

Diversity and Inclusion: Supporting Racially and Ethnically Underrepresented Students in Higher Education
By Rachelle Winkle-Wagner and Angela M. Locks

Fundraising and Institutional Advancement: Theory, Practice, and New Paradigms
By Noah D. Drezner and Frances Huehls

Student Development Theory in Higher Education: A Social Psychological Approach
By Terrell L. Strayhorn

Law and Social Justice in Higher Education
By Crystal Renee Chambers

Qualitative Inquiry in Higher Education Organization and Policy Research
By Penny Pasque and Vicente Lechuga

American Higher Education: Issues and Institutions
By John R. Thelin

Contemporary Issues in Higher Education
Edited by Marybeth Gasman and Andrés Castro Samayoa

For more information about this series, please visit:
www.routledge.com/Core-Concepts-in-Higher-Education/book-series/CCHE

Contemporary Issues in Higher Education

Edited by

Marybeth Gasman and Andrés Castro Samayoa

Routledge
Taylor & Francis Group

NEW YORK AND LONDON

First published 2019
by Routledge
52 Vanderbilt Avenue, New York, NY 10017

and by Routledge
2 Park Square, Milton Park, Abingdon, Oxon, OX14 4RN

Routledge is an imprint of the Taylor & Francis Group, an informa business

© 2019 Taylor & Francis

The right of Marybeth Gasman and Andrés Castro Samayoa to be identified as the authors
of the editorial material, and of the authors for their individual chapters, has been asserted
in accordance with sections 77 and 78 of the Copyright, Designs and Patents Act 1988.

Library of Congress Cataloging-in-Publication Data
Names: Gasman, Marybeth, editor. | Samayoa, Andrés Castro, editor.
Title: Contemporary issues in higher education /
edited by Marybeth Gasman and Andrés Castro Samayoa.
Description: First edition. | New York : Routledge, 2019. |
Series: Core concepts in higher education | Includes bibliographical references.
Identifiers: LCCN 2018036540 | ISBN 9781138344600 (Hardback) |
ISBN 9781138344617 (Paperback) | ISBN 9780429438127 (eBook) |
ISBN 9780429796104 (Web PDF) | ISBN 9780429796098 (ePub) |
ISBN 9780429796081 (Mobi/Kindle)
Subjects: LCSH: Education, Higher–Social aspects–United States. |
People with social disabilities–Education (Higher)–United States.
Classification: LCC LC191.94 .C66 2019 | DDC 378.73 2 23
LC record available at https://lccn.loc.gov/2018036540

ISBN: 978-1-138-34460-0 (hbk)
ISBN: 978-1-138-34461-7 (pbk)
ISBN: 978-0-429-43812-7 (ebk)

Typeset in Minion
by Out of House Publishing

CONTENTS

SERIES EDITOR'S INTRODUCTION

It is with great pleasure that I serve as a coeditor of the *Core Concepts in Higher Education* series, published by Routledge, with Marybeth Gasman and Ed St. John, two scholars deeply committed to social justice. The series is particularly important at this point in history given its commitment to produce critical scholarship in higher education that captures our most important challenges, from the past to the future of American higher education.

Contemporary Issues in Higher Education, edited by Marybeth Gasman and Andrés Castro Samayoa, is a rare gift of a book in the scholarly world in that it both reminds us of barriers and walls not yet crossed as well as providing a powerful foreshadowing of issues we will need to contend with as a society built on the promise of education as the ultimate engine for social mobility. A key goal of the book is to center the experiences of student populations who have heretofore not received primary attention in scholarship from our field by amplifying the voices of those who stand to benefit the most from our collective efforts to improve colleges and universities. Of major importance is the promise to illuminate invisible voices and the intersectionality they bring to research and public policy debates. With advances in data amidst the greatest demographic transformation in the nation entering the K-20 school systems of the nation, understanding what "contemporary" means to families, stakeholders, educators, and future generations is a critical contribution that requires careful and honest documentation. The editors achieve this goal.

Gasman and Samayoa are a multigenerational team of editors and scholars helping to curate new scholarly and policy priorities for the nation at a time when evidence-based research may be considered a secondary concern. They do this through the integrity of representative research and methods which will only make us a stronger community of higher education scholars and practitioners.

I commend them on this unique and powerful contribution.

Stella Flores
Associate Professor of Higher Education
New York University

PREFACE

WHY A "CONTEMPORARY ISSUES" BOOK NOW?

We are living in a fraught political moment in the United States that deeply affects the well-being of the students we are committed to serving. For some years, researchers and practitioners in higher education have now eschewed the misguided image of the average college student as a middle-class U.S. citizen aspiring to enroll in a four-year residential college immediately after their high school experience. On the contrary, the demographics for students across college campuses is changing: students are now older, enroll across two- and four-year programs, and belong to a more racially diverse community of aspiring graduates. These shifts are indicative of the growing opportunity and access to postsecondary education in the United States for individuals across multiple social demographics, from age to socioeconomic status. Yet, as practitioners and researchers in the field, we must also contend with the persistent inequities that plague students' opportunities to thrive during their postsecondary trajectories. Students must now navigate collegiate environments with waning public investments in support of their scholarly pursuits. Similarly, those who aspire to receive their postsecondary education must also experience campus environments with a heightened presence of bigoted acts against specific groups of students and dangerous policing of speech on campus and beyond.

The various chapters in this collection are situated at the crossroads of these multiple issues and speak to the complex dimensions that we need to understand in the shifting role of higher education in the United States. We offer this collection of essays as points of departure to clarify current issues affecting our field, and offer fresh perspectives by current scholars who articulate how policy, demographic, and institutional changes affect the everyday practices of those who work in higher education.

A primary goal in this particular volume is centering the experiences of student populations who have heretofore not received primary attention in scholarship from our field. The various contributors in this collection demonstrate how colleagues in our field can amplify the voices of those who stand to benefit the most from our collective efforts to improve colleges and universities.

HOW IS THIS BOOK STRUCTURED?

In order to address the various domains of interest in this book, we have divided authors' contributions into two sections. First, in Part I, "Emerging Challenges & Opportunities in the Higher Education Policy Landscape," we consider macro perspectives affecting institutional decision-making and processes in higher education, from colleges' credentialing procedures to the current demographic changes in students' enrollments and future demographic projections. Authors in Part I encourage us to think about institutions of higher education as social actors that are simultaneously responsive to shifts in social attitudes, as well as constitutive of them. The chapters in Part I advance our understanding on a wide range of issues—from the critical importance of place-based analyses to understand students' potential educational trajectories to the need for developing our collective commitment to combating sexual violence on campus through responsive institutional policies.

Secondly, in Part II, "Amplifying the Visibility of Specific Student Populations," we focus on authors whose scholarly work begins from students' vantage points, with a particular focus on students who have often been rendered invisible in prior scholarship. Our field has a wealth of texts engaging issues of race, economic disparity, gender inequity, and sexuality. We supplement prior scholarship that uses the salience of specific social identities by highlighting the work of scholars whose work advances our intersectional understanding of multiple populations. Some authors focus on students whose experiences are defined by precarious circumstances—from those who have no homes, to those who are undocumented. We do not suggest, however, that we should move away from the powerful analysis that is offered when we focus on students' identities. Rather, we wish to amplify the visibility of other communities that have not been foregrounded in contemporary literature.

OVERVIEW OF CHAPTERS

We begin the book with a chapter by Maurice Shirley and Stella Flores titled "The Demography of Pathways to Higher Education for Critical Populations," which dives into the changing demographics in the nation and the impact of these changes on higher education. Shirley and Flores provide a brief overview of youth in foster care, the school-to-prison pipeline, and immigrant students—topics that other contributors further expand throughout the collection.

Next, we move to feature work by Nicholas Hillman and William 'Casey' Boland. Their chapter, titled "Geography of College Choice," presents a typology around college choice, demonstrating how various sectors across the country, in fact, offer few options for students' future collegiate opportunities. Hillman and Boland urge us to consider that the availability of public institutions is uneven across the nation, with some communities having several options nearby while others have few, if any. In doing so, they offer a compelling case against the myth of equitable choices available for students across racial and ethnic groups to aspire for upward social mobility through their access to higher education.

Manuel González Canché writes about 'big data' in his chapter titled "Challenges and Opportunities in the Use of Big and Geocoded Data in Higher Education Research and Policy." Following Hillman and Boland's chapter, González Canché offers a valuable contribution to researchers aspiring to make use of big data to answer higher education's pressing questions. He explains to the reader that big data has the potential to (re)define college access and offers practical steps to craft sophisticated and meaningful research questions that advance the field.

Sexual violence on college campuses is a salient issue for anyone working within higher education today. In her chapter "Sexual Violence on College Campuses," Susan Marine provides an important overview of the topic, spends time defining rape culture and sexual violence and its causes, and discusses rape prevention and healing processes for survivors on college campuses.

Jason L. Taylor, in his chapter, "The New Credentialing Landscape," helps the reader to understand the complicated world of credentialing that has surfaced in the last decade. As few individuals can acquire jobs that will ensure they earn a living wage without a credential, policymakers and foundations have been pushing to increase the number of individuals that earn them. This push has created a rather complicated landscape that most higher education scholars are unfamiliar with, yet it is crucial to understanding degree attainment across the spectrum. Taylor's chapter focuses on the primary stakeholders in the credential space and its implications for higher education.

In "Vigorous Civility: Aspirations for Free Expression on Campus," Frederick M. Lawrence helps the reader understand the challenge of free expression on college campuses in what many would call one of the most tumultuous times. These challenges are coming from both the left and right and involve students, faculty, administrators, and invited speakers. In the midst's of our society's hyper-polarization, Lawrence argues for a clarification of our democracy's core values and a better, more inclusive, understanding of free expression college campuses.

The collective "Children of the House of 'Pay It No Mind'" (established by scholars Z. Nicolazzo, Dafina-Lazarus Stewart, and Romeo Edward Jackson) contribute a chapter titled "Refuting Contemporaneity: Trans* Experiences In, Out, and Beyond Higher Education" that not only provides an overview of trans* collegians in higher education, but helps the reader to understand the complexity and intersectionality of trans* issues within the higher education context.

In "Understanding Islamophobia on College Campuses," Shafiqa Ahmadi, Darnell Cole, and Monica Prado provide the reader with a comprehensive overview of Islamophobia, especially within the college context. More specifically, they concentrate on Muslim students' experiences; stereotypes and exclusion; and internalized oppression and student identity development. Given what is happening across the nation in the age of Trump, the authors also discuss the recent Muslim bans and the way faculty and campus administration can support Muslim students.

An often-overlooked aspect of today's college campuses is the homeless population that pursues higher education. Jarrett Gupton and Jennifer Trost, in their chapter, "Students Experiencing Homelessness on College Campuses," define homelessness on college campuses for the reader, delving into the causes of homelessness as well as the barriers that exist on campuses for homeless students. Of most importance, the chapter explores what higher education institutions can do to support homeless students and ensure their success.

In their chapter, "Currently and Formerly Incarcerated Students," Debbie Mukamal and Rebecca Silbert discuss California's work with formerly incarcerated students as a case study from which other states can learn. Realizing that mass incarceration has done immense damage to the state's families, local communities, and economy, the state has reached across the spectrum, including to its higher education system, to address the fallout from mass incarceration. The authors discuss how California is folding these students into its higher education system and the advantages to this approach for other states interested in repairing the damage caused by our prison systems.

Susana M. Muñoz and Yuri Hernández Osorio, in their chapter, "UndocuTrends in Higher Education," tackle an important and timely issue, providing an overview of the undocumented population in higher education. Moreover, they provide a deep discussion of issues of social activism, self-identity, and disclosure of immigration status among undocumented students. Given the Trump administration's views on immigration, the status of undocumented students is under constant threat. Muñoz and Hernández Osorio provide the reader with an in-depth discussion of deportations, sanctuary campuses, and increased anti-immigration movements that have an impact on college campuses.

Lastly, Cynthia Hess, Lindsey Reichlin Cruse, Barbara Gault, and Mary Ann DeMario from the Institute for Women's Policy Research examine how colleges and universities can better design interventions to support single mothers in college. In their chapter, "Understanding Single Mothers in College: Strategies for Greater Support," the authors use data from the National Postsecondary Student Aid Study to explore how single mothers have distinct outcomes in their financial borrowing, time usage, and support from colleges through different initiatives at federal and local levels.

We hope that the issues raised in this book will spark conversation and change within and among readers as it is vital that both current scholars and budding scholars are aware of the complexities involved in our nation's higher education institutions.

HOW TO USE THIS BOOK

We have envisioned graduate students, early career professionals, and scholars in the field of higher education as our audience for this text. At the end of each part, you will find suggested discussion questions for this book crafted by the editors and authors of each chapter. We invite you to use these as guiding questions for courses or for book clubs within your institution's specific functional unit. These guiding questions offer readers an opportunity to frame discussions in which they can engage following their reading, as well as inviting readers to consider avenues for future research and engagement. Our hope is that, through these chapters, readers can both expand the horizons of their knowledge while cultivating connections with peers within their institution and beyond. Indeed, we invite you to engage and connect with other readers of this text across other contexts by using the hashtag #AmplifyingHEissues on social media to find individuals who are also making use of this collection.

In curating a collection with scholars from a variety of disciplinary dispositions, we found it important to maintain the specific nomenclature and terminology used by authors rather than standardizing these across chapters. Readers will note that some authors use different ways to discuss racial and ethnic categories, genders, and other social identities. We encourage readers to note the various nomenclatures adopted by authors as meaningful representations of the plurality of perspectives in our field and to trace these usages to examine how different conventions afford new ways of understanding the various social identities we interrogate in our field.

PART I

EMERGING CHALLENGES AND OPPORTUNITIES IN THE HIGHER EDUCATION POLICY LANDSCAPE

1

THE DEMOGRAPHY OF PATHWAYS TO HIGHER EDUCATION FOR CRITICAL POPULATIONS

MAURICE SHIRLEY AND STELLA M. FLORES

The United States has experienced a significant shift in population demographics over the past decade. Not only has the total U.S. population increased by 16 million individuals since 2010 but the percentages of underrepresented racial groups and immigrants have also increased (U.S. Census Bureau, 2017). Standing on the precipice of change and evolution of America's population, the terms "minority" and "majority" will be redefined and look drastically different than what they have been for the past two centuries. This has been seen with the introduction of new, complex terms such as "minority–majority" and "majority–minority," which both attempt to describe the new makeup of the U.S. population. These new terms will extend far beyond the concept of race and into other identities such as immigrant status, religious affiliation, and age. With such tremendous growth of these identities, in terms of total numbers, it is predicted that no one identity will be the "majority" by 2040. The beginning of this phenomenon was first observed in 2011 when for the first time in U.S. history the number of births for racial minority groups outnumbered the number of births for the White population in a given year (Frey, 2014). What is more compelling and must be monitored is the increase in K-12 enrollment, the beginning of the K-20 education pipeline. The National Center for Education Statistics (NCES) projects major increases in enrollment for the K-12 sector for several states. Locations such as Washington, DC (42 percent increase), North Dakota (28 percent increase), Utah (18 percent increase), Texas (14 percent increase), Florida (13 percent increase), and Arizona (13 percent increase) are among those that are projected to experience the most growth by the year 2026.

Demographic shifts in the overall U.S. population are expected to be simulated in the postsecondary education sector over the next several years. Colleges and universities have experienced an increase in the proportions of underrepresented racial populations, immigrant students, English language learners, non-traditional students, international students, and low-income students, which can be attributed to growth in the U.S. population, labor market requirements, and key policy interventions that have increased access to higher education for these students. While colleges and universities have welcomed a larger percentage of underserved student populations, current policy efforts and postsecondary practices are likely not enough to truly support and serve the changing demographics of higher education.

This chapter explores key shifts in student demographics of colleges and universities, issues facing the increasing number of underrepresented student populations, and unknown factors that warrant greater attention for postsecondary leaders and stakeholders. Even further, we highlight several trends in student populations we believe are important not only in terms of demographic shifts facing higher education in the United States but policy relevance at the institutional, state, and federal levels. These trends include the shift in Black[1] student enrollment by numbers and institutional type, the growing importance of the Latino population as the new majority in many school districts, the increase of immigrant student populations entering postsecondary education, the growing plight of low-income students in the increasingly expensive endeavor known as college, the complex school-to-prison pipeline, and the growing presence of other key groups (i.e., international students, foster youth, etc.) that are becoming more noticeable within higher education.

UNDERSTANDING RACE

Black Migration to Community Colleges

One aspect of comprehensively assessing the demographic shifts of Black students in higher education is understanding where Black people live in the United States. Of the 310 million people residing in the United States in 2010, 12 to 13 percent identified as Black or African American. Of these 40 million Black citizens, 11 million were under the age of 18 and over half lived in the states of Georgia, New York, Florida, Texas, California, North Carolina, Illinois, and Maryland (U.S. Census, 2011). This is critical due to the importance of building strong pipelines from the K-12 education sector to the postsecondary sector. These eight states that house the majority of Black citizens, and potentially the majority of future Black college students, should serve as points of investment to further ensure Black students successfully complete high school, gain admittance to quality postsecondary institutions, and graduate within a reasonable timeframe after enrolling. When we speak of investing in these states, we must consider multi-tier approaches which include policies which promote Black student success at every grade level of education, quality schooling that will reduce the need for remediation in college, financial investment, extracurricular opportunities, and many more levers that promote healthy living in safe environments.

While understanding where the United States' Black population is concentrated and how to begin investing in the educational pipeline for years to come is necessary, we must also focus on how current college student enrollments have changed over the past several decades. As of 2015, Black students constituted 13.5 percent, or 2.3 million, of total undergraduate enrollment, a 65 percent increase from 2000 (McFarland et al., 2017). For the past few decades, postsecondary education has not only observed an increase in the number of Black students but also changes in where these students enroll. Historically, Black Colleges and Universities (HBCUs) used to enroll roughly 17 to 25 percent of the Black college student population in 1980 as compared to 7 to 10 percent in 2015 (Anderson, 2017). HBCUs are now enrolling a larger number of White and Hispanic students. HBCUs, which were once all Black institutions, are now estimated to be 75 percent Black and 25 percent other racial categories. Some HBCUs in Texas and Alabama no longer have student bodies that are predominantly Black and report that the majority of their students are Latino. Now, institutions such as community colleges are serving a greater number of Black students. Community colleges across the United States have noted a consistent increase in Black student enrollment since 1994. Studies on college completion for Black students have noted students who start college at two-year institutions are less likely to attain a bachelor's degree (Doyle, 2009; Long & Kurlaender, 2009). If community colleges are slated to serve the majority of Black students, greater investment in these institutions will be needed to support Black students and ensure these students attain a degree at their community college and/or successfully transfer to four-year baccalaureate degree-granting institutions. Colleges will likely need to shift programming and policies that attend to the needs of Black students more directly.

Understanding where Black college students attend college will be critical in how postsecondary institutions serve students in the years to come. Black students are more likely to identify as low-income and often enter college with less academic preparation than their White counterparts. Cokley, Obaseki, Moran-Jackson, Jones, and Vohra-Gupta (2016) note that African American high school graduates are less academically prepared for college than any other racial or ethnic group. This is partially attributed to the lack of access to Advanced Placement (AP) and International Baccalaureate (IB) courses. Black students who have access to AP/IB courses are also less likely to be encouraged to enroll in these courses in order to be academically prepared for college (College Board, 2013). Additionally, courses such as Algebra II that extend beyond introductory and basic math courses are not available in an estimated 25 percent of high schools that serve a significant portion of Black and Latino[2] high school students (Cokley et al., 2016). For these students, postsecondary education will need to bear the weight of providing tangible avenues to ensure they can enroll and persist to graduation. Tangible avenues include summer bridge programs, learning communities, and accelerated courses (Melguizo, Kienzl, & Kosiewicz, 2013). Additionally, community colleges will need a significant amount of support and resources to provide a robust curriculum, maintain suitable retention rates, and provide financial aid to further reduce costs associated with attending college if Black students continue to enroll at community colleges at the same rate as observed in past years. For other institutional types, an equal amount of focus on the success of Black students will be needed as well, especially for predominantly white institutions (PWIs) who recruit and enroll Black students from low-income neighborhoods and/or underserved high schools.

While we are able to evaluate trends of college enrollment and completion of Black students from past years, we are only able to speculate what the future may hold for this population. Action from voters, parents, policymakers, postsecondary leaders, and other key stakeholders could further dictate future outcomes of Black students in postsecondary education, especially on issues such as Affirmative Action or any form of equity program at the institutional level. Of similar importance is how these decisions will play a role in the college completion of Black students as well as their chances for quality employment prospects upon entering the labor market. In sum, the educational demographic outcomes of Black and other underserved students will not be a responsibility of the postsecondary sector alone. Postsecondary institutions and the secondary education sector will need to work in deep collaboration to prepare students for the academic rigor of college by facilitating a smoother transition into the postsecondary education sector and ultimately provide the skills for successful entry and sustainability in the labor market.

Latino Students

The Hispanic population in the United States has experienced rapid growth and now makes up a significant portion of the U.S. population and postsecondary student population. As of 2015, the Hispanic population constituted 17.5 percent (or 56.6 million) of the U.S. population, making them the largest minority group in the United States. Studies from the Pew Research Center highlight that the Latino population has experienced an average of 2.8 percent growth per year since 2007. The majority of this growth has been observed in the Southern and Western regions of the United States with California and Texas experiencing the most growth. Although California and Texas experienced the most growth in Latino populations during these years, states such as New Mexico, Arizona, Nevada, and Florida have populations where more than 20 percent identifies as Latino. While the South and the West experienced the greatest amount of growth of the Latino population, the Midwest and the Northeast still observed a notable increase in the Latino population. If current population trends continue to hold true, the Latino population is projected to increase by 6 percent, from 18 percent in 2015 to an estimated 24 percent in 2065 (Cohn, 2015). These trends are most aptly exhibited by the fact that many of the nation's largest school districts are now a majority Latino.

With total population growth also comes increased numbers of college-eligible students. Between 1993 and 2014, the high school dropout rate for Latino students decreased from 33 percent to 12 percent and the college enrollment rate increased from 22 percent to 35 percent (Krogstad, 2016). This 13-percentage point increase in college enrollment surpassed the increase enrollment rates for Black students (8 percent) and White students (5 percent). Of importance, however, is that demographic growth does not always translate into policy success. That is, in many locations more Latinos in college may mean there are just more Latinos rather than that efforts to increase college enrollment have been effective in their goals. Understanding the difference between growth that would have occurred on its own as a result of birth rates versus an effective college access strategy is a struggle many jurisdictions are still grappling with without proper evaluation methods.

While the number of Latino students entering college has been impressive, Latino students still lag behind White, Asian, and Black students in postsecondary attainment. Students who identify as Latino, on average, reflect a multitude of additional identities that include different countries of origin, as well as but not limited to being low-income, immigrants, English language learners, first generation, and academically underprepared for college. Latinos have the potential to have the greatest impact on educational institutions across the nation. What's more notable is, contrary to current beliefs, future students who identify as Latino are more likely to be native-born Latino and not immigrants. Immigrant background, however, is not generationally far from many student realities. Many Latino students have parents and/or grandparents who are immigrants to the United States.

While we consider Latinos as a cohesive group for the purposes of differentiating these students from other distinctive groups such as White students, Black students, and Asian students, the division and diversity within the Latino population has to also be considered as higher education prepares to better serve Latino students in the next decade, especially in the state context. The Latino student population consists of a multitude of countries, cultures, points of view on education, and a host of other influencers that separate students within this race categorization from one another. In terms of college participation, Latino subgroups experienced an increase in college enrollment at both two-year and four-year institutions for individuals between the ages of 18 and 24 within the span of five years (2008 to 2013). More specifically, the following Latino subgroups have had notable increases: Mexican (from 24 percent to 32 percent), Puerto Rican (from 31 percent to 34 percent), Dominican (from 36 percent to 41 percent), and Salvadoran (from 27 percent to 35 percent) (Musu-Gillette et al., 2016). College enrollment rates for South American and Central Americans have increased from 49 percent to 53 percent and from 25 percent and 32 percent, respectively. Although current data highlights the current trend of access and enrollment for these populations, few datasets can appropriately track these students by student origin to better understand their persistence and degree attainment rates.

If higher education is serving more of these students, the discourse on their participation and attainment will have to be modified to address these subgroups specifically. Simply referring to Latino students will not be sufficient much longer. A more detailed conversation that speaks directly to students' nationalities will become a necessity given different histories of immigration entry and state response to these students. For example, the experience of Dominican-origin students in New York will likely vary from that of the Mexican-origin student in Texas. On the other hand, the influx of Mexican-origin students to the New York City college system may or may not have some similarities with other Latino groups in the area although the integration period for the Mexican-origin students will be shorter and likely different from previous groups in the area.

Previous research has also highlighted the difference in academic performance and needs for students who identify as Mexican as compared to Guatemalan, Colombian, Peruvian, Puerto Rican, and Dominican (Leinbach & Bailey, 2006). While there are achievement and opportunity gaps between Latino and White students, there are also gaps between ethnic groups within the Latino population. Higher education stakeholders will need to conduct research to better understand the differences between these subpopulations and also start thinking about how to create policies and practices that further enhance the college experience for these students.

While these identities alone do not explain why Latino students face lower graduation rates, they do however provide additional explanation for the college attainment gap as each of these identities have unique obstacles that further complicate Latino student persistence and completion. Alternatively, the larger Latino story is not always negative. Recent research indicates that when these statuses are supported by interventions such as quality schooling or parental education, academic achievement is higher than some other groups (Clotfelter, Ladd, & Vigdor, 2009; Flores, Park, Viano, & Coca, 2017). The rate of growth of this population, along with its status of becoming the majority student population in the nation's largest district, make addressing the needs of this diverse population as a policy priority a necessary condition to increasing the educational attainment of the nation as a whole.

Asian Americans and Pacific Islander Students

Asian Americans and Pacific Islander (AAPI) populations have also contributed to the growth of the total number of students in the postsecondary education sector. The 2016 Census highlighted AAPIs as the fastest growing population in the United States, increasing about four times faster than other racial groups. The Asian population in the United States is estimated to more than double, from 6 percent (about 20.3 million) in 2015 to an estimated 14 percent (about 40 to 45 million) in 2065 (Cohn, 2015; U.S. Census Bureau, 2016). This population is also estimated to constitute the largest immigrant population, from 26 percent in 2015 to 38 percent in 2065, surpassing the Latino immigrant population (Cohn, 2015). This growth has also been reflected in the postsecondary education sector. Between 2000 and 2010, AAPI student enrollment increased from 846,000 to 1.1 million (29 percent) and remained relatively constant from 2010 to 2015 (McFarland et al., 2017).

The AAPI narrative differs from all other racial groups as these students are commonly misconceived as not having many barriers in higher education due to their high college participation and attainment rates (Teranishi & Kim, 2017). This often leads to research not focusing on subpopulations of students within the AAPI and/ or the intersection of identities (i.e., identifying as Asian American and low-income). Due to the lack of research and information on the students who identify as AAPI, these students are also forgotten when policies are developed to aid underserved populations in access, persistence, and completion of higher education, and are often excluded from discussions on equity (Teranishi & Kim, 2017). While AAPIs are often considered to be high academic achievers and have high college enrollment rates (Park & Hossler, 2015), students in these populations often face the same obstacles (i.e., financing higher education) as other racial groups, especially those who identify as immigrant and international students. Immigrant and international populations will be further detailed later in this chapter.

In many cases, AAPI students perform better on several academic measures (i.e., test scores, GPA, etc.) and have experienced attainment rates greater than that of Whites, Blacks, and Latinos, but are equally susceptible to adversity based on income, immigration status, quality of high school, ethnicity, etc. Several subgroups within the AAPI student population do not experience the same amount of access and enrollment compared to other subgroups. For example, the Bhutanese (20 percent), Burmese (28 percent), and Cambodian (41 percent) subgroups have lower enrollment rates than that of Chinese (75 percent), Japanese (72 percent), Korean (69 percent), and Asian Indian (68 percent) subgroups (Musu-Gillette et al., 2016; Park & Hossler, 2015). Typically dubbed the "model minority," AAPI students among struggling subgroups are being forgotten in the narrative of how well AAPI students are faring in terms of access and attainment of higher education.

As AAPI student populations are expected to maintain relatively high rates of college participation, institutional leaders and policymakers must begin exploring and researching these populations and their subpopulations in greater depth. Disaggregation of data and student experiences for these populations is one feasible approach to better understanding these students in the years to come. Similar to the Latino population, Asian student populations consist of unique subpopulations that should be further researched and focused on as the Asian student population increases in numbers in higher education. Because AAPI students are dispersed throughout the United States, research must also explore in which areas different subpopulations are concentrated and if those areas play a role in college choice, enrollment, persistence, and attainment. While we have seen advances in data disaggregation at the national level, state-level datasets are not always as robust with the exception of links to language of origin for students in English Learner programs, such as in Texas and a few other states (Flores, Batalova, & Fix, 2012). We know Asian populations are no longer primarily concentrated in immigrant gateway cities such as San Francisco, Los Angeles, New York City, Houston, and Chicago but have slowly migrated since the early 2000s to the interior West, South East, and New England regions of the United States due to high costs of living in gateway cities, job opportunities, and other factors (Frey, 2014). It may be possible that these factors also play a role in the college enrollment and completion story for AAPI students. Lastly, research to understand how language and family influences AAPI student participation in the postsecondary education sector may prove to be highly valuable for institutional leaders and higher education stakeholders when allocating resources, developing academic intervention initiatives, and providing services to enhance the college experience for AAPI students. In sum, improved data quality is an ongoing debate but remains essential to formulating more appropriate public policy and programmatic decisions for serving the students within this population that are most in need.

American Indian and Alaska Native Students

American Indian and Alaska Native (AI/AN) students are another population within higher education which deserves considerable attention when discussing pathways to higher education in the United States, mainly because they are often excluded from relevant conversations and research dedicated to increasing enrollment, persistence, and completion rates of underrepresented racial groups. Overall, these students make up approximately 1 percent of the total U.S. college student population (U.S. Department of Education, National Center for Education Statistics, 2016). Similar to other student populations, there has been a noticeable increase in the number of AI/AN students enrolled in postsecondary education, although not as great of an increase as compared to other student populations. From 2003 to 2013 the percentage of AI/AN students (ages 18 to 24) increased from 18 percent to 32 percent (Musu-Gillette et al., 2016). While these populations have experienced an increase in enrollment, there are unique factors and issues that complicate college persistence and have some influence on college completion rates. The factors include but are not limited to being academically underprepared for college, difficulty financing their college education, social isolation, and cultural differences (Hunt & Harrington, 2010; Keith, Stastny, & Brunt, 2016). These factors contribute to American Indian and Native Alaskan students having lower college completion rates than that of other racial groups (i.e., Whites, Blacks, Latinos, and Asians).

Tribal Colleges/Universities (TCUs), two-year public institutions, and four-year public institutions have traditionally enrolled the largest percentages of AI/AN students who attend college (NCES, 2008). What is most notable is the 23 percent increase in the number of AI/AN students who enroll and attend TCUs between the years 2001 and 2006. The majority of the TCUs in which these students enrolled were located in 12 states across the Midwest and the West (NCES, 2008). These states include Alaska, Arizona, Kansas, Michigan, Minnesota, Nebraska, New Mexico, North Dakota, Oklahoma, South Dakota, Wisconsin, and Wyoming. As enrollment trends continue in these states, policies and resources dedicated to facilitating retention and completion for these populations will become even more important than they are now. Addressing issues of academic preparedness (i.e., academic tutoring and college entrance test prep) will prove to beneficial in students gaining access and persisting through college (Brayboy, Fann, Castagno, & Solyom, 2012; Guillory, 2009; Keith et al., 2016). Also, state and institutional leaders can work to develop programs, both academic and social, and curriculum that better serve AI/AN needs (Wolf, Butler-Barnes, & Zile-Tamsen, 2017). These programs include but are not limited to programs that focus on increasing family involvement with education, college counseling, college outreach, and accelerated learning opportunities (i.e., Advanced Placement and International Baccalaureate course).

The U.S. Census Bureau (2016) estimated that 26.6 percent of American Indians and Alaska Natives were in poverty in 2015, which was the highest rate of poverty of any racial group in the United States; the national average was 14.7 percent. Additionally, the 2016 Census reported the median household income for American Indian and Alaska Natives was $38,530 in 2015 while the national average was $55,775. A postsecondary degree could provide these populations with greater access to higher-paying jobs and careers to earn a livable wage, access to better health care, and many other resources that may not be currently available. Working to increase college persistence and completion for individuals who identify as American Indian or Alaska Native is a necessity and will become even more pressing as enrollment continues to increases with each year that passes. However, we acknowledge that solutions cannot come from policymakers alone and without participation from American Indian or Alaska Native communities. A long history of exclusion and abuse of this community is deeply intertwined in the nation's history of educating indigenous populations (Brayboy et al., 2012). With the lowest participation rate in postsecondary education as well as in education policy circles broadly, strategies to increase American Indian or Alaska Native postsecondary participation will require a multi-sector, multi-jurisdictional, and generational investment beyond what we have provided as a nation to date.

Concluding Thoughts on Race

Although we focus broadly on Black, Latino, Asian, and American Indian populations in this chapter, their subgroups and ethnic origins are as much a part of the achievement story as well. What may be extremely helpful in better serving these students is to approach research and conversations on college success with an understanding of successes among these populations and how factors contributing to said success can be used to aid in the success of other student populations. Although racial groups are highly nuanced, there may be some similarities between groups (i.e., Asian immigrants and Latino immigrants) that we could learn from to enhance educational outcomes for both populations. Even though leaders and stakeholders have been working to advance the development of services and practices to serve underrepresented students in postsecondary education, our current practices and policies will need to be updated and constantly evaluated as the nation continues to move toward a greater demographic change. Improvements in data quality and use is one solution but so is the need to understand that ensuring the availability of equitable opportunity for those with less resources and policy representation is a win for states and the nation as a whole.

IMMIGRANT STUDENTS

In 2015 there was an estimated 61 million immigrants and their children living in the United States, an increase of roughly 18.4 million over a 15-year timespan (Camarota & Zeigler, 2016). For the most part, this increase has been consistent for the past four decades. What is more compelling is that children who have at least one parent who is an immigrant make up 30 percent of all immigrants (Camarota & Zeigler, 2016). These children will play a significant role in higher education with each year that passes. In 1970, immigrants and their children accounted for one in every fifteen U.S. residents but currently account for an estimated one in every five U.S. residents. If the current trend continues, it is estimated that this population will account for one in every three U.S. residents by the year 2040 (Suárez-Orozco, 2001). The growth is mostly reflected in the states of California, Texas, New York, New Jersey, Illinois, Arizona, Massachusetts, Maryland, Pennsylvania, Georgia, North Carolina, Washington, and Virginia. These states represent all regions of the United States that critically impact the economy and society and are also ranked in the top-20 list of largest states by population, which will be highly reflected in the number of representatives in Congress. To be more specific, immigrants in the United States may begin directly influencing the number of representatives each state is allotted in the House of Representatives, which is based on state population counts. If the states mentioned previously continue to grow due to the increase in the immigrant population, these states will experience increased influence over federal policies that affect both the K-12 and postsecondary education sectors. Due to the incentives for students to attend college in their state of residence (i.e., in-state tuition costs, being closer to family, etc.), these states may also begin experiencing an increase in the number of immigrant students on the college campuses which exist within their borders.

Immigrant students can generally be categorized into two distinct groups, legal immigrants and undocumented immigrants, although there are clear variations and associated advantages (or disadvantages) in the process toward legalization and/ or citizenship. While both populations are growing and will command substantial attention as they grow, undocumented students continue to face uncertain futures despite temporary policy interventions as seen in continued debates over the Deferred Action for Childhood Arrivals (DACA) program. Since 2000, the number of undocumented students who have entered postsecondary education each year has consistently increased (Casner-Lotto, 2018). In 2000 there was an estimated 5.9 million college-educated immigrants and by 2014 there was an estimated 10.5 million college-educated immigrants. Some of the individuals represented in these numbers were educated in a country other than the United States but the significant portion of individuals were educated within the U.S. system of higher education (Zong & Batalova, 2016). While policies and practices have been implemented over the years to successfully facilitate college enrollment for undocumented students (i.e., the Immigration Act of 1990), there are numerous factors that further complicate immigrant students' ability to enter the postsecondary education sector and also attain their degree. Such factors include attending under-resourced high schools, failure to complete high school, legal concerns, language barriers, college affordability, and aversion to delaying salary earnings from full-time employment, among many others.

Undocumented students currently comprise less than 5 percent of all eligible college students in the United States. Although they are a small population in size as compared to other demographics, their rate of increase (roughly 50,000 in 2005 and 65,000 in 2015) solidifies the necessity to focus on the success of these students, especially since they have been noted as being some of the brightest and most talented college-eligible students. UCLA's Center for Labor Research and Education published a report in 2007 which highlighted that undocumented students often do very well in school, with the majority of them being honor students, student leaders, and athletes with high academic achievement. Despite their ability to achieve, undocumented students' success is typically halted because they cannot access higher education and/or sustained, if any, legal employment. Given the presence of these high-achieving students, increasing access to higher education for these individuals could have significant benefits on society (i.e., increased civic engagement, decrease in crime, etc.) and the U.S. economy (i.e., highly skilled labor force, increase in GDP, etc.).

Despite these enormous challenges, the study of immigrant students in higher education over the last 20 years has still yielded very clear messages. When students, undocumented and legal, are given the academic and policy opportunities to succeed, they do so at rates higher than many of their native student counterparts (Baum & Flores, 2011; Flores, 2010; Kao, 1999). In the interim, federal policymakers are facing great debates over whether to extend the opportunities of undocumented students and remove privileges from legal students. However, the jurisdictions that are most likely to feel the impact of the benefits and consequences of lost immigrant human capital are the states. While immigration will remain largely a federal issue, the impact of immigrant students in school systems and the economy will likely determine a state's ability to make use of its human capital in far deeper terms than have been described. In sum, with the observable increase in the number of immigrants or children of immigrants within the United States in the K-20 pipeline, but especially in higher education, leaders and stakeholders cannot afford to let these students fall behind in college completion due to issues of access and resources. Doing so would further perpetuate inequality in education attainment, health, and access to quality employment, and will ultimately generate a larger proportion of the U.S. population that is undereducated.

YOUTH IN FOSTER CARE

In addition to understanding how the makeup of the U.S. college student population is changing by race and immigrant status, other identities also play a crucial role and will continue to emphasize the need to provide resources and services that are conscious of these trends. More specifically, foster youth are becoming increasingly noticeable in higher education. This population of students have been present in the postsecondary education sector for decades but policies and practices to promote success in higher education have not been sufficiently keeping up with the notable growth. This is partly attributed to the lack of knowledge on these students as well as their representation in educational debates. Similar to other groups, the identity of foster youth is not typical in many datasets, leading to an underinvestment or under identification of their importance in the story of the underrepresented student in the United States.

Current research notes that children who are in foster care are less likely to graduate from high school and are even more unlikely to enroll in college if they do happen to graduate from high school (Cohn & Kelly, 2015; Courtney et al., 2007; Day, Dworsky, Fogarty, & Damashek, 2011). In 2016 there were roughly 415,000 foster youth in the United States. Of those 415,000 youth, it is estimated that only 46 percent earned a high school diploma and 3 percent earned a bachelor's degree (Hernandez, Day, & Henson, 2017; Sarubbi, Parker, & Sponsler, 2016). Comparatively, foster youth are more likely to drop out of college within their first year than their peers who have not been in foster care (Day et al., 2011). Even more alarming is if a foster youth persists beyond one year of college, they are still at greater risk of not completing college. However, the dismal college attendance and completion rates are not due to a lack of motivation and/or aspiration on the adolescent's part. Studies have found that over 70 percent of young adults ages 15 to 19 aspire to attend college (Day, Riebschleger, Dworsky, Damashek, & Fogarty, 2012). As postsecondary education continues to enroll foster youth, interventions which aim to retain this population and enable persistence to completion will be vital.

Former foster youth experience greater barriers to succeeding in postsecondary education than many other student populations and are considered to be one of the most vulnerable student populations in both K-12 and postsecondary education (Bruce, Naccarato, Hopson, & Morrelli, 2010). This is primarily due to the fact that foster youth also identify as low-income, often have insecure living accommodation, and inconsistent educational backgrounds (Bruce et al., 2010; Stone, 2007). Currently there are 23 states that have implemented tuition waiver programs which aim to increase access and retention in postsecondary education for former foster care youth who aspire to attain a postsecondary credential (Hernandez et al., 2017). While these programs aim to provide assistance to foster youth, they vary in eligibility requirements (i.e., number of years spent in foster care, adoption status, GPA, etc.) which can inadvertently exclude many foster youth who need the aid and resources the most. The call is not to remove these waiver programs. Instead, it is to reconsider eligibility requirements for foster youth (Cohn & Kelly, 2015; Hernandez et al., 2017). Focusing on a K-16 pipeline approach may also prove to be feasible since barriers to education associated with this population tend to be rooted in inconsistency with housing, alternating guardianship, not attending the same school on a consistent basis, and socioeconomic status. Training of caseworkers and foster care guardians on the college-going process and resources available to the foster youth in their care could provide students with more knowledge about college and may further reduce financial burdens on the student while in college. Collaboration between high schools and postsecondary institutions with the intent to motivate and prepare foster youth through mentorship, test prep, and information sessions would bring positive benefits to this population (Cohn & Kelly, 2015). Increasing federal aid for all states to fund tuition waiver and additional resources programs for foster youth could enable more states, in addition to the 23 currently providing tuition waiver programs, to serve more students who are or have been a part of a foster care system in the United States (Hernandez et al., 2017).

The main issue in addressing issues of access, persistence, and completion for foster youth is that the size of this population pales in comparison to the size of other populations, which draws less attention to these students. Often, resources (i.e., funding) are dedicated to serving as many students as possible. As a result, resources tend to be funneled to populations and groups of students that exist in greater numbers. When considering the hundreds of thousands of foster youth spread across the 50 states, there may not be enough students concentrated in one area or district who identify as a foster youth to garner significant attention. Regardless of size, this population deserves ample attention, support, and resources to develop viable pathways to higher education.

SCHOOL-TO-PRISON PIPELINE

While higher education is experiencing significant growth in terms of a growing number of students enrolling in college, an increased number of new postsecondary institutions, and the development of new majors, there's a current trend that is becoming more noticeable and potentially concerning. The school-to-prison pipeline has become more commonplace than many scholars and leaders could have ever imagined. The U.S. prison system grew by more than 1.5 million people in the span of 30 years. Much of this growth has been attributed to policing in schools, zero-tolerance policies, and other initiatives to reduce crime in the K-12 sector that have introduced many students to the justice system in the form of juvenile detention centers and adult correctional facilities (Redfield & Nance, 2016; Simmons-Reed & Cartledge, 2014). In 2015, California (6,726), Texas (4,299), Florida (2,853), Pennsylvania (2,826), Ohio (2,163), Indiana (1,563), Michigan (1,554), Illinois (1,524), and New York (1,386) contained more than half of all juveniles (ages 0 to 17) held in detention centers in the United States (Puzzanchera, Sladky, & Kang, 2017). Overall in 2015 there were roughly 48,000 juveniles in detention centers, a decrease from 2013 (54,148) and 2010 (70,793). While the total number of juveniles in detention centers has been decreasing, these totals do not include the number of youth who were tried as adults and are incarcerated in federal and state penitentiaries. The incarceration of youth and young adults under the age of 18 impacts low-income and underrepresented students at greater rates than other students. On average, Black students are three times more likely to be suspended and expelled from schools than White students (U.S. Department of Education Office for Civil Rights, 2014). Furthermore, studies have shown that Black men are five times more likely to be incarcerated than White men but 2.5 times more likely than Latino males, and Black women are twice as likely to be incarcerated than White women (Morsy & Rothstein, 2016; NAACP, 2017).

The school-to-prison pipeline may potentially have significant ramifications on the postsecondary education sector for one critical reason: the loss of talent in the admissions and enrollment processes. Students who fall within this categorization may have the potential to do well in K-12 and ultimately enroll in college but are often halted due to strict policies on behavior. One key point highlighted by scholars is that this group of students is less likely to graduate from high school and continue on to college due to falling behind in class as a result of suspensions and being sent to juvenile detention centers (Gregory, Skiba, & Noguera, 2010; Noguera, 2003). Once students fall behind in classes and testing benchmarks, it becomes increasingly impossible for them to achieve the level of academic preparedness to enter the postsecondary sector. Because many of these students identify as racially underrepresented, higher education may soon observe a continued disappearance of these student populations, which will exacerbate issues of inequality not only in higher education but in the U.S. society and economy.

Not only are students more likely to be underprepared for college if they have been suspended or spent time within the criminal justice system, but if they decide to go to college their criminal record could have a deleterious effect on access to college, especially postsecondary institutions that are viewed as high-quality, rigorous, and/

or selective. While debate over reviewing criminal background records during the postsecondary admissions process is ongoing, future students with a criminal history may find it difficult to gain access to higher education. If they are accepted to college, many may not be eligible for federal and/or state financial aid, which the majority of college students use to cover the cost of tuition, books, food, living, etc. Without financial aid at the federal and state levels, these students will be less like to complete college due to financial obstacles and hardship.

To facilitate participation in the postsecondary education sector, the government will have to remove barriers that limit college access and do not support college completion. In states such as New York and North Carolina, the age of 15 is the upper age for youth to be tried as juveniles. At the ages of 16 and 17, youth who are charged with criminal offenses are automatically tried as adults. New initiatives implemented by the Governor and state legislature have begun to evaluate and design a plan to reform the justice system to further reduce the number of juvenile incarcerations and to also raise the age level at which a juvenile can be tried as an adult. North Carolina has also tried to raise the age limit but has not had any success. Colleges and universities will also need to make changes to policies and practices to facilitate greater participation and attainment for students who may have criminal histories. Some options are to reduce the amount of influence a criminal background has on the admissions process, reconfigure financial aid practices to make students with a criminal history eligible for financial aid, and provide academic support to assist students who may be underprepared for college as a result of school suspension or incarceration. While it is ideal to decrease the number of students who are suspended and incarcerated during the K-12 experience, colleges and universities will need to make changes previously noted to accommodate students who currently have criminal records. Further thinking about the Kindergarten-to-college pipeline (K-16), the postsecondary education sector could and should begin working with the K-12 sector to reconceptualize how to address school violence in ways that do not permanently impair students' future college and employment prospects.

CONCLUSION: THE CONSEQUENCES OF NOT ATTENDING TO CRITICAL POPULATIONS

The United States has one of the most diverse populations in the world, with every group making important contributions to the growth of the nation. While every group deserves proper educational attention, we have discussed populations that are at the current forefront of policy significance given their historic and future demographic growth (Black, Latino, Asian, and immigrant students) as well as groups who are at the center of our perhaps most forgotten humanitarian mission of educational development (American Indian, foster youth, and students caught in the school-to-prison pipeline). This focus does not mean that others do not need attention. Instead, we hope, it invokes educators and policymakers to understand the consequences of not attending to certain groups as essential to the moral fabric and economic development of the nation.

What are the consequences of not responding to the demographic realities of the most underserved students? The National Center for Education Statistics (NCES) projects a decline in Black student enrollment in postsecondary education over the next decade. If this projection becomes a reality, the United States will be facing a significant and familiar problem of an undereducated Black population, which could pose significant ramifications for the Black community as a whole, U.S. society, and the national economy. In regard to Latino students, Texas is now a state in which the Latino student is the majority student in its K-12 system and other states will soon follow. The discourse on politely including the issues of the Latino student in educational programming and policy is outdated. Including Latino students' issues as a primary issue of concern and reality at every level is now a policy priority for the educational well-being of the nation. Finally, we cannot forget whom we leave behind in the examination of foster youth and students caught in the school-to-prison pipeline. Our educational interventions, while many, are often designed to fit a two-parent, English-speaking, stable home environment student. We do not know enough about the most disadvantaged in our nation's schools with this framework and more attention to our most vulnerable youth, as these demographics show us, is not only necessary but will set the stage for who we are as caretakers of our nation's students.

QUESTIONS FOR DISCUSSION

1. What are the consequences for higher education institutions if they do not prepare for and respond to the changing demographics in the nation?
2. What arguments can be used to convince higher education practitioners to further consider the needs of students beyond those with two parents, who are English-speaking and from stable homes?
3. What kinds of unforeseen and unexpected issues will result from there being no majority identity by 2040?

NOTES

1 The terms African American and Black will be used interchangeably in this chapter.
2 The terms Hispanic and Latino will be used interchangeably in this chapter.

REFERENCES

Anderson, M. (2017). *A look at historically black colleges and universities as Howard turns 150*. Pew Research Center. Retrieved from www.pewresearch.org/fact-tank/2017/02/28/a-look-at-historically-black-colleges-and-universities-as-howard-turns-150/.

Baum, S., & Flores, S. M. (2011). Higher education and children in immigrant families. *The Future of Children*, *21*(1), 171–193.

Brayboy, B., McK. J., Fann, A., Castagno, A. E., & Solyom, J. A. (2012). *Postsecondary education for American Indian and Alaska Natives: Higher education for nation building and self-determination.* San Francisco, CA: Jossey-Bass.

Bruce, E., Naccarato, T., Hopson, L., & Morrelli, K. (2010). Providing a sound educational framework for foster youth: A proposed research agenda. *Journal of Public Child Welfare*, *4*(2), 219–240.

Camarota, S. A., & Zegler, K. (2016). *Immigrants in the United States: A profile of the foreign-born using 2014 and 2015 Census Bureau data.* Center for Immigration Studies. Retrieved from https://cis.org/sites/cis.org/files/immigrant-profile_0.pdf.

Casner-Lotto, J. (2018). *News and resources for colleges serving undocumented students.* Retrieved from www.cccie.org/outreach/resources-for-colleges-serving-undocumented-students/.

Clotfelter, C. T., Ladd, H., & Vigdor, J. (2009). The academic achievement gap in grades 3 to 8. *The Review of Economics and Statistics*, *91*, 398–419.

Cohn, D. (2015, October 5). *Future immigration will change the face of America by 2065.* Pew Research Center. Retrieved from www.pewresearch.org/fact-tank/2015/10/05/future-immigration-will-change-the-face-of-america-by-2065/.

Cohn, S., & Kelly, R. (2015). *Information packet: Foster youth attending college.* National Center for Child Welfare Excellence at the Silberman School of Social Work. Retrieved from www.nccwe.org/downloads/info-packs/CohnandKelly.pdf.

Cokley, K., Obaseki, V., Moran-Jackson, K., Jones, L., & Vohra-Gupta, S. (2016). College access improves for black students but for which ones? *Phi Delta Kappan*, *97*(5), 43–48.

College Board. (2013, February 13). *The 9th annual AP report to the nation.* Retrieved from http://bit.ly/1LQBokT.

Courtney, M. E., Dworsky, A., Cusick, G. R., Havlicek, J., Perez, A., & Keller, T. (2007). *Midwest evaluation of the adult functioning of former foster youth: Outcomes at age 21.* Chicago, IL: Chapin Hall Center for Children at the University of Chicago.

Day, A., Dworsky, A., Fogarty, K., & Damashek, A. (2011). An examination of post-secondary retention and graduation among foster care youth enrolled in a four-year university. *Children and Youth Services Review*, *33*(11), 2335–2341.

Day, A., Riebschleger, J., Dworsky, A., Damashek, A., & Fogarty, K. (2012). Maximizing educational opportunities for youth aging out of foster care by engaging youth voices in a partnership for social change. *Children and Youth Services Review*, *34*(5), 1007–1014.

Doyle, W. R. (2009). The effect of community college enrollment on bachelor's degree completion. *Economics of Education Review*, *28*(2), 199–206.

Flores, S. M. (2010). State "dream acts": The effects of in-state resident tuition policies on the college enrollment of undocumented Latino students in the United States. *The Review of Higher Education*, *33*, 239–283.

Flores, S. M., Batalova, J., & Fix, M. (2012). *The educational trajectories of English language learners in Texas.* Washington, DC: Migration Policy Institute.

Flores, S. M., Park, T. J., Viano, S. L., & Coca, V. M. (2017). State policy and the educational outcomes of English learner and immigrant students: Three administrative data stories. *American Behavioral Scientist*, *61*(14), 1824–1844.

Frey, W. H. (2014). *Diversity explosion: How new racial demographics are remaking America.* New York, NY: Brookings Institution Press.

Gregory, A., Skiba, R. J., & Noguera, P. A. (2010). The achievement gap and the discipline gap: Two sides of the same coin? *Educational Researcher*, *39*, 59–68.

Guillory, R. M. (2009). American Indian/Alaska Native college student retention strategies. *Journal of Developmental Education*, *33*(2), 12–38.

Hernandez, L., Day, A., & Henson, M. (2017). Increasing college access and retention rates of youth in foster care: An analysis of the impact of 22 state tuition waiver programs. *Journal of Policy Practice*, *16*(4), 397–414.

Hunt, B., & Harrington, C. F. (2010). The impending educational crisis for American Indians: Higher education at the crossroads. *Indigenous Policy Journal*, *21*(3).

Kao, G. (1999). Psychological well-being and educational achievement among immigrant youth. In D. J. Hernandez (Ed.), *Children of immigrants: Health, adjustment, and public assistance* (pp. 410–477). Washington, DC: National Academy Press.

Keith, J. F., Stastny, S. N., & Brunt, A. (2016). Barriers and strategies for success for American Indian college students: A review. *Journal of College Student Development, 57*(6), 698–714.

Krogstad, J. (2016). *Key facts about how the U.S. Hispanic population is changing.* Pew Research Center. Retrieved from www.pewresearch.org/fact-tank/2016/09/08/key-facts-about-how-the-u-s-hispanic-population-is-changing/.

Leinbach, D., & Bailey, T. (2006). *Access and achievement of Hispanics and Hispanic immigrants in the colleges of the City University of New York.* New York, NY: Community College Research Center.

Long, B. T., & Kurlaender, M. (2009). Do community colleges provide a viable pathway to a baccalaureate degree? *Educational Evaluation and Policy Analysis, 31*(1), 30–53.

McFarland, J., Hussar, B., de Brey, C., Snyder, T., Wang, X., Wilkinson-Flicker, S., … Hinz, S. (2017). *The Condition of Education 2017* (NCES 2017-144). U.S. Department of Education. Washington, DC: National Center for Education Statistics. Retrieved from https://nces.cd.gov/pubsearch/pubsinfo.asp?pubid=2017144.

Melguizo, T., Kienzl, G., & Kosiewicz, H. (2013). The potential of community colleges to increase bachelor's degree attainment rates. In L. W. Perna & P. Jones (Eds.), *The state of college access and completion* (pp. 115–139). New York, NY: Routledge.

Morsy, L., & Rothstein, R. (2016). *Mass incarceration and children's outcomes: Criminal justice policy is education policy.* Washington, DC: Economic Policy Institute.

Musu-Gillette, L., Robinson, J., McFarland, J., KewalRamani, A., Zhang, A., & Wilkinson-Flicker, S. (2016). *Status and trends in the education of racial and ethnic groups 2016* (NCES 2016-007). Washington, DC: U.S. Department of Education, National Center for Education Statistics. Retrieved from https://nces.ed.gov/pubs2016/2016007.pdf.

NAACP. (2017). *Criminal justice fact sheet.* Retrieved from www.naacp.org/criminal-justice-fact-sheet/.

National Center for Educational Statistics (NCES). (2008). *Status and trends in the education of American Indians and Alaska Natives: 2008.* Retrieved from https://nces.ed.gov/pubs2008/nativetrends/highlights.asp.

Noguera, P. A. (2003). Schools, prisons, and social implications of punishment: Rethinking disciplinary practices. *Theory Into Practice, 42*, 341–350.

Park, E., & Hossler, D. (2015). Understanding student college choice. In D. Hossler & B. Bontrager (Eds.), *Handbook of strategic enrollment management* (pp. 49–76). San Francisco, CA: Jossey-Bass.

Puzzanchera, C., Sladky, A., & Kang, W. (2017). *Easy Access to Juvenile Populations: 1990–2016.* Retrieved from www.ojjdp.gov/ojstatbb/ezapop/.

Redfield, S. E., & Nance, J. P. (2016). *School-to-prison pipeline.* Prepared by the American Bar Association Joint Task Force on reversing the school-to-prison pipeline.

Sarubbi, M., Parker, E., & Sponsler, B. A. (2016). *Strengthening policies for foster youth postsecondary attainment. Special Report.* Washington, DC: Education Commission of the States.

Simmons-Reed, E. A., & Cartledge, G. (2014). School discipline disproportionality: Culturally competent interventions for African American males. *Interdisciplinary Journal of Teaching and Learning, 4*(2), 95–109.

Stone, S. (2007). Child maltreatment, out-of-home placement and academic vulnerability: A fifteen-year review of evidence and future directions. *Children and Youth Services Review, 29*(2), 139–161.

Suárez-Orozco, C. (2001). Afterword: Understanding and serving the children of immigrants. *Harvard Educational Review, 71*(3), 579–590.

Teranishi, R., & Kim, V. (2017). The changing demographic landscape of the nation: Perspectives on college opportunities for Asian Americans and Pacific Islanders. *The Educational Forum, 81*(2), 204–216.

U.S. Census Bureau (2011). *The Black population: 2010.* Retrieved from: www.census.gov/prod/cen2010/briefs/c2010br-06.pdf.

U.S. Census Bureau (2016). *Facts for features: Asian/Pacific American heritage month: May 2016.* Retrieved from www.census.gov/newsroom/facts-for-features/2016/cb16-ff07.html.

U.S. Census Bureau (2017). *Current Population Survey 2017.* Retrieved from www.census.gov/programs-surveys/cps.html.

U.S. Department of Education, National Center for Education Statistics. (2016). *Digest of education statistics, 2015* (NCES 2016-014).

U.S. Department of Education, Office for Civil Rights (2014). *Civil rights data collection. Data snapshot: School discipline.* Washington, DC. Retrieved from https://ocrdata.ed.gov/downloads/crdc-school-discipline-snapshot.pdf.

Wolf, P. S., Butler-Barnes, S. T., & Zile-Tamsen, V. (2017). American Indian/Alaskan Native college dropout: Recommendations for increasing retention and graduation. *Journal on Race, Inequality, and Social Mobility in America*, *1*(1), 1–15.

Zong, J., & Batalova, J. (2016). *College-educated immigrants in the United States.* Migration Policy Institute. Retrieved from www.migrationpolicy.org/article/college-educated-immigrants-united-states.

2

GEOGRAPHY OF COLLEGE CHOICE

NICHOLAS HILLMAN AND WILLIAM CASEY BOLAND

Geography plays a central role in shaping opportunity in the United States. The magnitude of this relationship is strong, where the chances of escaping poverty or gaining upward mobility depend largely on where one lives (Chetty, Hendren, Kline, & Saez, 2014). Communities with the highest levels of social and economic inequality have the lowest mobility rates, resulting in a complex set of social forces creating and reinforcing inequality. There is no single solution to reversing intergenerational inequality, but colleges and universities play an important role to that end. For example, Chetty, Friedman, Saez, Turner, & Yagan (2017) recently found that low-income students attending open-access colleges tend to earn more than their parents, suggesting these institutions are uniquely situated to promote upward mobility. This is consistent with the high levels of intergenerational mobility found in other open-access public college settings (Attewell & Lavin, 2007).

Unfortunately, the distribution of open-access public institutions is uneven across the United States, where some communities have several options nearby while others have few. This distribution matters for promoting upward mobility, but it also requires researchers and policymakers to rethink traditional beliefs about the college choice process. Traditional college choice theories focus almost exclusively on the *process* of college opportunity—gathering information, searching for colleges, and submitting applications—when the focus ought to prioritize the *geography* of college opportunity. If a student needs to stay close to home due to family or work commitments, then what good is it for them to know a college hundreds of miles away is a "better match"? After all, most college students (66 percent) enroll somewhere within just 25 miles of their permanent home address (U.S. Department of Education, 2013).[1]

Because of this, college choice literature and policies that stem from it should focus on the local higher education market in which students make their choices. Or as Turley (2009) says, "stop treating the college choice process as though it were independent of location and start situating this process within the geographic context in which it occurs" (p. 126). By doing this and taking stock of the different markets in which students make choices, we can generate new solutions to longstanding problems facing educational inequality. We can also come to view colleges in a new light, particularly if they are the sole institution serving their local community.

The goal of this chapter is to describe four different types of local higher education markets that can be found across the United States: deserts, refuges, mirages, and oases. We provide examples of each of these markets and discuss how college choice is likely to differ according to where one lives. We also discuss how state and federal policymakers could help build the capacity of public colleges operating in communities with the fewest alternatives available.

THE GEOGRAPHY OF COLLEGE CHOICE

Most students attend open-access colleges and universities close to home that admit more than 90 percent of applicants. Using data from the U.S. Department of Education's Integrated Postsecondary Education Data System (IPEDS), Table 2.1 shows fall undergraduate degree-seeking enrollments by college selectivity. Approximately 57 percent of public sector students enroll in an open-access institution admitting 90 percent of all applicants; nationwide, half of *all* undergraduate degree-seeking students attend these institutions. In the private non-profit sector, colleges tend to be more selective and most students attend an institution admitting less than 75 percent of applicants.

As technology and travel expenses have fallen over time, students have become more mobile in their search for colleges (Hoxby, 1997; Long, 2004). However, the most mobile students tend to be those from more advantaged social backgrounds and from racial/ethnic majority groups (Niu, 2014; Shaw, Kobrin, Packman, & Schmidt, 2009). Most students do not cast wide nets when applying for colleges, as shown in

Table 2.1 Undergraduate enrollment by institutional selectivity

	Percent admitted				Total
	<50%	50% to 75%	75% to 90%	90%+	
Public two-year	7,046	26,804	5,919	5,592,463	5,632,232
Public four-year	1,006,268	2,671,341	1,464,012	1,210,913	6,352,534
Private non-profit	720,636	996,807	432,442	482,898	2,632,783
Total	1,733,950	3,694,952	1,902,373	7,286,274	14,617,549

Table 2.2 Distribution of undergraduate students' distance from home, by sector

	Miles from home			
	0–24	25–49	50–99	100+
Public two-year	83%	9%	4%	4%
Public four-year	57%	11%	12%	20%
Private non-profit	41%	10%	11%	38%
Total	66%	10%	7%	17%

recent analyses of recent high school seniors where the majority (56 percent) applied to only one or two places (Avery, Howell, & Page, 2014; National Center for Education Statistics, 2017). Therefore, the image of a highly mobile student shopping around for several colleges is not representative of the typical college student. Most students attend a college located within commuting distance from home, as displayed in Table 2.2.

Most students attending community colleges and public four-year universities are within 25 miles of home. Alternatively, nearly half (49 percent) of all students attending private non-profit universities travel at least 50 miles from home. This is in part due to the profile of students who enroll in each sector, where private non-profit institutions draw both from a wider applicant pool and select students who are more likely to fit the "traditional" view of a college student living on campus, enrolling full time, and not caring for dependents (Ehrenberg, 2012; Perna, 2010). In the public sector, students are less likely to fit this description and consequently place and the location of college becomes an important part of the college choice process (Turley, 2009). These differences are drawn along lines of race and class, where students most affected by geography and those attending open-access institutions tend to be lower-income and Latino or Black (Kirst, Stevens, & Proctor, 2010).

When communities have colleges nearby, they tend to have higher college participation rates and educational attainment rates. Earlier studies examining the role of community college location on college access established this relationship (Card, 1993; Kling, 2001; Rouse, 1995). Further research extended this work by documenting how proximity to college is particularly important for members of underrepresented communities and that the location of college can impose costs on these communities (Briscoe & De Oliver, 2006; Turley, 2009). The location of colleges varies by state and region, yet researchers consistently find negative relationships between distance to college and enrollment (Do, 2004; Franklin, 2013; Griffith & Rothstein, 2009). Distance also shapes educational opportunities through familial and cultural commitments keeping students close to home, especially for students from rural, Latino/a, or Black families (Ali & Saunders, 2008; McDonough, Antonio, & Trent, 1997; Perez & McDonough, 2008).

College choice is a highly localized decision. Knowing a college hundreds of miles away offers a "better match" would be of little utility for a student who needs to stay close to home for college. Unfortunately, college choice theories say little about this context and, in its absence, we are left to believe that geography matters very little in shaping educational opportunities. If geography does not matter, then all students would be highly mobile and policymakers simply need to provide better information to help students make better matches. Instead of trying to match students to better colleges located far away, we should meet students where they are by first understanding the different types of local markets from which they choose colleges. Understanding these differences can help us reconceptualize college choice in ways that are relevant to today's college students, particularly for students of color and from low-income families whose choices are shaped largely by their local options. Doing so will also help us reimagine policy solutions that span far beyond informational interventions to reverse educational inequality.

LOCAL HIGHER EDUCATION MARKET TYPES

We define a local higher education market by first using the U.S. Department of Agriculture's commuting zone classifications. Like metropolitan and micropolitan statistical areas, commuting zones are clusters of counties that have a high degree of economic integration. This is measured with U.S. Census Bureau journey-to-work records that (unlike metro/micropolitan areas) include every county in the United States. Since students choose a college based on its proximity to home and work, these 709 commuting zones represent the "local" community from which students might search for a college. Using IPEDS, we match every Title IV degree-granting institution that is not primarily online to its respective commuting zone.

Two defining features of a local higher education market are displayed in Figure 2.1. The horizontal axis represents the total number of colleges located in a commuting zone. The left side of this continuum represents commuting zones with the fewest alternatives nearby, where prospective students either have no or only one alternative from which to choose. On the right side of this continuum are commuting zones

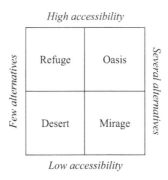

Figure 2.1 Typology of local higher education markets

that offer multiple alternatives, places where students have a wider array of options from which to choose. But just because a college is nearby does not make it accessible: students must first apply and get accepted. Therefore, the vertical axis represents the selectivity of each college in the commuting zone, where the top side of the continuum represents the most accessible institutions that have open-access admissions. On the bottom of the vertical axis are the most selective, and thus least accessible, institutions.

Based on these two criteria, we can start to draw sharp contrasts across local higher education markets. Starting in the bottom-left quadrant are "deserts" where there are either no colleges nearby or the only local options employ stringent admission standards. People living in these communities have *no* options if they need to stay close to home for college. However, if even just one of the local options were an open-access college, then this community would be classified as a "refuge." In the top-left quadrant are communities where there are few alternatives, but there is a single open-access institution nearby. This institution will serve a distinct role in promoting education and upward mobility since it is the only option available to local residents. In both quadrants, students have limited options to "shop around" for college, limiting the utility of traditional college choice theories.

Traditional college choice theories have more utility when a student lives in an educational "oasis," represented in the top-right quadrant. In these communities, people will have several open-access colleges nearby and may face difficult choices when deciding which college to attend. Informational interventions will likely help these students navigate the local marketplace in ways that would be of less utility in places where options are few (or nonexistent). In this search process, a student may find several colleges located nearby. But if the college is highly selective and a student is not admitted/admissible, then this is no true alternative from which a prospective student can choose. In these places, college choice is a "mirage," where there appears to be several colleges, but they are largely inaccessible. The next section applies this typology to illustrate more precisely how local higher education markets vary across the country. Understanding these differences is a critical step in efforts to update and extend college choice theory for today's college students who are increasingly place-bound.

APPLYING THE TYPOLOGY

Desert. Across the country, approximately one in four commuting zones (n=172) have *no* public colleges or universities. These deserts may have non-profit or for-profit institutions, but there are no public options available. Prospective students living in these communities must either travel far distances for college, enroll online, or attend a more expensive private institution. Each of these alternatives presents challenges that could further exacerbate educational inequality—students may face additional travel costs, receive suboptimal quality from distance education, or pay more for attending a private institution. Not only are public options unavailable, but the alternatives impose additional costs for prospective students.

The five-county commuting zone of Storm Lake, Iowa, is an example of an education desert. Located in the northwest corner of the state, this commuting zone has a labor force of 40,687 with a regional economy mostly focused on the agriculture industry, specifically meat packing (U.S. Census Bureau, 2010a). Common of deserts, median household income is below average at $47,823.70 though higher than the desert average ($42,898.30). Reflecting the region's primary economic driver, a substantially higher than average percentage of the labor force is within manufacturing (22.2 percent). Deserts tend to be in non-metropolitan areas and Storm Lake is no exception, with 68 percent of its population living in suburban counties and 32 percent in rural counties. Deserts also tend to exhibit lower college degree attainment. Storm Lake represents the average at roughly 18 percent of residents having obtained a bachelor's degree or higher.

According to the U.S. Department of Education, there are only two colleges located in this commuting zone: Buena Vista University and Faust Institute of Cosmetology. These colleges are relatively small, enrolling 2,114 and 18 undergraduate students, respectively. Buena Vista University is a private non-profit four-year university that surely serves some portion of local residents seeking higher education. Yet it is a moderately selective (64 percent of applicants are admitted) and a relatively expensive university where published tuition and fees for the 2016–2017 academic year were $32,210, which could cause sticker shock for many local prospective students (U.S. Department of Education, 2017a). The Faust Institute of Cosmetology is open access and only enrolls 18 undergraduates, charging $12,950 in tuition.

The absence of any public broadly accessible higher education institution likely contributes to the area's lower degree attainment rate and higher levels of poverty. Many such commuting zones rely on industries offering positions that do not need a credential beyond high school. Yet as most economists predict, many such industries will continue to shrink in the face of the explosive growth of employment in sectors requiring postsecondary degrees (Carnevale, Smith, & Strohl, 2010). To address these challenges, states may seek new ways to partner with private institutions located in deserts to help expand accessible and affordable opportunities to more residents. Alternatively, states may seek ways to deliver high-quality opportunities through partnerships with other public universities around the area. In either case, prospective students living in education deserts have no public options from which to choose.

Oasis. Opposite of a desert is an oasis, or a commuting zone with a bounty of public postsecondary options. An oasis has *more than one* open-access institution, including community colleges or four-year institutions admitting at least 90 percent of its applicants. Approximately a quarter of all commuting zones fall into this category (n=189) and these oases tend to be large metropolitan areas on the East and West Coasts as well as urban centers scattered throughout the country, including St. Louis, MO, Phoenix, AZ, and Chicago, IL. Within these communities there certainly could be pockets of deserts but, on average, these are places where residents are most likely to have the luxury of shopping around from multiple public options.

The four-county commuting zone of San Jose, California, is an example of an oasis. Located south of San Francisco, it encompasses a large metropolitan area with a labor force of over 1.3 million people and a median household income of $68,402, both of which are higher than the average oasis. The San Jose commuting zone has long attracted immigrant populations and is more racially/ethnically diverse than the average oasis, with a population that is 38 percent White, 31 percent Hispanic, 28 percent Asian, 3 percent African American, and 0.3 percent American Indian.

There are 33 colleges operating in this commuting zone, with the majority being in the public sector (11 public two-year and 8 public four-year). There are also several non-profit private four-year (14) and for-profit schools (10). The San Jose commuting zone has a highly educated population with approximately one-third of adults obtaining a bachelor's degree or higher. The San Jose commuting zone is the product of a coordinated statewide approach to higher education. California was among the first states to create a statewide system designed to increase access to higher education, while maintaining a commitment to advanced education and research activity (Callan, 2009; Douglass, 2000). The system affords California with many commuting zones that can be considered oases. States with similar public systems also boast many open-access two- and four-year institutions, especially New York. That does not mean a state lacking a unified public system cannot have an oasis. It also does not mean that California and New York do not have deserts. Yet it does appear that a confluence of metropolitan areas and statewide systems of higher education would predict a larger number of oases.

Mirage. A mirage is a place with *multiple* public options but *few* are open access. A public four-year university may be in the commuting zone, but if it is highly (or even moderately) selective, then it may not be accessible to local students. In these places, it may appear that opportunities are vast, but the only public open-access option is a community college. Without a broadly accessible four-year university, community colleges will be a more common starting point for students pursuing a bachelor's degree here and the local public four-year institution(s) will likely recruit students nationally rather than locally. Mirages comprise 18 percent of all commuting zones (n=124). Mirages can be found throughout the United States, but are primarily located in the Midwest and the South. States including several mirages include Kentucky, Mississippi, Georgia, Missouri, and Michigan.

The commuting zone surrounding Charlotte, North Carolina, represents a mirage. This might come as a surprise, given the city's growth. Charlotte was among the most quickly expanding U.S. cities between 2004 and 2014, during which time it gained nearly 1,000,000 new residents (U.S. Census Bureau, 2010b). The city is the second largest financial center in the U.S., being home to Bank of America and Wells Fargo. Clearly, Charlotte has become a major metropolitan cornerstone of the country.

But Charlotte also ranks last in a recent analysis of upward mobility in the United States (Chetty et al., 2014). Children born in low-income families tend to stay there, and this is likely a function of its local higher education market. Charlotte lacks any open-access four-year institutions. It is home to the University of North Carolina at Charlotte, a key public university, but it is largely inaccessible to local residents. In Fall 2015, the school admitted 63 percent of those applying (U.S. Department of Education, 2017a). The only other public four-year institution in the commuting zone is across the state line, Winthrop University in South Carolina, and it admits a similar percentage of applicants. Rather than having several open-access public universities nearby, the Charlotte commuting zone has eight community colleges, 13 private non-profit colleges and 10 private for-profit chains.

The Charlotte commuting zone labor force is nearly 1.1 million, with a median household income slightly higher than other mirages ($46,508.20 compared to $42,301.90). We might expect a large metropolitan commuting zone such as Charlotte to have high educational attainment levels, but only about one in five residents have a bachelor's degree or higher; this number is about the same as the commuting zone's childhood poverty rate where one in five youth are in poverty.

The economy of Charlotte and its surrounding community is driven in large part by industries requiring a minimum of a bachelor's degree. However, Charlotte's educational marketplace has limited options for pursuing a bachelor's degree, especially for local residents who must stay close to home because of family or work obligations. If they are not admitted to UNC-Charlotte or their credits do not transfer from the community colleges, their postsecondary opportunities become limited very quickly. The mix of colleges operating in mirages will surely vary across the country, yet all will face similar challenges where there may be several community colleges but no accessible four-year public universities in which to pursue a baccalaureate degree. To address these challenges, policymakers may seek ways to enhance the transfer experience, broaden local participation in the public four-year university, or even promote place-based programs to help make the selective public university more within reach to local residents.

Refuge. Opposite of a mirage is a refuge, or a commuting zone where the *only* public option is a single open-access institution—either a community college or a four-year public institution admitting more than 90 percent of applicants. Residents within such a commuting zone have no other accessible public option beyond this single institution. Over a third of commuting zones are refuges (n=224). Refuges are often located in the Great Plains and Southwest, similar to deserts; however, refuges tend to be larger than deserts, with a mean labor force around 65,000.

The four-county commuting zone of Eagle Pass-Uvalde, Texas offers an example of a refuge. Located on the Rio Grande, Eagle Pass is a border community between the United States and Mexico, with the town center of Uvalde nearly 80 miles to the north and east. This commuting zone covers a large area and has a labor force of approximately 47,000, and a racial/ethnic composition that reflects its location along the Mexican border: 88 percent of the commuting zone's residents are Hispanic. The commuting zone's median household income of $30,683 is far below the national average and its childhood poverty rate (40 percent) is far above.

This makes having an affordable public college nearby all the more crucial for upward mobility. And Southwest Texas Junior College serves this function as the area's only public open-access institution. This college enrolls 7,423 students, with more than half enrolled full time. The most popular associate's degree is in the Liberal Arts and Sciences, General Studies, and Humanities (430 enrolled in 2015), and the school awarded most of its certificates in Mechanical Repair Technologies/ Technicians (U.S. Department of Education, 2017b). As would be expected given the racial composition of the Eagle Pass commuting zone, Southwest Texas Junior College receives federal funding via Title V of the Higher Education Act as a Hispanic Serving Institution (HSI). While students from Southwest Texas Junior College transfer to four-year institutions (18.9 percent of students entering in Fall 2010 and then transferred within six years), there are no four-year degree-granting institutions in this commuting zone (Texas Higher Education Coordinating Board, 2017). There is not a public option for students who must stay close to home but would like to pursue a bachelor's degree.

Public open-access colleges operating in refuges are workhorses that serve as an engine of opportunity for the local community. But when their academic programs are limited to a few narrow options or if the college does not have capacity to meet rising local demand, state policymakers may seek creative ways to help promote opportunities in these communities. Perhaps investing in instruction so community colleges could offer bachelor's degrees or enhancing cross-sector collaborations between public and private colleges would be a way to promote opportunities in refuges. Minimally, policymakers should be careful to not advance high-stakes policy regimes that could disproportionately affect the sole public college serving as a refuge for their local residents who have no public open-access alternatives.

CONCLUSION

The goal of this chapter is to offer a closer examination of local higher education markets to help illustrate the important role geography plays in educational opportunity. Prospective students living in deserts or refuges do not have public open-access alternative from which to choose. And those living in oases or even mirages may have several options, even if those options are highly selective or unaffordable. In either case, the chapter illustrates how place shapes educational opportunities. College choice theory could benefit from a closer examination of the role of geography, and public policy could also benefit from considering more closely the unique role each campus has in their local higher education market. Incorporating geography more closely into theories and policies bearing on college choice should result in a more accurate and culturally aware diagnosis of the causes of educational inequality. Assuming all students are mobile or that colleges are somehow independent of their local communities will misrepresent the realities of how students decide where to attend college. Framing conversations in this new way may make it easier to see that unequal opportunity structures are likely the cause of educational problems, rather than students' "poor choices" or "undermatching."

This leads to the second goal of this chapter, which is to offer a way forward for thinking about the geography of college opportunity. If a state or community is interested in promoting upward mobility and educational opportunity, it would do well by taking an inventory of the local higher education marketplaces. If there are communities that are currently not well served by public options or if those public options do not have the capacity to meet local demands, then policymakers may seek ways to intervene. Many colleges are the only (or one of few) local option nearby, making them the workhorses serving local needs that would otherwise not be met. This is important for policymakers seeking to hold colleges more accountable for outcomes—be careful not to unfairly penalize a public college that is the only option for local residents. For example, a federal or state accountability policy that withholds resources from colleges not meeting certain performance outcomes may disproportionately burden colleges that currently serve as refuges. By penalizing these institutions, students living nearby might end up enrolling in more expensive and riskier for-profit colleges or they may even opt out of higher education altogether. To avoid this, policymakers would benefit from adjusting accountability metrics according to the local contexts in which a college operates. Similarly, policymakers may find it promising to invest in open-access colleges currently serving underserved communities that have the fewest choices nearby as a strategy to increase mobility or educational attainment levels.

By offering a typology of local higher education markets, we hope to illustrate with more clarity the various ways geography can shape educational opportunities. Geography can be destiny in higher education when opportunities are richly available in some communities and are unavailable in others. Asking students to "shop around" for better colleges is not feasible for those who need to stay close to home because of work or caring for dependents. Suggesting these students are making suboptimal educational choices without considering the local market in which those "choices" are made will do little to advance our understanding of college access and opportunities.

This chapter shows the many ways geography shapes opportunities and highlights the important role public open-access colleges can play when their communities have few or no colleges nearby to help educate our increasingly diverse nation. To expand opportunities and promote upward mobility, researchers and policymakers can bring geography more squarely into conversations to gain new ideas on how to solve longstanding educational problems.

QUESTIONS FOR DISCUSSION

1. Despite much fanfare on the part of state and federal policymakers, much of the empirical research on online education does not show much of a positive impact on low-income students and students of color. How could schools in a refuge or a desert better address the needs of students not within an easy commuting distance? What could policymakers do?
2. How might policymakers diagnose and solve problems related to access, affordability, and completion within each quadrant of the typology? To what extent does each quadrant present its own unique policy challenges and opportunities?
3. Many state policymakers argue that college credentials below the baccalaureate level (e.g., associate's and certificates) suffice for employment in local economies. Why would these credentials not be an adequate amount of education for the future U.S. workforce?
4. Remember back to when you applied to college. How many colleges did you apply to and how far away were these colleges from your hometown? What factors affected your decision? Did distance from home or work play any part in your college choice process?

NOTE

1   Data excludes students enrolled exclusively online (variable name "ALTONLN2" in the National Postsecondary Student Aid Survey).

REFERENCES

Ali, S. R., & Saunders, J. L. (2008). The career aspirations of rural Appalachian high school students. *Journal of Career Assessment, 17*(2), 172–188. doi:10.1177/1069072708328897.

Attewell, P., & Lavin, D. (2007). *Passing the torch: Does higher education for the disadvantaged pay off across the generations?* New York, NY: Russell Sage Foundation.

Avery, C., Howell, J. S., & Page, L. (2014). *A review of the role of college applications on students' postsecondary outcomes. Research brief.* College Board. Retrieved from http://eric.ed.gov/?id=ED556466.

Briscoe, F. M., & De Oliver, M. (2006). Access to higher education: A conflict between landed interests and democratic ideals. *Education and Urban Society, 38*(2), 204–227.

Callan, P. M. (2009). *California higher education: The master plan and the erosion of college opportunity.* San Jose, CA: National Center for Public Policy and Higher Education.

Card, D. (1993). *Using geographic variation in college proximity to estimate the return to schooling* (Working Paper No. 4483). Cambridge, MA: National Bureau of Economic Research. Retrieved from www.nber.org/papers/w4483.

Carnevale, A., Smith, N., & Strohl, J. (2010). *Projections of jobs and education requirements through 2018.* Washington, DC: Georgetown University Center on Education and the Workforce.

Chetty, R., Friedman, J., Saez, E., Turner, N., & Yagan, D. (2017). *Mobility report cards: The role of colleges in intergenerational mobility.* Retrieved from www.equality-of-opportunity.org/papers/coll_mrc_paper.pdf.

Chetty, R., Hendren, N., Kline, P., & Saez, E. (2014). Where is the land of opportunity? The geography of intergenerational mobility in the United States. *The Quarterly Journal of Economics, 129*(4), 1553–1623.

Do, C. (2004). The effects of local colleges on the quality of college attended. *Economics of Education Review, 23*(3), 249–257.

Douglass, J. (2000). *The California idea and American higher education.* Stanford, CA: Stanford University Press.

Ehrenberg, R. G. (2012). American higher education in transition. *The Journal of Economic Perspectives, 26*(1), 193–216.

Franklin, R. S. (2013). The roles of population, place, and institution in student diversity in American higher education. *Growth and Change, 44*(1), 30–53.

Griffith, A. L., & Rothstein, D. S. (2009). Can't get there from here: The decision to apply to a selective college. *Economics of Education Review, 28*(5), 620–628.

Hoxby, C. M. (1997). *How the changing market Structure of U.S. higher education explains college tuition* (Working Paper No. 6323). Cambridge, MA: National Bureau of Economic Research. Retrieved from www.nber.org/papers/w6323.

Kirst, M. W., Stevens, M. L., & Proctor, C. (2010). Broad-access higher education: A research framework for a new era. In *Report of the conference on Reform and Innovation in the Changing Ecology of Higher Education: Inaugural Strategy Session (Stanford University)* (pp. 7–8). Retrieved from https://cepa.stanford.edu/sites/default/files/Research%20Framework%2004-01-11.pdf.

Kling, J. R. (2001). Interpreting instrumental variables estimates of the returns to schooling. *Journal of Business & Economic Statistics, 19*(3), 358–364.

Long, B. (2004). How have college decisions changed over time? An application of the conditional logistic choice model. *Journal of Econometrics, 121*(1), 271–296.

McDonough, P. M., Antonio, A. L., & Trent, J. W. (1997). Black students, Black colleges: An African American college choice model. *Journal for a Just and Caring Education, 3*(1), 9–36.

National Center for Education Statistics. (2017). *High School Longitudinal Study of 2009.* Retrieved from https://nces.ed.gov/surveys/hsls09/.

Niu, S. (2014). Leaving home state for college: Differences by race/ethnicity and parental education. *Research in Higher Education, 56*(4), 1–35.

Perez, P. A., & McDonough, P. M. (2008). Understanding Latina and Latino college choice: A social capital and chain migration analysis. *Journal of Hispanic Higher Education, 7*(3), 249–265.

Perna, L. (2010). Understanding the working college student. *Academe, 96*(4), 30–32.

Rouse, C. E. (1995). Democratization or diversion? The effect of community colleges on educational attainment. *Journal of Business & Economic Statistics, 13*(2), 217–224.

Shaw, E. J., Kobrin, J. L., Packman, S. F., & Schmidt, A. E. (2009). Describing students involved in the search phase of the college choice process: A cluster analysis study. *Journal of Advanced Academics, 20*(4), 662–700.

Texas Higher Education Coordinating Board. (2017). *Regional data for 2016.* Retrieved from www.txhighereddata.org/reports/performance/regions/.

Turley, R. N. L. (2009). College proximity: Mapping access to opportunity. *Sociology of Education, 82*(2), 126–146.

U.S. Department of Education. (2013). *2011–12 National Postsecondary Student Aid Study (NPSAS:12): Student financial aid estimates for 2011–12.* Washington, DC: National Center for Education Statistics. Retrieved from http://nces.ed.gov/pubsearch/pubsinfo.asp?pubid=2013165.

U.S. Department of Education. (2017a). *National Center for Education Statistics. Institutional Characteristics Component.* Retrieved from https://nces.ed.gov/ipeds/datacenter/CDS.aspx.

U.S. Department of Education. (2017b). *National Center for Education Statistics, Completions Component.* Retrieved from https://nces.ed.gov/ipeds/datacenter/CDS.aspx.

U.S. Census Bureau (2010a). *QuickFacts: Storm Lake city, Iowa.* Retrieved from www.census.gov/quickfacts/fact/table/stormlakecityiowa/PST040217.

U.S. Census Bureau (2010b). *QuickFacts: Charlotte, North Carolina.* Retrieved from www.census.gov/quickfacts/fact/table/charlottecitynorthcarolina/POP060210.

3

CHALLENGES AND OPPORTUNITIES IN THE USE OF BIG AND GEOCODED DATA IN HIGHER EDUCATION RESEARCH AND POLICY

MANUEL GONZÁLEZ CANCHÉ

In order to better discuss challenges and opportunities in the use of big data in higher education research and policy, one should begin by establishing differences and similarities between information and data. One of these similarities is the overlap of time periods in which the level of expertise required to handle information and data issues resulted in the establishment of disciplines that were called "information science" and "data science." These time periods are referred to as the "information age" and "big data age." The consensus regarding the former is that it goes from 1970 to the present day, whereas the big data age goes from 2001 also to the present day. Notably, the establishment of both periods can be linked to publications that coined the terms "information science" (Borko, 1968) and "data science" (Cleveland, 2001). From this view, it is evident that while the term "big data" has recently gained major media attention it is certainly not new. Similarly, the rate at which information has continuously been expanding is also not a recent phenomenon. Indeed, information science, as a discipline, was established in the late 1960s to address the need to store and classify the ever fast-growing amount of information "for optimal storage, retrieval, and dissemination" (Borko, 1968, p. 5). That is, information science emerged to satisfy the need to process information for optimal accessibility and usability, which is a need that prompted the emergence of data science, with the main difference in the types of inputs they both handled.

The inputs that data science and information science handle are their single most important point of departure from one another. While information science deals with processing information, this information, however, constitutes what is commonly referred to as sources of knowledge, including books, journals, and other forms of published material. This is the main reason why information science is traditionally associated with processes, methods, and strategies implemented in libraries to ease access to information. Similar to the need leading to the creation of information science, the current availability of large amounts and sources of data prompted the need to develop innovative ways to collect, prepare, analyze, and visualize unprocessed information. Different from the inputs feeding information science, the raw information that data scientists typically manage consists of a large number of structured or unstructured data points that are traditionally referred to as "big data." From this view, like the need to create information science, our modern society has seen the emergence of data science, which advocates for the use of computer science and statistics as tools to learn from data (Cleveland, 2001).

While both information science and data science share the goal of using information and data, respectively, they fundamentally differ in their inputs to reach their goals and, consequently, their means and strategies to do so. Whereas information science deals with sources of knowledge, data science deals with pieces of information that may or may not be processed or even structured. Indeed, the clearest difference between now and the emergence of information science half a century ago is that in our current society, virtually everyone is continuously adding bits and pieces of data that can be processed to become information that can then be analyzed. Given that, as mentioned, virtually everyone is actively contributing to this data-generating process, the amount of unprocessed information to be handled is the largest in the history of mankind and the pace at which it keeps expanding is becoming faster. From this view, non-trivial challenges of the big data era consist of affording the means to store unprocessed and processed data, which require computing power capable of handling millions of bits being constantly generated. A related challenge is the technical training required to conduct data science, which is conceptualized as the process of turning "raw data into understanding, insight, and knowledge" (Wickham & Grolemund, 2016, para. 1).

Another important difference between information and data science is that the ultimate goal of the latter is to generate valuable knowledge and insight that could potentially take us a step closer to knowing the true value of a population parameter by compiling and analyzing massive amounts of information. In the case of information science, its goal is simply to facilitate the access to information. It is important to note that big data should not be reduced to information at the population level. While one of the aspirations of big data users is precisely to gain a solid inferential understanding of the population, a dataset built from a single speech (e.g., press conference, debate, etc.), for example, can become high dimensional by reaching hundreds or thousands of rows and columns. In this case, the analytic process will still involve specialized skills and knowledge, but no inferential gains will be accrued from this high dimensionality.

In sum, it can be said that the information age, and its corresponding information science discipline, mostly deal with published processed material that needs to be stored and classified for optimal retrieval. In the case of the big data age and data science, the input to be processed is originally unstructured. An important skill and knowledge required in this science is the initial process of structuring these raw pieces of data into structured databases that can later be analyzed through statistical procedures.

As the title of the chapter suggests, its main point of concern focuses on big and geocoded data issues. Even though a subsection below defines geocoded data, for now it is worth noting that geocoded data typically is big data that results from the intersection between latitude and longitude coordinates on the earth's surface with some attribute that is measurable. This measured attribute is typically referred to as a variable or indicator. What differentiates these indicators and variables from common datasets are their link to the earth's surface. Once this information is stored (e.g., geocoded), analysts can use these georeferenced data to generate maps using geographical information systems procedures, and/or to conduct inferential analyses using spatial statistics or spatial econometric analyses (see González Canché, 2014, 2017c, 2018 for examples of these procedures in higher education research).

Considering the main focus of this chapter then, its purpose is to discuss challenges and opportunities regarding the use of big and geocoded data in higher education policy and research. The focus on higher education policy and research is strategic as the mere analysis of big and geocoded data does not warrant that the research findings have relevant and/or timely recommendations and implications from policy- and/ or decision-making perspectives. From this view, the chapter is structured around sections designed to highlight challenges and opportunities that may threaten the policy relevance resulting from analysis of big and geocoded data in higher education research. The chapter highlights the significance and importance that critical analytic decisions have on the sorts and the scope of the inferences to be reached. Examples of these decisions involve the selection of the level of analysis (e.g., county-, zip code-, block-level), the definition of college access rates using sources of big and geocoded data, and the identification of neighboring structures typically employed in spatial econometrics and geographical information systems. The chapter relies on visual displays to exemplify the topics presented. The discussion section addresses recommendations for the use of big and geocoded data, which can be summarized as follows: (a) big data and sophisticated methods without relevant research questions constitute a wasted opportunity; (b) the importance of incorporating more than one analytic sample as validity and robustness checks; (c) the relevance of testing for effect heterogeneity; and (d) prioritization of relevance of research questions over the use of big and geocoded data. The sources of big and geocoded data include the U.S. Census American Community Survey and the National Center for Education Statistics's Integrated Postsecondary Education Data System. The chapter closes by emphasizing that given the availability of large amounts of data, graduate programs in [higher] education should prioritize investment in the development of researchers' critical-analytic skills. This training will not only make them more marketable, but will also benefit the field in general. Having mentioned this, note that the sources of data discussed herein refer to sources of information that, for the most part, have been pre-cleaned or at least can be accessed in conventional data frames format, with rows denoting units and columns denoting variables. This chapter does not deal with data inputs that are truly unstructured, as the level of expertise to deal with these pieces of information cannot be addressed in a single chapter. Instead, the focus of the chapter is on providing researchers and researchers in training with guidance and advice in the use of big and geocoded data critically.

THE IMPORTANCE OF MAKING CRITICAL ANALYTIC DECISIONS AND STUDYING RELEVANT TOPICS

The purpose of this section is to discuss examples of the manners in which analytic decisions involving big and geocoded data have important implications in terms of the scope of the inferences made. The first subsection deals with levels of data offered by the U.S. Census and the corresponding decisions and challenges that analysts may face when handling these data estimates. The second subsection moves the discussion to census-level data across the contiguous United States. Given that both subsections focus on issues related to college access, before beginning with the discussion and in line with the notion of finding research topics that are relevant, it is worth noting that the analysis of access issues remains an important and timely endeavor, especially in the present time when the availability of big and geocoded data can potentially help enrich our understanding of factors affecting its variation.

Education beyond high school is a topic of great public concern as policy decisions made in this area significantly affect millions of families with high school graduates every year. While access to college is not the solution to all the problems young people may face, failing to positively impact access to education beyond high school may not only serve to exacerbate the widening socioeconomic gap in the United States, but would also reinforce the potential negative implications associated with no college enrollment, particularly in regard to unemployment, poverty, and crime (Baum, Ma, & Payea, 2010; Matthews, 2010). On the other side of the spectrum, following a positive externality perspective (McMahon, 2009), providing access to postsecondary education to as many youth as possible is an investment that benefits individuals, communities, states, and the entire United States in general. Considering these reasons, this section offers critical viewpoints that may help identify new topics on college access using big and geocoded data and/or even (re)define college access lenses typically employed in higher education research. The overarching goal of selecting college access is to highlight its continuous contemporaneous relevance in higher education research, despite current emphasis on issues of completion and success in higher education. In short, the issue of access is not solved yet and big data can be used to improve our understanding on factors affecting its variation.

U.S. CENSUS AMERICAN COMMUNITY SURVEY AND HIGHER EDUCATION CENSUS DATA

Access to sources of big data such as the U.S. Census American Community Survey (ACS) represents a unique opportunity for higher education research. Analysts, researchers, and graduate students interested in higher education issues may greatly benefit from employing the ACS data either as a standalone source or to complement other data sources by merging ACS data with IPEDS, for example (see González Canché, 2014, 2017c, 2018 for examples of this approach). In continuing with information about ACS data, note that its levels of aggregation range from county, zip code tabulation areas, tracts, block groups, and blocks. From this view, one of the first methodological questions analysts should ask is regarding the level of analysis at which their research questions will be or need to be conducted. This question is not trivial as it has both conceptual and practical implications. This is so because their inferences will be a function of the level of aggregation selected. Conceptually speaking, analyses that use the county as the unit of analysis will virtually ignore the variation coming from hundreds or potentially thousands of census blocks configuring such a county. Accordingly, inferences with county-level estimates will not enable analyses of variation at the block level, for example. To be more specific, let us use a relatively small county called Santa Cruz, located in California, as an example to describe the implications resulting from using different levels of analyses.

Figure 3.1 shows Santa Cruz county with its borders and surrounding neighboring counties in northern California. Let us assume that a researcher decides to simply analyze the effect of a program implemented at the county level within the state of California. In this case, only counties that implemented such a policy would be the "treated" units of analyses, whereas all the remaining counties within the state would be considered part of the control group. This approach is commonly used in the higher education literature, but at the state level, wherein some states implement a given policy and non-policy-affected states are used as control units. From this view, in addition to the incapability of measuring within-county, or within-state level of variation by using aggregated units of analysis, another challenge consists of sample size issues. For example, analyses that are conducted at the state level in the contiguous United States consist of the 48 adjoining U.S. states plus Washington, DC, therefore rendering 49 units of analysis, if researchers decide to retain Washington, DC in the analytic sample. Going back to the California example, the number of counties is 58, which once again will result in a limited number of units of analysis when conducting analyses at the county level within the state of California. One strategy to address this limitation is

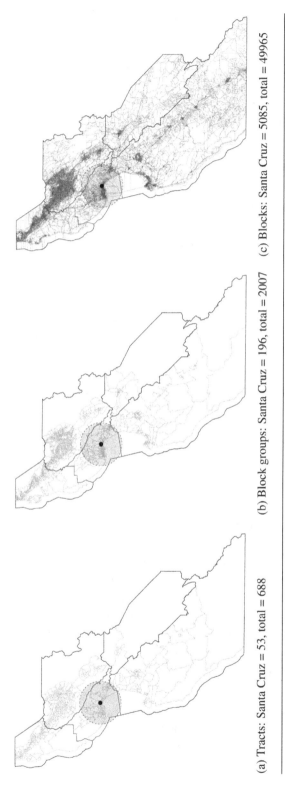

(a) Tracts: Santa Cruz = 53, total = 688   (b) Block groups: Santa Cruz = 196, total = 2007   (c) Blocks: Santa Cruz = 5085, total = 49965

Figure 3.1 Santa Cruz, the only county that implemented the small incentive policy is shown with its borders. Estimates were obtained from the U.S. Census ACS data estimates at the tract, group blocks, and block levels using the table number B15001 to build a dataset that is longitudinal in nature, that is, that has repeated measures on the indicators of interest across states or counties, over time. In the case of country-level analyses, wherein the unit of interest is each state, if analysts add a second time period and retain Washington, DC in the analytic sample, then the number of units will double, reaching 98. With three time periods, the number will be 147, and so on and so forth. A similar notion is applied to the observation of counties configuring a given state over time. A second method to deal with limited number of units consists of using ACS data estimates at smaller units of analysis. For example, instead of analyzing the contiguous United States relying on state-level estimates, researchers may access county-level estimates that configure each state across the United States. This approach will render information on 3,225 counties configuring the 48 states in the country. Similarly, if the analysis involves a single state, like California for example, instead of analyzing its 58 counties, researchers may decide to analyze the blocks configuring each county. Depending on whether the analysis is (a) across the contiguous United States or (b) in a given state, this approach not only addresses limited sample size issues but also enables testing for variation taking place within a given state or within a given county of interest, respectively, as discussed next.

As briefly stated above, the ACS data estimates allow for more detailed analyses that in addition to addressing sample size issues have a clear spatial component, which enables testing for spatial dependence issues (see González Canché, 2014, 2017c, 2018). More specifically, Figure 3.1 shows three levels for which ACS data estimates can be retrieved. In each of the three sub-figures contained in Figure 3.1, the borders indicate limits for which estimates might be available. For example, Figure 3.1(a) shows the census tract-level limits, Figure 3.1(b) shows census group blocks, and Figure 3.1(c) shows census block borders. In the first case, the number of tracts configuring Santa Cruz county is 53, which would indicate that instead of treating Santa Cruz as a single unit, researchers could potentially measure a given county-level program impact across the 53 tracts that are part of this county. If analysts decide to zoom in the analyses at the group block level, then the number of units available in Santa Cruz will be 196. Finally, at the smallest level, which is the census block, the number of available units for analysis in Santa Cruz is 5,085. From this perspective, it is then clear that sample size issues in cross-sectional datasets (i.e., measured at a single point in time) are not a concern when moving the analyses beyond the census tract level. Moreover, the 2015 data dictionary shows that the number of variables and indicators available surpasses 30,000.[1] If one considers that a relatively small and single county, such as Santa Cruz, is configured by more than 5,000 census blocks, then one may soon realize that the dimensionality of these data represents an important challenge in terms of computing power required to manipulate this massive amount of information.

A related challenge when dealing with ACS data consists of the nature of the information ACS conveys. ACS data are estimates and as such there is no guarantee that the information contained is an accurate representation of the population it is supposed to measure (see Glenn [2016] for an ample discussion of ACS and its use in the programming language R). While this is a non-trivial issue, the most straightforward manner to deal with it is simply to recognize that these estimates have a "center and spread" (Glenn, 2016, p. 3) and therefore are not exact numbers and must not be treated as such. This is the main reason why the language employed in this section has been referring to ACS data as data estimates, rather than just ACS data.

At any rate, the discussion presented in this subsection was intended to depict the critical analytic decisions researchers should make when selecting the level of analysis. This decision implies both conceptual and practical implications as those depicted by the level of dimensionality related to zooming in in a given state or county. For example, to access the Santa Cruz data estimates at the census block level, one requires access to a compressed folder that has a weight of 435 megabytes and such a folder does not even include information on the 49,965 census blocks reflected in Figure 3.1(c). While 435 megabytes is not an unmanageable data size, imagine if a given research project requires access to all the census blocks contained in the state of California or even the entire region in which the state of California is located. In either one of these cases, the size of the data estimates to be retrieved will exponentially grow and this expansion will require data handling capabilities that are both computationally and monetarily expensive.

GEOCODED BIG DATA

The data format of the information contained in Figure 3.1 is called a shapefile, which is a data format that stores geocoded or spatial information along with attributes defining that geocoded information (ESRI, 1998). This data format is referred to as a shape given that the latitude and longitude coordinates can take one of the following forms: a point, a line, and area (also referred to as a polygon). Examples of a point information include the exact location of a college or university. For example, the University of Pennsylvania is located at the following coordinates: 39.943699, –75.197254, which, as shown in Figure 3.2, is reflected as a pin on the map. In this figure, one can also see that this university is also located in the state of Pennsylvania, which in a shapefile is stored as an area or polygon. Finally, a line can depict any of the rivers shown in Figure 3.2. The weight of a shapefile depends on the types of shapes it stores. The heaviest shapefile contains polygons as each polygon is configured by a collection of lines and each line is configured by a collection of points, each of which is linked to georeferenced information on the earth's surface.

Each shape has attributes, which are variables or factors that can help define each shape. For example, in the case of the University of Pennsylvania, this point can have the following attributes: (a) private not-for-profit, (b) four-year institution, (c) research intensive, (d) highly selective, among others. States (polygons) can be linked to attributes on (a) poverty levels, (b) college access rates, (c) median disposable income,

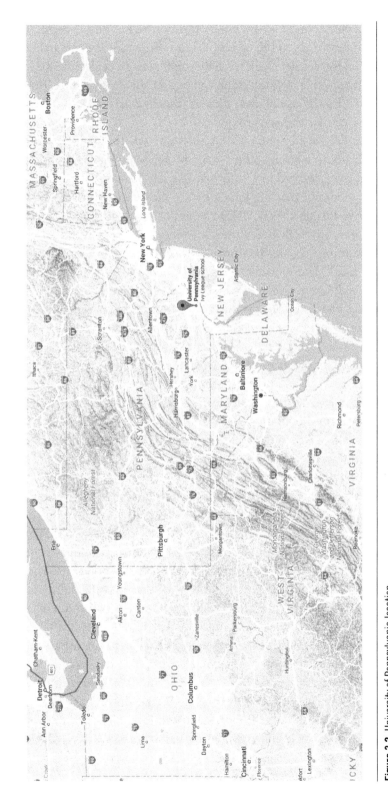

Figure 3.2 University of Pennsylvania location
Source: Google Maps.

(d) in-migration, etc. A line may be linked to information on (a) depth, (b) width, (c) length, etc. In returning to the case of Santa Cruz county, if researchers want to conduct analyses at the census block level, they will need to deal with 5,085 polygons, each of which with specific attributes that can be statistically analyzed. The following discussion exemplifies the use of ACS data to visually analyze differences in college access rates across gender and age groups.

Let us assume that we are interested in analyzing whether college access rates of high school graduates in a given county varies by gender and age groups. The county analyzed is Santa Cruz, located in California. The selection of this county is strategic as Santa Cruz is a county that implemented a policy that began providing a small monetary incentive (around $500 USD) to Santa Cruz high school graduates who enrolled in a community college within the county borders. Given that this county was the only one implementing this program among its neighboring counties and over time, Ruiz, Leigh, and González Canché (2018) implemented a geographically based difference in difference analysis, wherein Santa Cruz was considered the treated entity in that study. Figure 3.3 depicts the college-going rates of high school graduates in Santa Cruz and its neighboring counties over time. This type of representation is called cholorpleth maps, in which the polygons are assigned a given color intensity based on an attribute. In the maps shown in Figure 3.3 the color intensity is based on the proportion of high school graduates who did not enroll in college by gender and by age group (18–24 and 24–34 years of age). Readers interested in details regarding Ruiz et al.'s specification should directly consult that study. For now, it suffices to state that this small incentive was found to have a positive, but localized, effect on college access for both genders in the 18–24 age group.[2]

The visualization strategy implemented in this chapter, shown in Figure 3.4, is called a dot density map. This visualization technique builds upon the notion of a cholorpleth map. However, different from the cholorpleth technique, the dot density map creates a dot for a given unit in a polygon. The analytic decision that researchers need to make is whether they will have a one-to-one correspondence or if they will have a weight to reduce cluttering of information within polygons. For example, assume that a given polygon has an attribute with a value of 350. This can be the number of 18–24-year-old high school graduates who did not go to college. In this case, analysts may decide to plot 350 randomly distributed dots in that polygon to signal concentration or density of that attribute in that area. Yet, other analysts may decide to divide all these attributes by a scalar; let us assume this scalar is 10. In this case, each dot will represent 10 students, and the number of dots in the assumed polygon will be 35 instead of 350. The result of the dot density map shown in Figure 3.4 reflects information at the census block level and each dot represents a percentage point increase in high school graduates not accessing college in Santa Cruz, CA, according to ACS 2015 estimates.

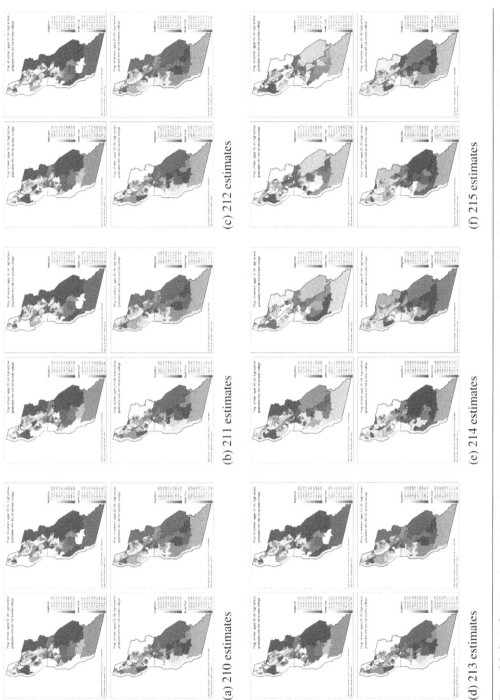

(a) 210 estimates   (b) 211 estimates   (c) 212 estimates

(d) 213 estimates   (e) 214 estimates   (f) 215 estimates

Figure 3.3 Santa Cruz, the only county that implemented the small incentive policy is shown with its borders. Estimates were obtained from the U.S. Census ACS data estimates at the census tract level using the table number B15001

Figure 3.4 Dot density map at the block level; each dot represents a percentage point increase in high school graduates not accessing college in Santa Cruz, CA, in 2015
Source: American Community Survey, 2015 estimates.

These maps, in addition, are separated by age group. Note that in the 18–24 age group, the concentration of male high school graduates who did not access college is overall more spread out and prevalent across the county. In the case of the 25–34 age group, this situation is reversed and women who finished high school or its equivalent and who did not enroll in college are more spread out and prevalent across the county. People interested in comparing these estimates to those presented in Figure 3.3 can zoom into Figure 3.3(f). This is a useful exercise as it soon will be clear that the cholorpleth approach does not reveal the same patterns as clearly as the dot density map does. While the information is the same, as it was obtained from the same source, the decision to use a visualization technique, over others, matters in terms of conveying information as clearly as possible. The main challenge in dealing with dot density maps is once again the level of dimensionality. Not only is the map showing information on 5,085 blocks, but also each block will have x number of dots to be iteratively plotted, which will create hurdles in terms of computing power to handle that massive amount of information. In the case of the cholorpleth maps, there is one value per polygon, which results in a less expensive computational approach.

SPATIAL DEPENDENCE

One of the main advantages of working with geocoded data consists of the possibility of testing whether the attributes under analysis are spatially dependent. Spatial dependence is an important issue given that the outcomes observed in a given point or polygon may be influenced by the outcomes of the neighboring points or polygons and vice versa.[3] In the case of polygons, one can establish a neighbor using three criteria: (a) polygons that touch in a given point are neighbors as shown in Figure 3.5(a), also known as Rook's approach; (b) polygons that share a border are neighbors, Figure 3.5(b), also shown as Bishop's approach; and (c) the combination of the previous two approaches, that is, polygons that either touch in a point, share a border or both will be considered neighbors. This is shown in Figure 3.5(c) and is referred to as Queen's approach (Bivand, Pebesma, Gomez-Rubio, & Pebesma, 2013). The Queen's approach is the most comprehensive neighbor identification strategy and its application at the state level is presented in Figure 3.5(d), wherein the state of Pennsylvania is used as the state of interest and the identification of six neighbors is presented. Figure 3.5(e) shows the rationale employed with dealing with points. In this case, researchers have to specify either a radius or simply identify closest entities to establish neighboring units. Specifically, Figure 3.5(e) shows the 1k or closest neighboring approach, wherein only the closest unit$_{it}$ to unit$_i$ is defined as a neighbor. In the case of gas station A and B, they are the closest to one another; accordingly, the double-arrow indicates that they are considered neighbors to one another. In the case of gas station C, its closest neighbor is gas station B, but since for gas station B, the closest is gas station A, gas station B does not have an arrow pointing to gas station C. If

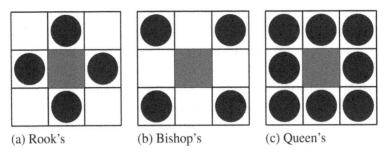

(a) Rook's   (b) Bishop's   (c) Queen's

State–level Neighboring Structure

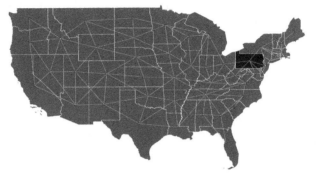

(d) Queen's specification to identify Neighbors at the state level—PA has six neighbors

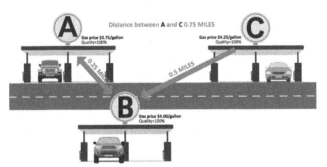

(e) Points, $1k$ specification

(f) $1k$ specification in higher education research; see González Canché (2014) for more information

Figure 3.5 Approaches used to define neighbors and spatial weight matrices

analysts decide to expand the number of neighbors to two, for example, then all gas stations shown in this figure will be neighbors. The main challenge of this identification approach consists of choosing the optimal number of neighbors that better capture spatial dependence and competition. When there is no previous evidence of this "optimal" decision, researchers may need to test for several specifications and see which one is associated with best model fit. See González Canché (2014) for an example in higher education research in which the author tested five specifications.

Once researchers have established a feasible rule to identify neighboring units, then they can test whether neighbors' outcomes are spatially dependent, but the discussion about strategies to test for this issue are beyond the scope of this chapter due to space limitations. For more information, see Bivand et al. (2013) and for recent examples in higher education research see González Canché (2014, 2017c, 2018).

USING BIG DATA TO POTENTIALLY HELP RE(DE)FINING COLLEGE ACCESS

This section takes advantage of big data estimates provided in Digest of Education Statistics (2011, 2012) and the U.S. Department of Education, Integrated Postsecondary Education Data System (2012a, 2012b). These estimates at the state level were accessed and merged into a single dataset that allowed computing the proposed college access estimates discussed herein. All data and codes are available upon request.[4]

(Re)Defining College Access

One measure of college access consists of dividing state i's number of recent high school graduates enrolling in college by the total number of high school graduates that state produced in a given academic year. For example, in the academic year 2009–2010 Alabama produced 48,166 high school graduates from public and private institutions (Digest of Education Statistics, 2011, 2012), of whom 28,330 or 59 percent enrolled in any form of Title IV eligible institutions in-state in the academic year 2010–2011 (U.S. Department of Education, Integrated Postsecondary Education Data System, 2012a, 2012b). At the national level, the percentage of the 3.41 million high school graduates enrolling in any form of Title IV eligible institutions in-state was 52.9 percent (1.8 million). These new enrollees are also referred to as recent high school graduates (RHG) as they enroll in college within 12 months of graduation. This measure, although straightforward, may be misleading in terms of real access to higher education provided by a given state. In that same academic year, a total of 953,000 non-recent high school graduates (NRHG; first-time degree-seeking students who enroll in college within 12 months of having graduated from high school) also enrolled in any form of college in the state where they graduated from high school or obtained their GED. However, by the metric used before, NRHG would not be accounted for in the computation of college access, as typical of studies on college access that deal with financial aid, for example (see Toutkoushian & Hillman, 2012, for an excellent summary of these studies).

While it would be ideal to see that more RHG find access to higher education immediately after graduation, the inclusion of NRHG in the computation of access should not be overlooked. NRHG students do occupy seats, pay in-state tuition, absorb monetary and non-monetary resources, and—perhaps more importantly— have the right to receive an education for the betterment of themselves, their families, and their communities. Ignoring them from our conceptualization of college access may hinder our understandings of the impact of resources disbursed by states to provide college education in different sectors, levels, and forms. More specifically, decisions about how to define college access have critical implications. For example, if college access is defined as the proportion of RHG enrolling in public in-state four-year institutions, this measure would only account for 817,000 of the 3.41 million high school graduates of 2009–2010 (which represents 23.9 percent). Under this view, the 34.4 percent of the total RHG freshman students who, on average, found access to college in the public two-year sector in the contiguous U.S. postsecondary education system in 2010–2011 would be discarded (IPEDS, 2012a, 2012b). This measure would also fail to account for 55 percent of the total number of non-RHG (952,820) who were welcomed by the public two-year sector that academic year (see Table 3.1). Moreover, our definition of access to postsecondary education could be further improved by accounting for enrollment beyond the public sector. As in the case of NRHG, ignoring the role that private two- and four-year colleges have in college access equates to assuming that these sectors have no role in providing access and/or that state financial aid disbursements have no effect whatsoever in variations of access to those sectors. Even though financial aid disbursements may indeed have no effect on access to these unexplored sectors, empirical evidence, practically absent, is needed to improve our understanding on the matter. In sum, this section of the chapter calls attention to the complex ways in which access to higher education in a given state can be measured and presents a conceptual framework in which the use of big data can serve to enhance our understanding of college access in a given state.

Proposed Framework

Researchers have traditionally excluded non-recent high school graduates from college access models, as well as high school graduates enrolling outside the four-year sector (once more, see Toutkoushian & Hillman, 2012, for an excellent summary on the current state of the topic). Considering that these exclusions may potentially mask the real measure of college access in a given state, the proposed model discussed herein offers a comprehensive view of college access indicators using census-level data provided by IPEDS. These data enable accounting for mobility patterns of first-time

Table 3.1 Distribution of students in-migrating to, remaining in, or out-migrating from state i in 2010–2011

	In-migrated			In-state			Out-migrated		
	$\mu\pi$	Min	Max	$\mu\pi$	Min	Max	$\mu\pi$	Min	Max
μ Total Recent HS Grad.	8873	1103	34000	36802	628	249894	7901	783	31666
$\mu\pi$ RHG	0.266[a]	0.062	0.93	0.781[d]	0.235	0.922	0.218[b]	0.077	0.764
4-year public RHG	0.447*	0.011	0.865	0.482†	0.102	0.803	0.359†	0.208	0.626
4-year priv. non-profit RHG	0.428*	0	0.967	0.125†	0	0.377	0.484†	0.222	0.732
4-year priv. profit RHG	0.018*	0	0.11	0.013†	0	0.04	0.029†	0.009	0.069
2-year public RHG	0.073*	0	0.357	0.344†	0	0.691	0.075†	0.008	0.301
2-year or less public/priv. RHG	0.031*	0.001	0.275	0.034†	0.011	0.176	0.051†	0.01	0.118
μ Total Non-Recent HS Grad.	3649	345	16833	19445	739	150148	2562	392	7256
$\mu\pi$ NRHG	0.266[c]	0.065	0.697	0.832	0.409	0.955	0.167[d]	0.59	0.044
4-year public NRHG	0.231**	0.03	0.864	0.157††	0.009	0.642	0.107††	0.032	0.275
4-year priv. non-profit NRHG	0.191**	0	0.567	0.037††	0	0.135	0.13††	0.046	0.324
4-year priv. profit NRHG	0.188**	0	0.774	0.071††	0	0.274	0.388††	0.152	0.658
2-year public NRHG	0.219**	0	0.668	0.546††	0	0.871	0.168††	0.061	0.558
2-year or less public/priv. NRHG	0.168**	0.005	0.563	0.186††	0.028	0.485	0.204††	0.059	0.469

[a]with respect to (wrt) hosted RHG, [b]wrt produced RHG, [c]wrt hosted NRHG, [d]wrt produced NRHG
*wrt in-migrated RHG, †wrt in-state RHG, **wrt in-migrated NRHG, ††wrt in-state NRHG
Source: IPEDS and Digest of Education Statistics.

degree-seeking students who are classified as RHGs and NRHGs. The mobility patterns included in this conceptualization account for retention (students who graduated in state *i* and enrolled in state *i*), in-migration (students who graduated in state *i′* and moved into state *i*), and out-migration (students who graduated in state *i* and moved out of-state to state *i′*) in a given academic year *t* and in a given state *i*, as discussed next.

Figure 3.6 exhaustively partitions the population of first-time degree-seeking college students hosted by a given state *i* in a given academic year. This figure also emphasizes the complex ways in which college access can be conceptualized and constitutes the college access framework of total college freshman in state *i* that is proposed in this chapter. As mentioned, every year a given state *i* produces *x* number of high school graduates represented by the partitions A, E, and F of Figure 3.6. From these RHG only partitions A and F enroll in college within 12 months of graduation; partition A does so in state *i* (in-state students), while students in partition F enroll in college out-of-state, which is typically referred to as out-migration of RHG. The portion of RHG of state *i* who did not enroll in college within 12 months of college graduation is captured by partition E. The sizes of these partitions vary from state to state and the actual estimates of each one can be obtained from survey data provided by IPEDS (2012a, 2012b, 2012c, 2012d). The corresponding distributions for the academic year 2010–2011 are presented in Table 3.1. Each partition of Figure 3.6 contains

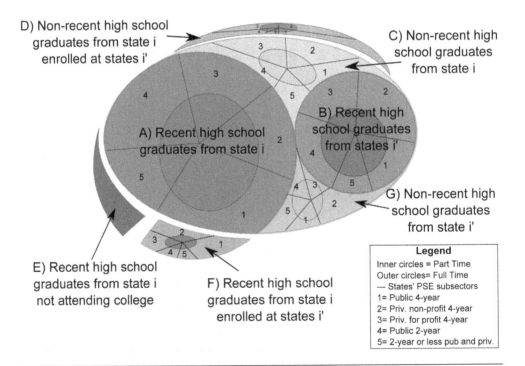

Figure 3.6 College access framework: Breakdown of total freshman in state i

an inner-darker circle along with internal divisions. The inner circle represents part-time freshman and the outer circle represents full-time freshman. The divisions represent the postsecondary sectors and levels that configure each state's higher education system within each partition. As mentioned above, the current state of the literature on college access and different forms of financial aid (Toutkoushian & Hillman, 2012) is founded upon traditional measures of college access which have considered only one or two triangles formed in the partition A. That is, college access is currently defined as the proportion of all RHG produced by state *i* who enrolled full time in public two- (subpartition A4) and/or four-year institutions in state i (subpartition A1). Scholars who included out-migration of RHG have also limited their analyses to either enrollment in public two- and four-year colleges out-of-state (sub-partitions F4 and F1, respectively) or on only merit-based aid (see Cornwell, Mustard, & Sridhar, 2006; Dynarski, 2000, 2008; Toutkoushian & Hillman, 2012; Zhang & Ness, 2010; Zhang, Hu, & Sensenig, 2013).

Figure 3.6 further shows that the total number of first-time freshman in a state *i* is not only composed by y number of RHGs (partitions A, B) and *z* number of NRHGs (partitions C, G); these *y* and *z* number of freshman in a state *i* are also comprised of resident (partitions A, C) and non-resident students (partitions B, G). Figure 3.6 also shows that all of these subgroups of first-time degree-seeking students (in-state, in-migrated, and out-migrated students) are distributed in different sectors and levels of that state's postsecondary education system. These sectors and levels are represented with numbers ranging from 1 to 5, where 1 is public four-year sector, 2 is private not-for-profit four-year sector, 3 is private for-profit four-year sector, 4- is public two-year sector, and 5 includes two years or less for-profit and not-for-profit sectors. As briefly stated above, an important limitation of current research consists of ignoring student out-migration that takes place outside the four-year public and private not-for-profit sectors. This issue is discussed and addressed by González Canché (2018) when dealing with student mobility in the non-resident student network.

Incorporating NRHG into Our Measures of College Access

While important, the inclusion of NRHG in the measures of college access is not a trivial endeavor. Going back to the first example, if recent high school graduates enrolling in college in state in year *t* (RHG_t) is used as the numerator and total RHG of that year *t* ($TRHG_t$) is the denominator ($RHG_t/TRHG_t$), the resulting proportion is obtained from dividing a fraction of the whole by its whole at time *t*. In the case of the contiguous United States, this represents 0.53, which is the result of dividing the 1,803,316 RHG_t who enrolled as first-time in-state students in Fall 2010 (as reported by the U.S. Department of Education, Integrated Postsecondary Education Data System, 2012a, 2012b) by the 3,411,354 $TRHG_t$ of spring of 2010 (as reported by the Digest of Education Statistics, 2011, 2012). Note that the denominator is obtained from the Digest of Education Statistics and the numerator is obtained from the U.S. Department of Education, Integrated Postsecondary Education Data System. Moreover, the U.S. Department of Education, Integrated Postsecondary Education Data System also provides information on the NRHG who enrolled in college in Fall 2010. Notably, these NRHG do not belong to the total of recent high school graduates in a given state in spring of 2010. Indeed, $NRHG_t$ were part of the TRHG at time $t - n$ ($TRHG_{t-n}$). The main issue here is that this total would be a function of going back n number of years and adding the fraction of $TRHG_{t-n}$ who never enrolled in college until time t. While this is not computationally expensive, it is currently impossible given that IPEDS surveys do not capture the high school graduation year of new NRHG entrants. To be more specific, the problem associated with pretending that RHG_t and $NRHG_t$ are part of the same whole (because they enroll in college the same academic year as reported by the U.S. Department of Education, Integrated Postsecondary Education Data System) is that dividing their sum by their assumed whole ($RHG_t + NRHG_t$)/$TRHG_t$ will result in an inflation of the real access to higher education in the contiguous United States. For example, in Fall 2010 there were 952,820 NRHGs across the contiguous United States who enrolled in the states where they attended high school. If we simply add them to the previous estimate we will have (952,820 + 1,803,316)/3,411,354, which results in an overall access rate of 0.81. Thus, omitting NRHGs mask access to higher education, but simply including them inflates access rates to higher education; the critical question is how to address this conundrum?

Even though solving the issue presented above is currently not possible, a reasonable solution may be to look at shifts in proportions of enrollments among different sectors for RHG_t and $NRHG_t$ separately, as shown in Table 3.1. For instance, from college access and financial aid perspectives, in looking at Figure 3.6 we could measure if different forms of aid shift proportions of enrollments within RHG_t and $NRHG_t$. That is, looking only at partition A at time t, which represents $RHGA_t$ who enrolled in-state at time t, one could start asking if specific forms of aid (merit, need, loans) impact the variation of the proportion of enrollments in the public four-year sector. Under this perspective, we would have that the total of partition A in a state i at time $_t$ (TA_{it}) could be the numerator of the subpartition A_{it} who enrolled in sector 1 ($A1_{it}$), which represents public, four-year colleges in-state i at time t. This rationale is presented in Table 3.1, wherein the national average proportion of RHG who enrolled in-state in the public four-year sector was 0.482. Similarly, the previous rationale could be extrapolated to the $NRHG_t$, where its total C in state i at time t (TC_{it}) would be the divisor of specific sectors we aim at examining. For example, also in Table 3.1, note that the public two-year sector was the most important attractor of NRHG enrolling in college in Fall 2010 with 0.546. Following this approach, researchers can envision studies designed to measure factors affecting these variations in proportions across RHGs and NRHGs.

In addition to looking at shifts in proportions within states, researchers could also analyze out-migration and in-migration patterns of RHG_t and $NRHG_t$. For example, it is possible to analyze if aid disbursements have any effect on reduction of out-migration for RHG_t enrolling in private four-year institutions out-of-state, which is the result of dividing the total subpartition $F2_{i't}$ by its total $TF_{i't}$, where the i'th subscript corresponds to any state i other than students' home state i. Finally, we can test if aid disbursements affect the in-migration of RHGC to specific sectors of state i. It could be that merit-based aid disbursements affect enrollment in the public four-year sector of out-of-state students ($B1_{i't}/TB_{it}$) while it has no effect on enrollments in the public two-year sector. For now, it is worth noting that the public four-year sector slightly attracts a larger proportion of RHGs than the private not-for-profit four-year sector (0.447 and 0.428, respectively) and that this difference expands when analyzing in-migration patterns of NRHGs attending these two sectors (0.231 and 0.191, respectively) with the public two-year sector becoming slightly more relevant than the private not-for-profit four-year sector in welcoming NRHGs in state (with 0.219).

DISCUSSION

The purpose of presenting these myriad possibilities in measuring and defining college access rates is not to over-complicate our conceptualization of this important issue, but to offer an innovative perspective that may enable more precise operationalizations using sources of big data critically. The sources are available; it is our obligation as higher education researchers to use them critically in the hope of moving our field forward.

This closing section further elaborates on challenges and opportunities related to the use of big and geocoded data in higher education research. The discussion is structured around topics that are intended to serve as a general guide for researchers who aim to conduct research using sources of big and geocoded data.

Big Data and Sophisticated Methods Without Relevant Research Questions Is a Missed Opportunity

The retrieval and use of big data implies the development of specialized skills and knowledge. As discussed in this chapter, the availability of sources of big data that can be used in higher education research opens up the possibility of being creative and innovative when conceptualizing and operationalizing issues in higher education research. Nonetheless, the use of big data and sophisticated methods just for the sake of using them could potentially translate into conducting research without policy implications and recommendations. Given the applied nature of higher education as a field of research, our community cannot afford to conduct research without such implications and recommendations.

The examples presented in this chapter, while descriptive in nature, dealt with an issue that has the potential to impact hundreds of thousands of students every year. This type of research is considered important, timely, and relevant, especially in the current context where the rhetoric about college in the United States has shifted to an emphasis on college completion and success rather than on college access. This shift, at least tacitly, may convey the notion that the access issue has been solved or is not important enough to warrant the continuation of analyses on ways to improve access rates in this country. Considering that access is the first step toward continuation and eventual degree attainment, the college completion goal requires boosting access, improving continuation, or both. Accordingly, the analysis of factors that may improve access remains relevant.

An important strategy that researchers could use to ensure that their topics of study involving big and geocoded data are relevant is to revisit influential manuscripts for which the scope of the research can be expanded with the use of big data. This approach should not be limited to replication exercises, but can expand on the questions posed by the original authors. As depicted in the college access framework discussed herein, researchers can create new indices across divergent sectors and levels to test factors affecting variation of those access indices, such as financial aid disbursements.

Once researchers have identified timely and relevant topics, the availability of big data usually enables creation of mutually exclusive analytic samples over time that enable inclusion of several samples in the same study. While this is a practice that is almost absent in higher education research, the incorporation of two analytic samples that come from the same population of interest enables testing for consistency and robustness of the results. For example, in a recent study, González Canché (2017a) created two analytic samples to test whether there is a wage penalty associated with initial enrollment in the two-year sector as opposed to initial enrollment in the four-year sector among scientists in STEM disciplines. Similarly, González Canché (2017b) also created two analytic samples on college-goers using two decades of information. These studies constitute two recent examples in which the author has relied on more than one main data source. In the case of González Canché (2017b), the author additionally incorporated big data sources at the state- and county levels, which served to illustrate how multiple data sources can be merged.

In addition to including several analytic samples, researchers could test for effect heterogeneity. The concept of effect heterogeneity serves to test whether the influence of a given variable, factor, or treatment has divergent impacts on participants based on their inherent characteristics, such as gender and ethnicity, for example. As seen in the access framework section, effect heterogeneity can also be applied to other characteristics, such as recent high school graduate status. In the case of the ACS data estimates, the examples discussed placed an important emphasis on gender and age groups. However, the richness typically associated with ACS data estimates enable researchers to test for effect heterogeneity based on ethnicity, as well. Typically, once analytic samples have been disaggregated based on gender, ethnicity, or its combination, then researchers can proceed to fit different models using the same specifications (i.e., same predictor, control, and outcome variables across models.). An example of this approach can be found in Webber and González Canché (2015), wherein the authors tested for intersectionality issues using quantitative methods.

An important consideration when dealing with geocoded data is that region of the country may have an important effect given the availability of college options. For example, Figure 3.7 contains two maps. Figure 3.7(a) is the result of measuring the average distance to all colleges or universities accredited to confer a valid degree or credential per ZCTA across the contiguous United States. Figure 3.7(b) is the result of iteratively measuring the distance of every ZCTA to its closest college or university that is accredited to confer a valid degree or credential across the contiguous United States. While these two definitions may appear similar, their implementation yields drastically different results. Figure 3.7(a) shows that all ZCTAs located on the west coast are the farthest away, on average, from every college and university in the contiguous United States. While this information is factually correct based on the definition used, it is incorrect given that it ignores the local availability of college options. This is the reason why Figure 3.7(b) is preferred as it clearly depicts zones in which the local availability of colleges better reflects the context that recent and non-recent high school graduates experienced based on their location. For example, note that the states of California and Washington have local availability of colleges and universities that were not captured by the definition presented in Figure 3.7(a).

CLOSING REMARKS: TRAINING AND CRITICAL THINKING

To close this chapter the following points summarize some guidance that has proven useful in the use of big and geocoded data.

- It is usually recommended to revisit cornerstone research incorporating big and geocoded data. This revisiting process involves addressing old important issues using new approaches and expanding on the scope that previous research was able to cover.
- When possible, researchers should incorporate more than one analytic sample as validity and robustness checks. This holds true even when analyzing survey and sample data, such as the one provided by the National Center for Education Statistics.
- Researchers should aim to test for effect heterogeneity as it is not realistic to assume that a given predictor variable of interest may impact participants with the same or very similar magnitude. Also, the disaggregation of analytic samples based on participants' attributes such as gender and ethnicity forces us to use critical lenses in [higher] education research.

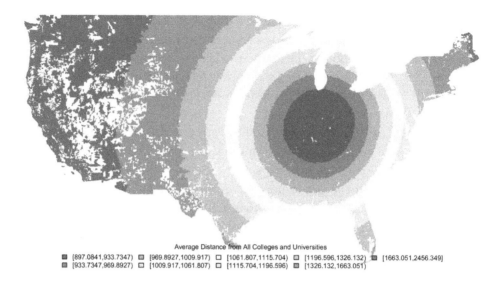

Average Distance from All Colleges and Universities

■ [897.0841,933.7347) ■ [969.8927,1009.917) □ [1061.807,1115.704) ■ [1196.596,1326.132) ■ [1663.051,2456.349]
■ [933.7347,969.8927) □ [1009.917,1061.807) □ [1115.704,1196.596) ■ [1326.132,1663.051)

(a) Mean distance from all colleges and universities

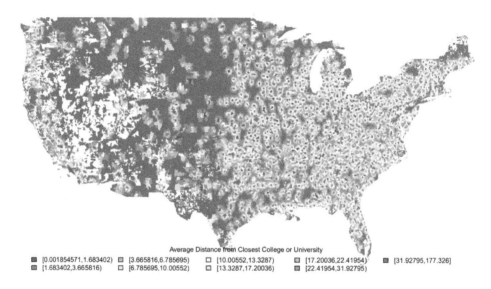

Average Distance from Closest College or University

■ [0.001854571,1.683402) ■ [3.665816,6.785695) □ [10.00552,13.3287) ■ [17.20036,22.41954) ■ [31.92795,177.326]
■ [1.683402,3.665816) □ [6.785695,10.00552) □ [13.3287,17.20036) ■ [22.41954,31.92795)

(b) Mean distance per each ZCTA from all colleges and universities

Figure 3.7 While factually correct, Map (a) may lead to biased conclusions by implying that students in the west coast, for example, are "isolated" in terms of local availability of college options. The dynamic algorithm that identifies Map (b) consistently rendered estimates that more accurately captured the actual availability of college options locally
Source: U.S. Census ACS, IPEDS. Code available upon request.

- Always prioritize relevance of research question over use of sophisticated methods and big data.
- The use of theory is crucial when using big data and sophisticated methods.
- Invest in development of your big and geocoded data management skills.

Big and geocoded data offers the possibility of improving our understanding of higher education issues. One of the most important recommendations the chapter offers is regarding the need to train researchers in the use of big and geocoded data. Overall, the message is clear: given the availability of large amounts of data, graduate programs in [higher] education should continue investment in the development of researchers' visual-display, data management, and statistical modeling skills. This training will not only make them more marketable, but will also benefit the field in general.

QUESTIONS FOR DISCUSSION

1. What are some of the pros and cons that the use of big and geocoded data might bring to [higher] education research?
2. Why would it be important to test for effect heterogeneity and differences in estimates by participants' characteristics (e.g., gender, race/ethnicity, socio-economic status)?
3. How are big data different and similar to geocoded data?
4. What are some of the critical analytical decisions discussed in the chapter and what are their potential implications?
5. What are some of the sources of big and geocoded data mentioned and used in the chapter?
6. Why should one prioritize relevance of the research questions over methodological sophistication?
7. What are some of the cornerstone research topics that you think could be readdressed using big and geocoded data?
8. What reactions do you have about the bullet points presented by the author; are there any points for which you would expand or disagree?

NOTES

1   This data dictionary is available from the US Census at the following link: www2.census.gov/programs-surveys/acs/summary_file/2015/documentation/user_tools/ACS2015_Table_Shells.xlsx
2   With these effects impacting high school graduates living within 12 miles from a community college.
3   This rationale also applies to lines; for example, the level of pollution in a river may be associated with the level of pollution of the river that is closest to it.
4   All coding schemes to replicate the proportions along with the survey data available online are available upon request. These computations include only students enrolling in Title IV eligible institutions in the contiguous United States.

REFERENCES

Baum, S., Ma, J., & Payea, K. (2010). *Education pays, 2010: The benefits of higher education for individuals and society.* Trends in Higher Education series. College Board Advocacy & Policy Center. Retrieved from https://trends.collegeboard.org/sites/default/files/education-pays-2010-full-report.pdf.

Bivand, R. S., Pebesma, E. J., Gomez-Rubio, V., & Pebesma, E. J. (2013). *Applied spatial data analysis with R.* Dordrecht, The Netherlands: Springer.

Borko, H. (1968). Information science: What is it? *Journal of the Association for Information Science and Technology, 19*(1), 3–5.

Cleveland, W. S. (2001). Data science: an action plan for expanding the technical areas of the field of statistics. *International Statistical Review, 69*(1), 21–26.

Cornwell, C., Mustard, D. B., & Sridhar, D. J. (2006). The enrollment effects of merit-based financial aid: Evidence from Georgia's HOPE program. *Journal of Labor Economics, 24*(4), 761–786.

Digest of Education Statistics. (2011). *Private elementary and secondary schools, enrollment, teachers, and high school graduates, by state: Selected years, 2001 through 2011 [Table 205.80].* U.S. Department of Education, Institute of Education Sciences, National Center for Education Statistics. Retrieved from http://nces.ed.gov/programs/digest/d13/tables/dt13_205.80.asp.

Digest of Education Statistics. (2012). *Public high school graduates, by state or jurisdiction: Selected years, 1980-81 through 2010-11 [Table 123].* U.S. Department of Education, Institute of Education Sciences, National Center for Education Statistics. Retrieved from http://nces.ed.gov/programs/digest/d12/tables/dt12_123.asp.

Dynarski, S. (2000). *Hope for whom? Financial aid for the middle class and its impact on college attendance* (Tech. Rep.). National Bureau of Economic Research. Retrieved from www.nber.org/papers/w7756.

Dynarski, S. (2008). Building the stock of college-educated labor. *Journal of Human Resources, 43*(3), 576–610.

ESRI. (1998). *Shapefile technical description, Jul. 1998.* Environmental Systems Research Institute [ESRI], Inc. Retrieved from www.esri.com/library/whitepapers/pdfs/shapefile.pdf.

Glenn, E. H. (2016). *Working with the American community survey in R: A guide to using the ACS package.* Dordrecht, The Netherlands: Springer.

González Canché, M. S. (2014). Localized competition in the non-resident student market. *Economics of Education Review, 43*, 21–35.

González Canché, M. S. (2017a). Community college scientists and salary gap: Navigating socioeconomic and academic stratification in the U.S. higher education system. *The Journal of Higher Education, 88*(1), 1–32. doi:10.1080/00221546.2016.124393.

González Canché, M. S. (2017b). Financial benefits of rapid student loan repayment: An analytic framework employing two decades of data. *The ANNALS of the American Academy of Political and Social Science, 671*(1), 154–182.

González Canché, M. S. (2017c). The heterogeneous non-resident student body: Measuring the effect of out-of-state students' home-state wealth on tuition and fee price variations. *Research in Higher Education, 58*(2), 141–183.

González Canché, M. S. (2018) Geographical network analysis and spatial econometrics as tools to enhance our understanding of student migration patterns and benefits in the U.S. higher education network. *The Review of Higher Education, 41*(2), 169–216. doi:10.1353/rhe.2018.0001.

Matthews, D. (2010). *A stronger nation through higher education.* Lumina Foundation. Retrieved from https://files.eric.ed.gov/fulltext/ED512538.pdf.

McMahon, W. W. (2009). *Higher learning, greater good: The private and social benefits of higher education.* Baltimore, MD: Johns Hopkins University Press.

Ruiz, R., Leigh, E., & González Canché, M. (2018). *Community college promise programs: A multi-site examination of program impacts on college access using a geographically-based difference-in-differences approach.* Research-Based Knowledge of College Promise Programs conference at the University of Pennsylvania. Retrieved from http://ahead-penn.org/content/improving-research-based-knowledge-college-promise-program.

Toutkoushian, R. K., & Hillman, N. W. (2012). The impact of state appropriations and grants on access to higher education and outmigration. *The Review of Higher Education*, *36*(1), 51–90.

U.S. Department of Education, Integrated Postsecondary Education Data System (IPEDS). (2012a). *IPEDS enrollments, residence and migration of first-time freshman: Fall 2010* [Survey data files EF2010C]. IPEDS Data Center. Retrieved from http://nces.ed.gov/ipeds/datacenter/data/EF2010C.zip.

U.S. Department of Education, Integrated Postsecondary Education Data System (IPEDS). (2012b). *IPEDS institutional characteristics, directory information* [Survey data files, HD2010]. IPEDS Data Center. Retrieved from http://nces.ed.gov/ipeds/datacenter/data/HD2010.zip.

U.S. Department of Education, Integrated Postsecondary Education Data System (IPEDS). (2012c). *Race/ethnicity, gender, attendance status, and level of student: Fall 2010* [Survey data files, EF2010A]. IPEDS Data Center. Retrieved from http://nces.ed.gov/ipeds/datacenter/data/EF2010A.zip.

U.S. Department of Education, Integrated Postsecondary Education Data System (IPEDS). (2012d). *Student financial aid and net price: 2010–11* [Survey data files, SFA1011]. IPEDS Data Center. Retrieved from http://nces.ed.gov/ipeds/datacenter/data/SFA1011.zip.

Webber, K. L., & González Canché, M. S. (2015). Not equal for all: Gender and race differences in salary for doctoral degree recipients. *Research in Higher Education*, *56*(7), 645–672.

Wickham, H., & Grolemund, G. (2016). *R for data science: Import, tidy, transform, visualize, and model data*. Newton, MA: O'Reilly Media, Inc. Retrieved from http://r4ds.had.co.nz/introduction.html.

Zhang, L., Hu, S., & Sensenig, V. (2013). The effect of Florida's Bright Futures program on college enrollment and degree production: An aggregated-level analysis. *Research in Higher Education*, *54*(7), 746–764.

Zhang, L., & Ness, E. (2010). Does state merit-based aid stem brain drain? *Educational Evaluation and Policy Analysis*, *32*(2), 143–165.

4

SEXUAL VIOLENCE ON COLLEGE CAMPUSES

SUSAN MARINE

Despite more than 30 years of sustained advocacy and prevention efforts by students, faculty, and student affairs administrators, the scourge of sexual violence on college campuses continues (Harris & Linder, 2017). The prevalence of sexual violence has not diminished during these decades of efforts to oppose it; current research suggests that more than one in four of all cisgender college women, roughly the same number of trans* and non-binary students, and one in nine college men will experience attempted or completed sexual assault during their years enrolled in college (Cantor, Fisher, Chibnall, & Townsend, 2015; Fisher, Cullen, & Turner, 2000; Koss, Gidycz, & Wisniewski, 1987). The commonplace occurrence of sexual violence should not inure us to its terrible impact. Indeed, because the effects reverberate across the lives of survivors as well as their friends and partners, all students' ability to flourish in college is threatened by the specter of the experience of rape. The harms caused to college communities by sexual violence thus are, or should be, of grave concern of all educators—faculty and student affairs professionals alike.

In this chapter, I will explore the early history of collective awareness about campus sexual violence, the causes and conditions that underlie its occurrence, and highlight the features of both the federal government's and various institutional responses to it. I will discuss the ongoing picture that is forming about how it can best be prevented, and will center the voices and experiences of survivors in understanding the significant impact sexual violence has on student lives and futures. Through unpacking these various facets of one of higher education's most sinister problems, I expressly intend to enlist all who hold leadership roles in higher education to better understand this complex problem, and to commit to its eradication.

SEXUAL VIOLENCE ON CAMPUS: AN OVERVIEW

Sexual violence—defined as any sexual act committed against someone without that person's freely given consent (Centers for Disease Control, 2014)—is alarmingly common among U.S. college students. Sexual violence on college campuses appears to be typified by several factors: The perpetrator is often known to the victim, and the abuse often takes place in the context of a date or other social gathering (Abbey, 1991; Wolitzky-Taylor et al., 2011); alcohol was used to either lower inhibitions (leading to heightened risk) or as a facilitative agent by perpetrators, or both (Gross, Winslett, Roberts, & Gohm, 2006; Lawyer, Resnick, Bakanic, Burkett, & Kilpatrick, 2010); and owing to these factors and others, survivors often do not recognize they have been assaulted or are likely to downplay the seriousness of the event (Hockett, Saucier, & Badke, 2016).

Until recently, the vast majority of studies of incidence and prevalence of campus sexual violence explicitly focused on the experiences of white, cisgender (typically, heterosexual) women and, to a far lesser extent, cisgender men. This is deeply problematic, given that studies indicate that between 14 and 58 percent of trans* and genderqueer individuals have experienced some kind of forced sexual contact, ranging from sexual touch to rape, in the course of their adult lives (Lombardi, Wilchins, Priesing, & Malouf, 2001; Marine, 2017). Additionally, static notions about who is typically victimized—with survivors routinely portrayed as white, cisgender, heterosexual women—are consistently foregrounded in both media depictions and research about sexual violence. To expand these narratives and images, critical scholars have recently explored the complex nexus of social identities (such as one's race, class, gender, and sexuality) as they influence experiences with sexual violence, demanding greater attention to be paid to intersectional frames and the power/privilege implications of identity on survivors' lives and agency (Harris & Linder, 2017). Despite the foreboding nature of this topic, hope lies ahead: For as long as there have been students (and faculty and staff) sexually violating others on college campuses, there has been resistance in the form of a slow-growing but deeply committed movement to hasten its end.

CAMPUS SEXUAL VIOLENCE: A MOVEMENT'S BEGINNING

The advent of the campus sexual violence prevention and response movement came 20 years after the community rape crisis movement began in the early 1970s (Collins & Whalen, 1989). The roots of these movements are largely attributed to the consciousness-raising activities so common in that era: Women were coming together in small groups and sharing stories of sexual harassment, assault, stalking, and interpersonal violence, and were astonished to find these incidents were far more common than they thought (Rose, 1977). The principles unifying activists in the early sexual violence movement centered on advancing women's bodily safety and autonomy in a sexist culture, and recognition of sexual violence as a universally applied means of subordinating women (Brownmiller, 1975; Wasserman, 1973).

In the late 1980s, awareness and visibility of campus rape suddenly spiked as a result of Mary Koss and colleagues' nationwide, large-sample study documenting the fact that 26 percent of college women endured unwanted sexual contact (Koss, Gidycz, & Wisniewski, 1987). Prior to this study, the frequency of sexual violence was not well understood, but the data were undeniable: Campus rape was an everyday occurrence for far more students than previously thought. Survivors like Katie Koestner, who were willing to publicly disclose their experiences in the media, also heightened visibility of the issue (Gibbs & Monroe, 1991). The Violence Against Women Act (VAWA) of 1990, introduced into law by Senator Joe Biden of Delaware and signed into law in 1994, initially focused on increased lighting and surveillance in public areas, funding for law enforcement and for battered women's shelters, and the establishment of a policy task force at the federal level to examine trends in gender-based violence prevalence and incidence (Lopez, 1990). Title IV of this act specifically "authorize[d] the Secretary of Education to make, on a competitive basis, grants to and contracts with institutions of higher education for rape education and prevention programs" (United States Congress, n.d.). Later iterations of the bill allocated additional funding to conduct a nationwide baseline study on the prevalence of campus sexual violence, to identify and combat dating violence on campus, to formalize standards for the adjudication of sexual violence on college campuses, and to address campus sexual violence in specific populations, including LGBTQ communities (Seghetti & Bjelopera, 2012).

With each successive reauthorization, VAWA demonstrated that sexual violence on campus was becoming a priority for the government to address. The federal government's recent attention on holding colleges accountable for compliance with Title IX mandates has renewed interest in this problem and its varied yet inchoate solutions (Marine & Nicolazzo, 2017; McCaskill, 2014). In response to the interest of the federal government, over the course of the last three decades, many colleges have developed mechanisms to respond systematically to the occurrence of sexual violence, including revised policies and protocols, sexual violence response teams, and hiring therapists who specialize in crisis response (Fisher, Daigle, & Cullen, 2009; Karjane, Fisher, & Cullen, 2005). Additionally, colleges built programs to foster awareness about sexual violence among students, and to teach them about strategies they could enact to reduce the occurrence of rape. Although these programs raised awareness of sexual violence then, and remain focused on this today, we now understand that prevention of rape can only be enacted by perpetrators, while those who are victimized (and their allies) can only enact behaviors properly understood to reduce risk (Lonsway et al., 2011).

Even as these improvements took place, campuses were rife with reports of mishandling of reported incidents. Both survivors and assailants began suing their colleges for malfeasance, citing negligence in the process due to biased or underprepared adjudicative boards, an inconsistently applied standard of evidence, or unclear procedures for appeal of decisions (Bernstein, 1996; Perez-Peña, 1994). Thus, even as rape on campus became more visible, and responses from the federal government more robust, a student's experience with reporting sexual violence problematically depended on the resources which each individual college or university committed to the problem.

And yet, a movement was afoot to ensure greater consistency and accountability across institutions. Leadership from the Obama administration led to the release of the Dear Colleague letter in 2011 (Ali, 2011), placing campuses on notice that they had a legal obligation under Title IX to respond effectively, swiftly, and transparently to reports of sexual violence. By explicitly linking the issue to Title IX enforcement, the federal government effectively established sexual violence as a matter of gender equity and civil rights. By enacting federal law to respond to the civil rights violation inherent in a student's inability to pursue an education free from the threat of violence, the U.S. Department of Education declared sexual violence a clear form of gender-based discrimination. Shifting the discourse from sexual violence as an isolated criminal act with implications primarily for the survivor, to conceiving of it as a violation of a student's civil rights, meant that U.S. colleges and universities were now required to examine (and address) their policies, practices, and procedures (Henry & Powell, 2014). At issue was the need to more rigorously analyze and counter the social and cultural factors that contribute to widespread and pervasive gender discrimination, what Roberta Hall and Bernice Sandler (1982) termed "a chilly climate" on campus some 30 years earlier. The presence of IFC (historically white, interfraternity conference) fraternities and high-profile athletics programs provide damning evidence of rape culture on college campuses, with their heavy emphasis on hegemonic and competitive masculinities, the ritualized overconsumption of alcohol, the subsequent erasure of women's agency, and higher rates of sexual violence perpetration (Martin, 2016). Careful study of the problem was beginning to point to a much larger array of interconnected factors contributing to the occurrence of sexual violence on the college campus, now being termed rape culture.

DEFINING RAPE CULTURE

The term *rape culture* has been recently taken up by scholars and activists alike to name the social forces, patriarchal structures, and media-inscribed norms of violence and domination at work in the average campus's Saturday night party scene (Buchwald, Fletcher, & Roth, 2005; Henry & Powell, 2014). However, rape culture is not a new idea: Its contours deeply resonate with early rape crisis activists' appraisal of the factors driving the occurrence of sexual violence in society at large. Yet, despite decades of cultural critique by scholars, campus rape prevention educators, and students showing that addressing rape culture is the key to getting at the roots of ending sexual violence on college campuses, most colleges' approach to ending sexual violence is largely grounded in legal approaches and compliance with Title IX mandates. Scholars have noted that the compliance culture unwittingly ushered in by the 2011 Dear Colleague letter (Ali, 2011) and its mandates has unfortunately displaced concerns about student agency and safety, distracted from the larger task of culture change, and undermined approaches to responding to sexual violence as a coordinated community effort (Marine & Nicolazzo, 2017). On the positive side, students experiencing sexual violence, previously often suffering in silence, were now more visible and vocal as a result of the heightened awareness of Title IX protections, and thus suddenly a force to be reckoned with.

Arguably, compliance pressure increased the possibility, if not the actuality, of institutions holding the perpetrator accountable for a survivor's violation. It has ensured that many who have worked diligently to advance safety on their campuses can see progress. Yet, in order to interrupt the limited and one-dimensional framing of sexual violence advanced by compliance culture and mandates, it is essential to return to the root question: What are the causes of sexual violence on the college campus, and what can be done to reverse them?

SEXUAL VIOLENCE ON CAMPUS: CAUSES AND CONDITIONS

Rape culture is indeed a helpful construct to refer broadly to the set of sociocultural factors which underlie the occurrence of sexual violence on campus. But what are these factors, and how do they create a backdrop whereby perpetration is not only common, but tolerated? Researchers continue to grapple with the specific behavioral and social correlates of rape, but a few factors are consistently revealed in the research literature as correlated with its prevalence. These include the sanctioning of hegemonic masculinities, particularly among all-male social and athletic groups (Kimmel, 2008; Schwartz & DeKeseredy, 1997), the prevalence of alcohol use and abuse on college campuses (Sønderlund et al., 2014), the media's role in both supporting men's violence against women and promulgating indifference to rape (Grubb & Turner, 2012; Jhally, 2002), and the persistent disbelief and silencing of survivors (Jordan, 2011). Taken together, these factors create a perfect storm of thinking and acting in the campus context that makes the occurrence of sexual violence more likely, and responses to it often muted. While each of these factors taken alone play a role, college campuses appear to provide a ripe incubator for their full and concomitant flourishing.

Hegemony is a term popularized by Antonio Gramsci in the 1970s, referring to a system of dominance in which particular forms of behavior, values, or actions are considered more acceptable by the group in power within a society, and thus enforced and regulated. Hegemonic masculinity is the set of behaviors, norms, and actions associated with the idea that men's power and male dominance is the preferred social arrangement; men are thus entitled to take power in any way they see fit, including through force (Connell, 2005). Hegemonic masculinity is embodied on college campuses through the ascription of social power to men's groups, particularly fraternities and athletic teams, through the expectation that men can and should be sexually active (and aggressively so), and that by being sexually aggressive they can defensibly reassert their dominance (Kimmel & Davis, 2011). While colleges may disavow these realities, men's hegemonic (mis)behavior on college campuses is tacitly sanctioned, leading to social environments where sexual violence can flourish unchecked (Harper & Harris, 2010).

The difficulty in naming and reducing these behaviors lies in their almost universal conflation with the "campus party scene," and the ubiquity of alcohol use and abuse on college campuses. While sexual violence researchers and advocates regularly reaffirm that alcohol does not cause rape, it is unquestionably implicated in its prevalence on campus (Cantor et al., 2015; Fisher et al., 2000). The great majority of reported incidents of campus sexual violence involve incapacitation on the part of the victim, and intoxication or drug use on the part of the perpetrator, a fact that has remained unchanged despite significant campus efforts to reduce excessive drug and alcohol use (Abbey, 1991, 2002, 2011). Research suggests that alcohol plays a significant role for women, who may use it to reduce anxiety in social settings, as well as to disinhibit sexual exploration. Perpetrators view women who use alcohol as asking for or inviting sex, a phenomenon known as alcohol expectancy (Benson, Gohm, & Gross, 2007). They then may intentionally provide alcohol to a potential victim in order to facilitate rape, setting the stage not only for the encounter but for the likelihood of impaired memories following it. Alcohol and drugs thus influence the facilitation of rape through violence and coercion, while perpetrators use them as a scapegoat to explain away their aggression or to deny that sexual contact was non-consensual (Abbey, McAuslan, & Ross, 1998).

While abuse of alcohol is not universally implicated in the occurrence of campus sexual violence, its prevalence (coupled with the ubiquity of male-dominated social scenes) on most campuses reflects the predominant belief that partying in college is not only normative but a desirable and universally fun way to celebrate one's emerging adult independence (Ridburg, 2004). Images of the "typical" campus party scene promoted in alcohol advertising, popular films, music videos, and in other media suggest that getting bombed and hooking up are expected behaviors for undergraduates, particularly white, heterosexual students (Weiss, 2013). Sexual intimacy in young adulthood is synonymously associated with using alcohol or other drugs to lessen anxiety and release inhibitions, and many popular media images sidestep the complexity of gaining or giving consent in these situations (McNair, 2002). In both mainstream advertising and pornography alike, heterosexual men are portrayed as powerful to the extent that they are able to complete a sexual conquest; heterosexual women, powerful to the extent that they successfully resist men's advances yet secretly wish to fulfill them (Jhally, 2002). Lesbian, gay, bisexual, queer, and trans* identified individuals are invisible in commonly portrayed sexual scripts, or are parodied as both deviant and sexually insatiable (Peele, 2007).

And while such images belie the deep and varied complexity of the many ways that humans meet, interact, and connect through intimacy while in college, a phone camera snapshot or a brief seven-second video captured in a moment of vulnerability serves to obscure these complexities. The accessibility of social media sites like Snapchat and Instagram are used as evidence of a person's culpability (or innocence) in the court of public opinion that follows (Salter, 2013). Thus, both the mass media and an individual's social media circles often promote toxic messages regarding agency, sexual permissiveness, and boundary-crossing with significant traumatic effects (Rentschler, 2014).

Finally, rape culture's foundation is continually fortified through the ongoing and persistent disbelief expressed by many regarding the veracity of stories told by survivors. The public and private shaming many campus rape survivors experience serves as a detriment to coming forward and seeking justice; indeed, research suggests that fewer than 10 percent of sexual violence incidents are ever reported to any authority, and even fewer are brought to adjudication (Cantor et al., 2015). The experiences of survivors who come forward and tell their stories to campus officials, only to have their stories dismissed or minimized, is characterized as institutional betrayal, leading many survivors to detach from their campus communities, often never to return (Paul et al., 2013; Smith & Freyd, 2013). The isolation experienced by those who have survived sexual violence is thus compounded by a sense of abandonment from those charged with guiding, supporting, and protecting every student—including and especially faculty and student affairs educators.

SURVIVORS SPEAK: THE AFTERMATH OF SEXUAL VIOLENCE

Survivors of sexual violence experience a range of after-effects that impede their ability to connect with peers, to engage in college life, and to pursue academic work effectively. This often includes depression, anxiety, an inability to concentrate or focus, sleeplessness or intense fatigue, and a persistent sense of fear for one's safety known as hypervigilance. These after-effects comprise an array of symptoms often referred to as PTSD, or post-traumatic stress disorder (Arata & Burkhart, 1996). As described previously, the social pressures against speaking up about and reporting sexual violence are intense, and survivors are often silenced and socially punished for coming forward (Belknap, 2010). Survivors of campus sexual violence speak of turning their suffering inward, seeking solace through maladaptive coping mechanisms like alcohol use/abuse, food restriction, and self-harm (Clark & Pino, 2016). For others, the fury of the violation experienced can and does drive survivors to act affirmatively for their own healing. And while no two narratives of this aftermath are ever the same, attention to the voices of those who have come forward is essential and instructive for understanding the life-changing impact of sexual violence.

Survivors often speak of the ways their worlds are reduced after the experience, as intense fear of encountering the perpetrator shapes decisions about where to go and with whom. Iman Stenson, a survivor of sexual violence featured in the 2016 documentary *The Hunting Ground*, described that she felt "the campus getting smaller and smaller, as there were many places I didn't feel comfortable going" (Ziering & Dick, 2015). The larger sociocultural issues that promote tolerance for sexual violence often hang heavily over a survivor's life, shaping their sense of the futility of speaking up. Trey Malone was a campus rape survivor who took his own life after penning a suicide note in which he blamed:

> …a society that remains unwilling to address sexual assault and rape. One that pays some object form of lip service to the idea of sexual crimes while working its hardest to marginalize its victims. One where the first question a college president can pose to me, regarding my own assault is, 'Have you handled your drinking problem?' … Please listen to what I said about sexual assault … There are millions more just like me that need help and no, someone who is drunk cannot give consent. (McGuiness, 2012)

Campus sexual violence survivors frequently experience blame for what happened to them, borne of a misplaced belief that claiming an experience with violence somehow provides cultural capital. Wagatwe Wanjuki, a survivor of sexual violence and activist who was expelled from Tufts University after speaking out about her rape, described her experience with the consistent mistrust she faced as follows:

> There is no privilege to being a survivor; there is nothing to gain from being raped. The opposite is true: survivors have a lot to lose, including their privacy — in addition to the economic, emotional and psychological costs of the trauma they endured. Yet the assumption that people lie about being victimized prevails. (Wanjuki, 2014)

Surviving a sexual assault while in college can surface anxieties about one's other identities and the impact of the assault in solidifying them, as described by Micah, a queer transmasculine man. He lamented, "I would say there was a lot of shame in, with the statistics of, especially around trans* folks who are survivors, grappling with being one of those numbers" (Tillapaugh, 2017, p. 108). Becoming a number just as one is coming into one's own around an authentically reclaimed gender can set the process of self-acceptance back, as trans* survivors struggle to discern the trauma from the challenges of functioning healthfully in a deeply transphobic society.

These stories show the wide array of obstacles and barriers faced by sexual assault survivors as they attempt to regain a sense of safety and agency following a traumatizing event while in college. This trauma is compounded by the ways that survivors are responded to, the narratives others associate with their violation, and the ways that others' reactions can negate the most fundamental sense of one's worth in the world. Nowhere has this been more poignantly expressed than in the words of the woman raped by Stanford student Brock Turner. The utter devastation she experienced—and her resolve in naming it—is captured graphically in the words she directed to her rapist at his sentencing hearing:

> I collapsed at the same time you did. If you think I was spared, came out unscathed, that today I ride off into sunset, while you suffer the greatest blow, you are mistaken. Nobody wins. We have all been devastated, we have all been trying to find some meaning in all of this suffering. Your damage was concrete; stripped of titles, degrees, enrollment. My damage was internal, unseen, I carry it with me. You took away my worth, my privacy, my energy, my time, my safety, my intimacy, my confidence, my own voice, until today. (Baker, 2016)

PREVENTING RAPE: A MOVEMENT EVOLVES

It is evident, then, that the impact of sexual violence on students and college communities is enormous, and costs us much in terms of lost potential, lost energy, and lost faith. It stands to reason that the most important priority for leaders within an institution, and across postsecondary education, is to identify and engage with meaningful, effective strategies for prevention, and to doggedly pursue refining them through practice and research.

For most colleges, prevention of sexual violence is typified by several common practices, each of which contributes to, but does not ensure, prevention. The first is awareness-raising. Virtually all colleges engage their students, particularly their new first-year students, in annual, brief education about their sexual violence (often called sexual misconduct) policy, and the resources on campus for those who experience it (Karjane et al., 2005). Some institutions expand this awareness-raising activity by including discussion of the role that alcohol plays in sexual violence, as well as dispelling rape myths such as "women who say no really mean yes" and "sex is a legitimate form of repayment for taking someone out to dinner." Other colleges provide students with a peer-led theatrical performance or simulated scenario to help develop better understanding of the issues involved in campus sexual violence, as well as to develop greater empathy with survivors (McMahon, Postmus, Warrener, & Koenick, 2014).

Colleges and universities often couple this awareness-raising with an emphasis on actions students can take to interrupt or intervene in sexually violent or coercive situations with peers, a contemporary strategy known as bystander inter-vention (Banyard, Moynihan, & Plante, 2007). Bystander approaches, which focus on deploying students for social change within the typical campus party scene and its hazards, engage students in learning ways they can intervene by distracting a poten-tial perpetrator from his[1] goal, including verbally separating him from the potential victim, checking in with her to determine her willingness to be intervened with, and in some cases physically blocking or deflecting his access to her. Students learning bystander techniques generally practice them in the sterile environment of a campus lecture hall or auditorium, with peers who are unimpaired by alcohol. It is difficult to simulate the actual context of most campus rapes in this kind of training session. Importantly, rates of incidence of sexual violence likely will spike after a college commits to spreading bystander messages among all its students, as more students come forward due to the more supportive, aware context. Students may misre-port their experience as bystanders, and the preventative effects of doing so. Thus, the overall effectiveness of bystander approaches is an ongoing question (Banyard, Moynihan, Cares, & Warner, 2014).

Colleges also heavily rely on having widely published, comprehensive policies for the adjudication of sexual violence as a preventative tool. The tacit reasoning in this approach is that if sexual violence happens and is reported, having a meaningful, well-designed policy in response will ensure that perpetrators are identified and held accountable (Streng & Kamimura, 2015). While carefully constructed policies—which focus on due process and thoughtful review of evidence to determine culpability—can increase the likelihood that students are well served by the adjudication process, the fact that so few come forward in the first place almost ensures that policies will remain a benign substitute for true prevention. Because fewer than 10 percent of students will ever bring their complaint of sexual violence to a campus official for redress (Harris & Linder, 2017), such policies can only ever play a very small role in ending sexual violence on campus.

In order to truly enact preventative strategies that work, campuses can and must refocus their energy on reaching actual and potential perpetrators, engaging in the complex act of re-education to end the beliefs and behaviors that cause the problem (Berkowitz, 1994). While this belief has had longstanding currency in postsecondary education, its actualization—through policy, practice, and change strategy—has been elusive. Several factors contribute to this challenge. First, identifying who perpetrators are is an inexact science, since most of what we know about campus rape perpetrators is based on research conducted with serial offenders who are incarcerated (Fisher et al., 2009). Research on campus rape perpetrators, while promising in its early iterations, has been stalled and thus inconclusive regarding their motives and psychological profiles. Lisak and Miller's (2002) study on college men who admit to committing sexual violence but remain at large suggested that perpetrators act repeatedly, inten-tionally identifying and isolating victims in alcohol-infused social settings, and doing so with impunity. Subsequent research revealed that multiple perpetration did not characterize the behaviors of those (approximately 11 percent in a large sample) who admit committing sexual violence (Swartout et al., 2015); because rape perpetrators are more likely to commit rape only once, these researchers urged educators to initiate prevention approaches to reach these offenders before they arrive at college. However, this study also declined to identify the specific qualities inherent in identifying the 11 percent most in need of active intervention.

While research is informative for understanding these patterns and their meaning, some have disputed the idea that a small minority of men are solely responsible for committing rape on college campuses. Instead, they argue that most or all men are implicated in supporting (actively or implicitly) the culture that fosters sexual violence, with some men holding more responsibility for intervening due to their positionalities of power in society (Walton & Beaudrow, 2016). In current prevention conversations, talking about the roles of those who do not identify as men in prevention typically devolves into debates about whether women's behaviors are fair game for intervention, which is generally viewed as victim blaming by advocates and activists (Abbey, 2011). Research about the identities, behaviors, and proclivities of those who commit sexual violence against lesbian, gay, bisexual, queer, and trans* and non-binary students is completely absent from the literature, and thus our work to continue understanding prevention across student identities and communities is currently limited (Marine, 2017).

In place of a singular focus on identifying and reaching potential or actual perpetrators with prevention messages, other researchers have advocated for a more multi-tiered approach to creating rape-free campus cultures. The social justice paradigm of sexual violence prevention (Hong, 2017; Hong & Marine, 2018) reconceptualizes the role of campus leaders and students in ending sexual violence by focusing on naming and shifting the complex interplay of power and agency that undergirds all rape-supportive cultures. The primary contribution the model makes is to challenge the notion that sexual violence happens in a vacuum, equally impacting all and equally fomented by all. Instead, it centers prevention work in power consciousness—the ways that those with dominant social identities along lines of position, race, class, gender, and sexuality—have a disproportionate influence in norm-setting on college campuses, and thus in interrupting rape culture. In order to shift a campus culture toward healthier norms, all actors—students, faculty, administrators—must commit to actively shifting this power balance by refusing participation in compliance culture, and instead working toward more complex but more rewarding solutions. These solutions involve naming and changing both individual actions and systemic factors that contribute to rape culture. Ideas about to whom sexual violence happens, and what it looks and sounds like in survivor narratives, are complexified in order to avoid the temptation to conceive of violence as being represented by a single story (Adichie, 2009). Instead of training a select number of student leaders with broad and deep information about the causes and conditions underlying sexual violence, all students are perceived of as health opinion leaders, and provided with effective tools to influence change in their communities.

Leadership on the issue of anti-violence cultural transformation, typically deployed by one individual or office, is now spread across an institution's leadership, infusing every aspect of both the academic and co-curricular domains. Evidence of strong practices for changing culture are found both within and outside of the institutional context, and draw upon the wisdom and experience of community-based activities and grassroots movements. And the work of prevention and response is shared by many, and championed by many. Hong's (2017) model thus provides a power-conscious, multi-layered, transformational (as opposed to transactional) way of thinking about sexual violence on college campuses. It is a bold and fully engaging way to envision what it will take to create social change around ending sexual violence. It will, Hong (2017) suggested, require "care, competence, and moral courage" to build and implement (p. 32). But given the limited success we have had to date enacting traditional paradigms of prevention and change and actually reducing the incidence of sexual violence on college campuses, the benefits of doing so are potentially enormous. As Hong (2017) instructed:

> Moral courage exists at the intersection of three things: First, we as individuals and institutions must have a clear core or guiding principle to aspire to; second, some element of danger, threat, or risk to ourselves or those we care about is either implied or associated with implementing this principle. These two elements combined with the third – endurance, resilience, and tenacity to sustain our principled action through the risk, constitute moral courage. (p. 38)

CONCLUSION: HEALING AND CHANGE AS THE NEXT FRONTIER

Sexual violence on college campuses has been thus established as a persistent problem, with roots in both individual action and a larger social scaffolding that upholds domination in both direct and indirect ways. For the better part of three decades, college officials, researchers, and policy makers have grappled with the realities of sexual violence, without making significant headway in advancing its demise. Because institutions of higher education are considered to be one of the crown jewels of American democracy (Thelin, 2011), conferring social mobility through advancements in science and society, and a better life for hundreds of millions of people, it is a profoundly shameful reality that a preventable violent crime overshadows quotidian life on our campuses.

This chapter has provided an overview of the prevalence and incidence of sexual violence on the contemporary college campus, and has outlined the factors that contribute to its ongoing occurrence. The movement to end sexual violence, richly intertwined with the histories of grassroots activists and advocates, has gained new momentum through the recent emergence of campus survivor activist groups such as Know Your IX (2017) and SurvJustice (2017). The role of the federal government has also hastened significant awareness-raising and change, particularly through the implementation of the widespread systemic improvements detailed in the 2011 Dear Colleague Letter. While these changes promised significant advancements in the ways colleges respond to student survivors and their needs, an uncertain future lies ahead. The Trump administration's priorities, reflected in recent actions taken by Secretary of Education Betsy DeVos, include rolling back these advancements, calling instead for public comment and a potential revision of federal policy that colleges will be expected to enact. Early signs suggest these changes will tip the scales of justice in favor of the accused (Svrluga & Anderson, 2017), causing a fairly seismic shift in current policy and practice. Such shifts should serve to remind educators that creating cultural change around sexual violence is something each one of us is called to do, and that waiting for a federal solution to a deeply community-embedded problem is not the answer. As survivor activist Wagatwe Wanjuki (2017) opined, "Once administrators stop addressing sexual violence as yet another item on a checklist for compliance and start approaching sexual violence with a genuine desire to do the right thing, we will be able to take unprecedented strides in addressing sexual violence" (p. ix).

Instead, we are urged to stay informed, to focus on prevention practices grounded in evidence, and to keep our vision intently focused on the truth that through commitment to sustained, principled systemic change—coupled with a strong dose of moral courage—we will make progress in ending rape.

QUESTIONS FOR DISCUSSION

1. Given that there are a number of complex factors implicated in ending campus rape, where should faculty and student affairs educators focus change efforts?
2. How can the experiences and perspectives of survivors be centered in change work?
3. Given that trans* and non-binary students experience sexual violence at the same or greater rates than cisgender women, what can educators do to address this reality?
4. Does Title IX have utility in ending campus rape? How can the law best be leveraged to this end?
5. What are the strengths and challenges associated with the social justice paradigm?

NOTE

1 While bystander intervention programs acknowledge that sexual assault can happen among students of different genders, most campus sexual violence teaching tools and approaches generally over-rely on the "traditional scenario" of cis male perpetrator and cis female survivor (Marine & Nicolazzo, 2017).

REFERENCES

Abbey, A. (1991). Acquaintance rape and alcohol consumption on college campuses: How are they linked? *Journal of American College Health, 39*, 165–169.

Abbey, A. (2002). Alcohol-related sexual assault: A common problem among college students. *Journal of Studies on Alcohol, 14*, 118–128.

Abbey, A. (2011). Alcohol and dating risk factors for sexual assault: Double standards are still alive and well entrenched. *Psychology of Women Quarterly, 35*, 362–388.

Abbey, A., McAuslan, P., & Ross, L. T. (1998). Sexual assault perpetration by college men: The role of alcohol, misperception of sexual intent, and sexual beliefs and experiences. *Journal of Social and Clinical Psychology, 17*(2), 167–195.

Adichie, C. N. (2009). Chimamanda Ngozi Adichie: The danger of a single story [Video file]. Retrieved from www.ted.com/talks/chimamanda_adichie_the_danger_of_a_single_story?language=en.

Ali, R. (2011). *Dear colleague letter: Sexual violence* (April 4, 2011). Washington, DC: United States Department of Education. Retrieved from www2.ed.gov/about/offices/list/ocr/letters/colleague-201104.pdf.

Arata, C. M., & Burkhart, B. R. (1996). Post-traumatic stress disorder among college student victims of acquaintance assault. *Journal of Psychology & Human Sexuality, 8*(1–2), 79–92.

Baker, K. J. M. (2016, June 3). Here is the powerful letter the Stanford victim read aloud to her attacker. *BuzzFeed*. Retrieved from www.buzzfeed.com/katiejmbaker/heres-the-powerful-letter-the-stanford-victim-read-to-her-ra.

Banyard, V. L., Moynihan, M. M., & Plante, E. G. (2007). Sexual violence prevention through bystander education: An experimental evaluation. *Journal of Community Psychology, 35*(4), 463–481.

Banyard, V. L., Moynihan, M. M., Cares, A. C., & Warner, R. (2014). How do we know if it works? Measuring outcomes in bystander-focused abuse prevention on campuses. *Psychology of Violence, 4*(1), 101–115.

Belknap, J. (2010). Rape: Too hard to report and too easy to discredit victims. *Violence Against Women, 16*(12), 1335–1344.

Benson, B. J., Gohm, C. L., & Gross, A. M. (2007). College women and sexual assault: The role of sex-related alcohol expectancies. *Journal of Family Violence, 22*(6), 341–351.

Berkowitz, A. D. (1994). A model acquaintance rape prevention program for men. *New Directions for Student Services, 1994*(65), 35–42.

Bernstein, N. (1996, February 11). Civil rights lawsuit in rape case challenges integrity of a campus. *The New York Times*. Retrieved from www.nytimes.com/1996/02/11/us/civil-rights-lawsuit-in-rape-case-challenges-integrity-of-a-campus.html?pagewanted=all.

Brownmiller, S. (1975). *Men, women, and rape*. New York, NY: Simon & Schuster.

Buchwald, E., Fletcher, P., & Roth, M. (2005). *Transforming a rape culture* (revised ed.). Minneapolis, MN: Milkweed.

Cantor, D., Fisher, W. B., Chibnall, S., & Townsend, R. (2015). *Report on the AAU Campus Climate Survey on sexual assault and sexual misconduct*. Washington, DC: The Association of American Universities.

Centers for Disease Control and Prevention. (2014). *Preventing sexual violence on college campuses: Lessons from research and practice*. Retrieved from www.justice.gov/ovw/page/file/909811/download.

Clark, A. E., & Pino, A. L. (2016). *We believe you: Survivors of campus sexual assault speak out*. New York, NY: Holt Paperbacks.

Collins, B. G., & Whalen, M. B. (1989). The rape crisis movement: Radical or reformist? *Social Work, 34*(1), 61–63.

Connell, R. W. 2005. *Masculinities* (2nd ed.). Berkeley, CA: University of California Press.

Fisher, B. S., Cullen, F. T., & Turner, M. G. (2000). *The sexual victimization of college women*. U.S. Department of Justice, National Institutes of Justice and Bureau of Justice Statistics. NCJ 182369. Retrieved from www.ncjrs.org/pdffiles1/nij/182369.pdf.

Fisher, B. S., Daigle, L. E., & Cullen, F. T. (2009). *Unsafe in the ivory tower: The sexual victimization of college women*. Thousand Oaks, CA: Sage Publications.

Gibbs, N., & Monroe, S. (1991). When is it rape? *Time, 137*(22), 48–54.

Gross, A. M., Winslett, A., Roberts, M., & Gohm, C. L. (2006). An examination of sexual violence against college women. *Violence Against Women, 12*(3), 288–300.

Grubb, A., & Turner, E. (2012). Attribution of blame in rape cases: A review of the impact of rape myth acceptance, gender role conformity and substance use on victim blaming. *Aggression and Violent Behavior*, *17*(5), 443–452.

Hall, R. M., & Sandler, B. R. (1982). *The classroom climate: A chilly one for women?* Washington, DC: Association of American Colleges Project on the Status of Women.

Harper, S. R., & Harris III, F. (2010). *College men and masculinities: Theory, research, and implications for practice*. New York, NY: John Wiley & Sons.

Harris, J., & Linder, C. (2017). *Intersections of identity and sexual violence on campus: Centering minoritized students' experiences*. Sterling, VA: Stylus Publishing, LLC.

Henry, N., & Powell, A. (Eds.). (2014). *Preventing sexual violence: Interdisciplinary approaches to overcoming a rape culture*. New York, NY: Springer.

Hockett, J. M., Saucier, D. A., & Badke, C. (2016). Rape myths, rape scripts, and common rape experiences of college women: Differences in perceptions of women who have been raped. *Violence Against Women*, *22*(3), 307–323.

Hong, L. (2017). Digging up the roots, rustling the leaves. In J. C. Harris & C. Linder (Eds.), *Intersections of identity and sexual violence on the college campus: Centering minoritized students' experiences* (pp. 23–41). Sterling, VA: Stylus.

Hong, L., & Marine, S. (2018). Sexual violence through a social justice paradigm: Framing and applications. *New Directions for Student Services*, *161*, 21–33.

Jhally, S. (2002). Tough guise: Violence, media, and the crisis in masculinity [Video]. Amherst, MA: Media Education Foundation.

Jordan, J. (2011). Silencing rape, silencing women. In J. M. Brown & S. L. Walklate (Eds.), *Handbook on sexual violence* (pp. 253–286). London, UK: Routledge.

Karjane, H. M., Fisher, B., & Cullen, F. T. (2005). *Sexual assault on campus: What colleges and universities are doing about it*. Washington, DC: US Department of Justice, Office of Justice Programs, National Institute of Justice.

Kimmel, M. (2008). *Guyland: The perilous world where boys become men*. New York, NY: Harper Collins.

Kimmel, M. S., & Davis, T. (2011). Mapping guyland in college. In J. Laker & T. Davis (Eds.), *Masculinities in higher education: Theoretical and practical considerations* (pp. 3–15). New York, NY: Routledge.

Know Your IX (2017). *Know Your IX: Empowering students to stop sexual violence*. Retrieved from www.knowyourix.org/.

Koss, M. P., Gidycz, C. A., & Wisniewski, N. (1987). The scope of rape: Incidence and prevalence of sexual aggression and victimization in a national sample of higher education students. *Journal of Consulting and Clinical Psychology*, *55*(2), 162–170. doi:10.1037/0022-006X.55.2.162.

Lawyer, S., Resnick, H., Bakanic, V., Burkett, T., & Kilpatrick, D. (2010). Forcible, drug-facilitated, and incapacitated rape and sexual assault among undergraduate women. *Journal of American College Health*, *58*(5), 453–460.

Lisak, D., & Miller, P. M. (2002). Repeat rape and multiple offending among undetected rapists. *Violence and Victims*, *17*(1), 73–84.

Lombardi, E. L., Wilchins, R. A., Priesing, D., & Malouf, D. (2002). Gender violence: Transgender experiences with violence and discrimination. *Journal of Homosexuality*, *42*(1), 89–101.

Lonsway, K., Banyard, V. L., Berkowitz, A. D., Gidycz, C. A., Katz, J. T., Koss, M. P., Schewe, P. A., & Ullman, S. E. (2011). *Rape prevention and risk reduction: Review of the research literature for practitioners*. Retrieved from www.vawnet.org/applied-research-papers/print-document.php?doc_id=1655.

Lopez, R. (1990, 21 June). Women speak out on attacks. *The Chicago Tribune*. Retrieved from http://articles.chicagotribune.com/1990-06-21/news/9002200492_1_violence-against-women-act-violent-national-crime-rate.

Marine, S. B. (2017). For Brandon, for justice: Naming and ending sexual violence against trans* college students. In J. C. Harris & C. Linder (Eds.), *Intersections of identity and sexual violence on campus: Centering minoritized student's experiences* (pp. 83–101). Sterling, VA: Stylus.

Marine, S., & Nicolazzo, Z. (2017). Campus sexual violence prevention educators' use of gender in their work: A critical exploration. *Journal of Interpersonal Violence*. doi:10.1177/0886260517718543.

Martin, P. Y. (2016). The rape prone culture of academic contexts: Fraternities and athletics. *Gender & Society*, *30*(1), 30–43.

McCaskill, C. (2014). Sexual violence on campus. *Report, U.S. Senate Subcommittee on Financial and Contracting Oversight*. Washington, DC: United States Senate Archives.

McGuiness, W. (2012). Amherst College student's suicide note points blame at school administration for mishandling sexual assault. *The Huffington Post*. Retrieved from www.huffingtonpost.com/2012/11/08/amherst-college-student-suicide-note_n_2095386.html.

McMahon, S., Postmus, J. L., Warrener, C., & Koenick, R. A. (2014). Utilizing peer education theater for the primary prevention of sexual violence on college campuses. *Journal of College Student Development*, *55*(1), 78–85.

McNair, B. (2002). *Striptease culture: Sex, media and the democratization of desire*. New York, NY: Routledge.

Paul, L. A., Walsh, K., McCauley, J. L., Ruggiero, K. J., Resnick, H. S., & Kilpatrick, D. G. (2013). College women's experiences with rape disclosure: A national study. *Violence Against Women*, *19*(4), 486–502.

Peele, T. (2007). *Queer popular culture: Literature, media, film, and television*. London, UK: Springer.

Perez-Peña, R. (1994, June 1). Private colleges are criticized for their brand of justice. *The New York Times*. Retrieved from www.nytimes.com/1994/06/01/us/private-colleges-are-criticized-for-their-brand-of-justice.html?pagewanted=all.

Rentschler, C. A. (2014). Rape culture and the feminist politics of social media. *Girlhood Studies*, *7*(1), 65–82.

Ridburg, R. (2004). Spin the bottle: Sex, lies & alcohol featuring Jackson Katz & Jean Kilbourne [Documentary film]. Northhampton, MA: Media Education Foundation.

Rose, V. M. (1977). Rape as a social problem: A byproduct of the feminist movement. *Social Problems*, *25*(1), 75–89.

Salter, M. (2013). Justice and revenge in online counter-publics: Emerging responses to sexual violence in the age of social media. *Crime, Media, Culture*, *9*(3), 225–242.

Schwartz, M. D., & DeKeseredy, W. (1997). *Sexual assault on the college campus: The role of male peer support*. Thousand Oaks, CA: Sage Publications.

Seghetti, L. M., & Bjelopera, J. P. (2012). *The Violence Against Women Act: Overview, legislation, and federal funding*. Washington, DC: Congressional Research Service.

Smith, C. P., & Freyd, J. J. (2013). Dangerous safe havens: Institutional betrayal exacerbates sexual trauma. *Journal of Traumatic Stress*, *26*(1), 119–124.

Sønderlund, A. L., O'Brien, K., Kremer, P., Rowland, B., De Groot, F., Staiger, P., … Miller, P. G. (2014). The association between sports participation, alcohol use and aggression and violence: A systematic review. *Journal of Science and Medicine in Sport*, *17*(1), 2–7.

Streng, T. K., & Kamimura, A. (2015). Sexual assault prevention and reporting on college campuses in the US: A review of policies and recommendations. *Journal of Education and Practice*, *6*(3), 65–71.

SurvJustice (2017). Homepage. Retrieved from www.survjustice.org/.

Svrluga, S., & Anderson, N. (2017, September 7). DeVos decries 'failed system' on campus sexual assault, vows to replace it. *The Washington Post*. Retrieved from www.washingtonpost.com/news/grade-point/wp/2017/09/07/protesters-gather-anticipating-devos-speech-on-campus-sexual-assault/?utm_term=.3b178e35d7e8.

Swartout, K. M., Koss, M. P., White, J. W., Thompson, M. P., Abbey, A., & Bellis, A. L. (2015). Trajectory analysis of the campus serial rapist assumption. *JAMA Pediatrics*, *169*(12), 1148–1154.

Thelin, J. R. (2011). *A history of American higher education*. Baltimore, MD: Johns Hopkins Press.

Tillapaugh, D. (2017). "The wounds of our experience": College men who experienced sexual violence. In J. C. Harris & C. Linder (Eds.), *Intersections of identity and sexual violence on campus: Centering minoritized students' experiences* (pp. 101–118). Sterling, VA: Stylus.

United States Congress (n.d.). S.2754 Violence Against Women Act of 1990. Retrieved from www.congress.gov/bill/101st-congress/senate-bill/2754.

Walton, G., & Beaudrow, J. (2016). Tipping the Iceberg: Positionality and male privilege in addressing sexual violence against women. *Culture, Society and Masculinities*, *8*(2), 140–154.

Wanjuki, W. (2014). Believing victims is the first step to stopping rape. *The New York Times*. Retrieved from www.nytimes.com/roomfordebate/2014/12/12/justice-and-fairness-in-campus-rape-cases/believing-victims-is-the-first-step-to-stopping-rape.

Wanjuki, W. (2017). Foreword. In J. C. Harris & C. Linder (Eds.), *Intersections of identity and sexual violence on campus: Centering minoritized students' experiences* (pp. vii–xv). Sterling, VA: Stylus.

Wasserman, M. (1973, November). Rape: Breaking the silence. *The Progressive, 37,* 19–23.

Weiss, K. G. (2013). *Party school: Crime, campus, and community.* Boston, MA: Northeastern University Press.

Wolitzky-Taylor, K. B., Resnick, H. S., McCauley, J. L., Amstadter, A. B., Kilpatrick, D. G., & Ruggiero, K. J. (2011). Is reporting of rape on the rise? A comparison of women with reported versus unreported rape experiences in the National Women's Study-Replication. *Journal of Interpersonal Violence, 26*(4), 807–832.

Ziering, A. (Producer), & Dick, K. (Director). (2015). *The hunting ground* [Documentary]. Los Angeles, CA: Chain Camera Pictures.

5

THE NEW CREDENTIALING LANDSCAPE

JASON L. TAYLOR

In 2016, six well-known public universities established the University Learning Store, "a first-of-its-kind partnership of non-profit universities dedicated to delivering online, on-demand, skills-focused courses and credentials that meet the needs of 21st-century employees and employers" (University Learning Store, 2017a, para. 1). These university partners include institutions such as the University of Wisconsin, the University of California, Los Angeles, and the University of Washington, to name a few. The rationale for the establishment of the University Learning Store is evident from the website that indicates, "The world has changed. Gone are the days when a person could go to college for two or four years, graduate, and work for the same company until retirement" (University Learning Store, 2017b, para. 2). The website goes on to indicate that adults need ways to update their skills and that "they need clear, trusted ways to tell employers exactly what they know and are able to do" (2017b, para. 3).

The University Learning Store is indicative of a larger movement impacting higher education in the United States. This movement is characterized by a proliferation of new and innovative modes of learning, a cacophony of individuals and organizations poised to make a profit or get a competitive edge in the postsecondary landscape, and a fresh wave of credentials that are sold and purchased. All of this is, of course, within the context of a powerful national and state policy agenda focused on increasing college completion.

This chapter reviews the relatively new landscape of credentials that has emerged over the past several years. This burgeoning landscape of learning and credentials intersects with and impacts higher education in new ways. In some cases, colleges and universities have led the development of new credentials and modes of learning, and in other cases they are trying to find a seat at the table. The chapter begins with a summary of credentialing theory and the role that credentials play in education and society. The chapter then reviews the new landscape of credentials, describing what they are and how they work. This includes credentials such as certificates conferred through colleges and universities, massive open online courses, and badges and microcredentials. The chapter concludes with a discussion on the influence of this new credentials landscape on higher education.

CREDENTIALING

It is critical to situate this new credentials landscape within the literature on the role of credentials in American education and society. In his review of credentialing theory, Brown (2001) asserts that credentials have multiple meanings in society, including economic, cultural, and political. The economic meaning suggests that credentials reflect technical skills that translate to productivity in the workforce. That is, employers and recruiters seek candidates with credentials because credentials represent skills that are likely to result in a productive employee. Alternatively, the cultural and political meanings suggest that the relationship between credentials and economic productivity is weak, and that the primary purpose of credentials is exclusionary. That is, credentials are used as a mechanism to exclude individuals from higher social positions.

Brown and Bills (2011) note that there are many competing theories and metaphors used when describing the purpose and processes of credentialing. They argue that credentials are not monolithic and operate in different ways in different social contexts. Although credentials are closely aligned with the economy (Baker, 2011), Brown and Bills (2011) suggest that "credentials are explicit abstractions from substantive realities—they represent something else" (p. 136). Credentials provide a convenient way to assess and make a judgment about someone. They note that, "Credentials are sources of power for individual holders insofar as they effectively block substantive judgments about their actual abilities" (p. 135). Consider, for example, if you are at a social event and you are introduced to new acquaintances. Your new acquaintances ask about your educational and/or professional background, and you share that you have a graduate degree from Columbia University. This immediately provides your new acquaintance with information about you based on how society understands Columbia University and individuals with credentials from Columbia University.

Brown and Bills (2011) go on to describe the many organizational and social purposes of credentials such as:

> connoting the rationality of decision making, lowering the costs associated with painstaking examination of substantive qualifications by substituting standardized procedures, reducing the risks of failure in actual performances

by prefacing them with educational simulations that serve as practice, and providing codified information that can be readily communicated across disparate organizational spheres without exploring the substance of things. (p. 135)

These many purposes manifest in different ways and in different contexts, and as Baker and Bills argue, rather than seeking a dominant theory, it would be valuable to assess these different explanations and how they work collectively.

No doubt that these purposes manifest themselves in different aspects of society and life, but employment is arguably the dominant purpose for the new credentials landscape. In this context, Baker (2011) notes credential theory holds that "educational certification is a historical legitimatization of advantages that empower degree holders in occupational and organizational recruitment. Credential requirements for jobs are less concerned with concrete work skills than with demanding that recruits hold similar, school-taught cultural dispositions to incumbents of positions" (p. 20). Thus, what becomes valued is not actual competence or skills, but a credential that signals cultural and social affluence that is used for the purpose of excluding individuals from advantaged occupations.

Credentialing theory is relevant because new providers and credentials have entered the credentialing landscape. Advances in technology and the evolution of a more knowledge-based economy and society have democratized knowledge. Access to specialized knowledge and skills is no longer limited to ivory towers. Credentialing theory informs how we might make sense of this new credentialing landscape and how we might predict the outcomes of new credentials.

If we assume that credentialing theory is true—that is, that credentials are "more cultural and exclusionary than technical and efficacious" and "degree thresholds are more important in credentialed labor markets than are years of schooling or technical knowledge," then moving toward a more competency-based credentialism might be seen as a form of liberation. This assumes that credentials have historically not been based on a coherent set of competencies, but the move toward competencies would mean that recruiters not only have a signal of candidates' trustworthiness (i.e., a cultural or social marker), but they would have detailed information about their technical knowledge and skills that was previously unspecified.

THE NEW CREDENTIALS

Associate's degrees, bachelor's degrees, and graduate degrees have long been the currency in higher education. However, a new landscape of credentials is penetrating higher education. Credentials such as badges, certificates, massive online open courses (MOOCs), and microcredentials are increasingly occupying space in the higher education landscape. Because this landscape is quickly evolving, it is necessary to identify a framework to make sense of basic questions such as: What are credentials? What are their characteristics?

The Association for Career and Technical Education (ACTE) defines credentials as "a verification of an individual's qualification or competence issued by a third party with the relevant authority to issue such credentials" (Association for Career and Technical Education, 2017, p. 1). Their definition borrows from the Department of Labor and includes four primary credentials: certificate, certification, degree, and license.

On the one hand, the nature and meaning of postsecondary education credentials is relatively straightforward and clear. That is, associate's degrees and bachelor's degrees are well understood and accepted in the United States. As a recent report by the American Council on Education (ACE) notes, associate's degrees and bachelor's degrees are valid because they are conferred by accredited institutions, they have face validity, they have predictive validity because they are likely to lead to specific jobs and student success, and they are valuable due to their social and economic returns (Everhart, Ganzglass, Casilli, Hickey, & Muramatsu, 2016). Degrees are also portable in that employers often require them for jobs, and associate's degrees and bachelor's degrees are prerequisites for the next level of education (Everhart et al., 2016). These same characteristics largely apply to certificates offered by many community colleges and private colleges, although certificates are often more local, specialized, and less portable than associate's and bachelor's degrees. Some certificates at the sub-baccalaureate level are not well understood, but two-year institutions have been offering them for quite some time and they are often highly valued by local employers.

On the other hand, a new wave of postsecondary credentials has infiltrated American higher education and created questions not only about the nature and validity of these credentials, but also about the extent to which they align and compete with existing degrees and credentials. These credentials include not only well-defined and established degrees and certificates, but new professional and industry certificates, badges, MOOCs, online microcredentials, and even competency-based education programs. This new wave of credentials are often not well understood nor do they have the currency enjoyed by traditional degrees and certificates. And as recent literature suggests, although they offer more flexible modalities and perhaps more applicable skills, there is little evidence of their efficacy and minimal assurance of their quality (Brown & Kurzweil, 2017).

Because they are rapidly emerging and evolving, this new wave of postsecondary credentials is somewhat difficult to define and we lack a taxonomy that clearly defines them. However, in the following section is an attempt to organize and characterize some of the dominant credentials in this new and evolving landscape. Four primary categories of credentials are offered: (a) college- and/or industry-recognized certificates and certification; (b) badges and microcredentials; and (c) massive online open courses.

College- and/or Industry-recognized Certificates and Certifications

The terrain of certificates and certifications is muddy and complex. I characterize these as "college and/or industry-recognized" because a college or industry often delivers them and/or recognizes them. These certificates are typically earned through participation in a program or courses offered by a college, the result of which is a certificate that is conferred through the college. In some cases, an industry and/or employer will recognize the college credential as adequate for employment. In other cases, the employer (and sometimes state) will require an individual to complete an exam or other testing to receive an industry-recognized certificate or credential.

Research conducted by the National Center for Education Statistics (NCES) offered the following definition for educational certificates:

> A credential awarded by a training provider or educational institution based on completion of all requirements for a program of study, including course-work and tests or other performance evaluations. Certificates, as an academic award, are not time limited and do not need to be renewed. (Bielick, Cronen, Stone, Montaquila, & Roth, 2013, p. 5)

This NCES definition does not include a certificate earned outside of an education institution, but these are not uncommon.

Some literature and organizations distinguish between certificates and certifications (e.g., Bielick et al., 2013; Everhart et al., 2016). Certifications are defined as "awarded by private companies, nonprofit organizations, or government agencies to validate the certification holder's competence for practice in a given profession or trade" (Everhart et al., 2016, p. 32). Similarly, the National Center for Education Statistics defines a certification as:

> A credential awarded by a certification body based on an individual demon-strating, through an examination process, that he or she [sic] has acquired the designated knowledge, skills, and abilities to perform a specific job. The examination can be written, oral, or performance-based. Certification is a time-limited credential that is renewed through a recertification process. (Bielick et al., 2013, p. 5)

This definition of certification makes an important distinction between a credential delivered by postsecondary institutions and a credential offered by another entity (e.g., certification body). As noted in the definition, these certifications are often the gateway to employment, even if an individual has completed a postsecondary certifi-cate. The classic example is in nursing. Even though an individual receives a degree in nursing, they must pass the Nursing Clinical Licensing Exam, a certificate required for practicing as a nurse.

Despite this important distinction between certificates and certifications, neither are universally understood and portable. Even Everhart et al. (2016) acknowledge that certificate acceptance in the labor market is variable and regional, and that there are often competing certifications with inadequate transparency and sometimes limited portability depending on the region and employer. One example that blurs the line between a certificate and certification is in education. For example, if an individual wants to be a teaching assistant in Indiana, they must either complete two years of college, an associate's degree, or pass a state or local assessment (Indiana Department of Education, 2017). In this case, an individual can complete a credential issued by a postsecondary institution (e.g., associate's degree), but they can also successfully complete an exam and receive a state certification to be eligible for employment. All of this suggests that the landscape of college- and/or industry-recognized credentials is muddy.

A credential related to both a certificate and certification is a license. Bielick et al. (2013) define a license as:

> A credential awarded by a licensing agency based on pre-determined criteria. The criteria may include some combination of degree attainment, certifications, assessment, apprenticeship programs, or work experience. Licenses are time-limited and must be renewed periodically. (p. 5)

Similarly, Everhart et al.'s (2016) categorization includes only state licenses, which they note typically require some type of educational training, supervised practice, and testing, and that license criteria are often determined by a profession or trade. Survey cognitive interviews conducted by NCES suggest that the distinction between licenses and certifications was not clear (Bielick et al., 2013). And to further confuse this landscape, these terms are sometimes used interchangeably.

Prevalence of College- and/or Industry-recognized Certificates and Certifications

The prevalence of these credentials is difficult to ascertain, not just because of confusing definitions but because of inadequate data collection. Unlike traditional educational attainment, census data collection does not regularly collect information at this level, so existing data are only available from ad hoc surveys. In 2012, the U.S. Census conducted one such survey to understand what they labeled "alternative educational credentials" (Ewert & Kominski, 2014, p. 1). The data came from the Survey of Income and Program Participation (SIPP) administered in Fall 2012 to a representative sample of adults aged 18 and older. Alternative educational credentials were measured based on the NCES definitions of certification, license, and educational certificate (Bielick et al., 2013). They found that 22 percent of adults reported receiving a professional certification or license, and 9 percent reported receiving an educational certificate. Interestingly, professional certifications and licenses were most common among those individuals with advanced degrees such as master's degrees (45 percent), professional degrees (68 percent), and doctorate degrees (39 percent). Still, a sizeable proportion of adults with associate's degrees (30 percent), some college

(19 percent), or a high school diploma (14 percent) had earned a professional certificate or license. Educational certificates were more likely to be reported among those with associate's degrees (17 percent), followed by master's (14 percent) and professional degrees (14 percent). A recent NCES report based on the Adult Training and Education Survey found comparable data showing that 31 percent of the U.S. labor force had sub-baccalaureate certificates, credentials, or licenses (U.S. Department of Education, 2018). Among those without a postsecondary degree but who held one of these credentials, 56 percent had a license, 43 percent had a postsecondary certificate, and 21 percent had a certification (U.S. Department of Education, 2018). Based on these surveys, it is clear that these credentials are an important part of this new credentials landscape.

Badges and Microcredentials

The newest players in the credentials space are badges or microcredentials. Badges and microcredentials are more modular than a degree or certificate and often focus on a single competency. Much literature adopts Mozilla's definition of digital and open badges, which are characterized as "an online record of achievements, tracking the recipient's communities of interaction that issued the badge and the work completed to get it" (Mozilla Foundation, 2012, p. 3). Educause, an educational technology company, defines digital badges as "digital tokens that appear as icons or logos on a web page or other online venue. Awarded by institutions, organizations, groups or individuals, badges signify accomplishments such as completion of a project, mastery of a skill, or marks of experience" (Educause, 2012, p. 1). Since the 2011 launch of badges by Mozilla and with the participation by U.S. Secretary of Education Arne Duncan (Gibson, Ostashewski, Flintoff, Grant, & Knight, 2013), the Open Badges Community was formed and serves as a central agent to facilitate the badge movement. According to Open Badges (2017), open badges include the following information: "details about the organization issuing the badge, what the individual has done to earn the badge, the criteria that the badge has been assessed against, that the badge was issued to the expected recipient, the badge earner's unique evidence (optionally included), and when the badge was issued and whether it has expired" (para. 4). As noted by the U.S. Department of Education's Office of Educational Technology, badges and microcredentials allow for learning to happen at any time and in any location as well as the "portability of evidence of mastery" based on specific competencies (U.S. Department of Education, 2017, p. 65). Similarly, they allow for learning to occur in much smaller chunks than what is traditionally offered with a degree, certificate, or even a course. As Pursel, Stubbs, Choi, and Tietjen (2016) note, some students enroll and do not complete MOOCs (described below) because they only intend to learn a subset of skills; badges and microcredentials can fill this credential gap.

According to Gibson et al. (2013), the purpose of badges is threefold: (a) "Incentivize learners to engage in positive learning behaviors"; (b) "Identify progress in learning and content trajectories"; and (c) "Signify and credential engagement, learning and achievement" (p. 4). However, Grant (2016) notes that early research on badges suggests that badges are predominantly being used to promote positive learning behaviors or pro-social behaviors. A few of these behaviors include encouraging students to be creative and expressive, practicing time management, completing exams and providing helpful and timely instructor feedback, and promoting class attendance and participation, for example (Grant, 2016). This line of research is important for understanding the role and impact of badges in education and employment.

Given the novelty of badges and microcredentials, it is relevant to understand who is involved and how they work. Derryberry, Everhard, and Knights (2016) identify six primary stakeholders in the open badge ecosystem: learning providers, assessors, job seekers, employers, standards organizations, and endorsers. The traditional credential model involves learning providers (e.g., educational institutions), job seekers (e.g., students), and employers. However, because the badge system is an open system, other stakeholders play critical roles. One of those is the assessor who is responsible for assessing the articulated competencies in a consistent way, independent of how the learner achieved them. The learning provider may or may not be the assessor in an open badges model. Standards organizations also play a role, and as Derryberry et al. (2016) note, competencies or standards for employment badges are often based on industry standards, best practices, or other employer regulations. Finally, and arguably most critically in this new space, are the endorsers. Historically, state and federal governments, accreditation, professional organizations, and reputation serve as endorsement mechanisms for credentials in higher education. Derryberry et al. (2016) note that:

> Endorsers are organizations with the expertise to analyze the quality of specific badges, including how the badge is defined, the competencies it represents, its standards alignments, the process of assessing the badge earner, and the qualifications of the badge issuer to structure and evaluate the learning achievement represented by the badge. (p. 18)

Badges and microcredentials exist both within and outside of higher education. The Open Badges Community involves diverse stakeholders that issue badges, including private companies and employers, but it also includes government agencies, professional associations, and other communities of practice (Open Badges, 2017). Perhaps the bigger question is which organizations accept or legitimize badges and microcredentials in lieu of other credentials, and this is not opaque. Within higher education, however, many institutions are beginning to experiment with open badges. In a survey of 190 public and private colleges and universities conducted by Pearson and the University Professional and Continuing Education Association (UPCEA),

Fong, Janzow, and Peck (2016) found that about 20 percent of institutions offered digital badges.

The Education Design Lab recently launched the 21st Century Skills Badges, an effort intended to help "develop in-demand skills and streamline employers' hiring process" (Kierstead & Roth, 2018, para. 1). Twelve colleges and 50 employers partnered to develop the eight badges, which certify students in skills that employers seek: initiative, collaboration, creative problem-solving, critical thinking, intercultural fluency, empathy, oral communication, and resilience. This is just one of many examples of badges in the contemporary higher education landscape. Several studies and articles have highlighted the innovative use of badges and microcredentials in higher education, and it is likely that their use will continue to grow. Again, perhaps the bigger issue is how badges and microcredentials will be accepted and valued and by whom.

Massive Open Online Courses (MOOCS)

McAuely, Stewart, Siemens, and Cormier (2010) define a MOOC as "an online course with the option of free and open registration, a publically-shared curriculum, and open-ended outcomes. MOOCs integrate social networking, accessible online resources, and are facilitated by leading practitioners in the field of study" (p. 10). Perna et al. (2014) note that the first connectivist MOOC was launched in 2008 by Downes, Siemens, and Cormier and focused not just on using technology for learning but for networks of connections. The first MOOC that is in a traditional lecture format, and more common of the MOOC movement, was a course on Introduction to Artificial Intelligence, launched in 2011 at Stanford by Sebastian Thrun and Peter Norvig (Perna et al., 2014). What followed was an expansion of MOOCs that were free courses offered in partnership between venture capitalist-backed companies and many well-known universities. Upon their launch in 2011 and 2012, MOOCs generated excitement and they promised to be transformative. In a 2012 article in *The New York Times*, columnist David Brooks wrote about MOOCs calling them "The Campus Tsunami" (Brooks, 2012). Users who completed MOOCs were often, but not always, offered an opportunity to receive a certificate of completion.

It is difficult to track the prevalence of MOOCs because MOOCs are unregulated and not tracked by a government source. However, the website Class Central tracks MOOCs and found that in 2016, over 700 universities around the world offered more than 6,800 courses and enrolled 58 million students (Shah, 2016). The top five providers of MOOCs are Coursera, edX, XuetangX, FutureLearn, and Udacity (Shah, 2016). Similarly, the top five university providers are among the most well-known colleges and universities in the world: Stanford University, Massachusetts Institute of Technology, University of Pennsylvania, University of Michigan, and Harvard University (Shah, 2016).

Despite the proliferation of MOOCs, commentators and the literature have noted that MOOCs have failed to complete students and failed to deliver on their promise to expand access to education (Zemsky, 2014). For example, research has found that MOOC completion rates are often less than 12 percent of registrants (Cusack, 2014; Ho et al., 2014; Koller, Ng, & Chen, 2013; Perna et al., 2014).

Since these early efforts and studies, MOOCs have changed and increasingly offer opportunities for users to earn credentials or credits toward credentials. Shah (2016) reports that there are more than 250 credentials offered through MOOCs. These credentials come in different flavors and many of them come with a price tag. At one end of the spectrum is what looks like a traditional online degree program offered in partnership with a leading institution of higher education. An example of this is the Master of Business Administration (iMBA) offered as a partnership between the University of Illinois and Coursera. The program is completely online, includes 18 courses and 3 capstone projects, and costs approximately $22,000 (Coursera, 2017). The program looks and feels more like a traditional online program where students must apply and be admitted; they receive the exact same MBA degree received by students in the residential program (Coursera, 2017).

In the middle of the spectrum is the Global Freshman Academy, a partnership between EdX and Arizona State University (ASU). The academy describes itself as a "first of its kind collaboration that offers full university freshman level courses for credit" (EdX, 2017a, para. 1). The general education courses are open to anyone who wishes to enroll, but upon successful completion, students can pay $600 per course and receive transcripted credit from ASU. Credits that are transcripted can be applied toward a degree at ASU or transferred to another institution (EdX, 2017a).

At the other end of the spectrum are "micromasters" credentials offered by EdX in partnership with several universities and employers. EdX (2017b) describes this form of credential:

> MicroMaster programs are a series of graduate level courses from top universities designed to advance your career. They provide deep learning in a specific career field and are recognized by employers for their real job relevance. Students may apply to the university offering credit for the MicroMasters certificate and, if accepted can pursue an accelerated and less expensive Master's Degree. (para. 1)

As the name implies, the credentials are intended to be part of a larger master's degree, and individuals who successfully complete the program can pay between $600–$1400 per program.

No doubt that MOOCs have evolved from their initial development. As they continue to mature and evolve, we need new ways to define and understand them as well as measure their impact.

STAKING THE STAKEHOLDERS IN THE
NEW CREDENTIALS LANDSCAPE

This new wave of credentialing involves a variety of stakeholders who are involved in credentialing for different purposes. The web of stakeholders is intertwined, complex, and evolving. A 2013 portrait of MOOC players created by *The Chronicle of Higher Education* illustrates many of these stakeholders and their web (see Figure 5.1). Although the landscape has evolved and many other stakeholders have emerged in the certificate, badge, and microcredential space, this graphic illustrates that major stakeholders include private investors (both individuals and companies), private philanthropy, institutions of higher education, and faculty and innovators at institutions of higher education.

Although the landscape of stakeholders is diverse and complex, this section identifies some of the primary stakeholders and their motivations for engagement in

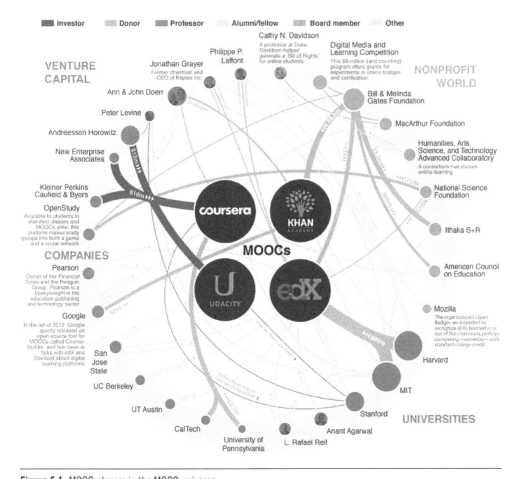

Figure 5.1 MOOC players in the MOOC universe

credentialing. Unfortunately, there is little empirical literature on these stakeholders and their motivations, and much more research is needed. I conceptualize and discuss the primary stakeholders in three categories: credential providers, credential facilitators, and credential gatekeepers. These are not necessarily mutually exclusive categories because many credential providers are also facilitators and some facilitators may also be gatekeepers. However, these three categories provide a useful way to make sense of the many stakeholders, their roles, and their motivations.

Credential Providers

One confusing aspect of this new landscape of credentialing is the entities that provide or issue the credentials. Most traditional credentials such as associate's degrees, bachelor's degrees, and graduate and professional degrees are provided and awarded by recognized and respected colleges and universities. Despite the emergence of new for-profit and non-profit organizations and new credential providers, colleges and universities remain the dominant providers of degrees, but they are also intimately involved in the delivery and provision of certificates, MOOCs, badges, and microcredentials. As noted above, prestigious universities such as Stanford University, Massachusetts Institute of Technology, University of Pennsylvania, University of Michigan, Harvard University, University of Illinois, and many others are strategic providers of MOOCs, badges, and microcredentials. Similarly, certificates are increasingly offered at the undergraduate and graduate levels by colleges and universities. According to the National Center for Education Statistics, the number of sub-associate certificates conferred by colleges and universities increased by 35 percent between 2004–2005 and 2014–15 (U.S. Department of Education Statistics, 2016).

The motivation for these institutions is likely threefold: innovation and access, competition, and revenue. Many traditional colleges and universities were leaders in the development of MOOCs (e.g., Stanford University). MOOCs were viewed as an innovation that could expand access to higher education (Zemsky, 2014). Innovation and access are core missions of many leading universities, so it is not surprising that they were motivating factors. Undoubtedly a second motivation for traditional colleges and universities is competition. As Stanford and other elite institutions lead in the development of MOOCs and microcredentials, more institutions have entered the space because they likely want to get a competitive advantage among their peers. This relates to the third motivation: revenue. In a context where public resources to higher education are decreasing and competition is flourishing, the delivery of new credentials offers a new potential revenue source for institutions. Given that several of these new credentials have shifted to a revenue-generating model (Shah, 2017), it is likely that others will follow. Although institutions are motivated by innovation and expanding access, the reality is that the technological and human resources and infrastructure needed to develop and deliver credentials comes at a cost that institutions may not be willing to absorb without a revenue source.

Speaking of revenue, a second contingent of credential providers are new companies that have emerged in the education technology space. The biggest players in this space are providers previously mentioned such as Coursera, EdX, and Udacity, and Khan Academy, for example. These credential providers, who are primarily in the MOOC and microcredential space—often as strategic partners with higher education institutions, governments, and non-profits—are private companies, some with a mission to earn a profit. Each has their own history, but as *The Chronicle of Higher Education* (2013) article shows, many of these companies were funded by a combination of venture capitalists, private companies, colleges and universities, and non-profits (philanthropic foundations). These providers are private companies who need a sustainable business model that generates revenue to survive or to profit.

Another contingent of providers are those who have entered the badge and microcredential space. The landscape of providers is a little messy and evolving, although there are some dominant players. Providers of badges and microcredentials are those that provide learning. However, as previously described, the badge learning providers are diverse and numerous, including private companies and industry, professional associations, communities of practice, and government agencies, to name a few. In other words, providers really include any entity that desires to share knowledge and skills with another entity or individual; the list is endless and diverse. Some of the existing badge issuers or providers include: Dallas Museum of Art, Educause, IBM, Michigan State University, NASA, New Milford High School, the Smithsonian National Museum of Natural History, the University of Illinois at Urbana-Champaign, and the YMCA of Greater New York, to name a few.

Credential Facilitators

Credential facilitators are those entities that do not directly provide or deliver credentials (or not exclusively), but their actions facilitate credentials. These actions are primarily manifested in fiscal, technological, and advocacy forms. Arguably one of the most significant credential facilitators from a fiscal perspective is venture capitalists, who take risks to invest money because of the promise of profits. According to EdSurge, education technology startups targeting postsecondary education and corporate training and learning raised $593 million in 2016 (Wan, 2016). This figure includes all types of education technologies (not just those directly related to credential production), but many of the players involved in the credentials space are included in this figure, and venture capitalists were big investors to early providers such as Coursera, EdX, and Udacity, for example (Hepler, 2013). These figures illustrate the significant role that private investors play in the credentialing space, and their motivation is to earn profit.

Private philanthropic foundations have also been incredibly influential in the facilitation of credentials. The extent of their participation is difficult to assess because there is no empirical literature on it, but they have thrown their money behind MOOCs as well as badges and microcredentials. As Figure 5.1 displays, early investors in MOOCs included the Bill & Melinda Gates Foundation and the MacArthur Foundation (Chronicle of Higher Education, 2013). The MacArthur Foundation invested heavily in a new non-profit in 2015 focused on digital learning and media (Herold & Doran, 2015). One of the first projects of the new venture was digital badges. In 2016, the Lumina Foundation, one of the largest private foundations that funds higher education, announced its impact investing program intended to help support its goal to increase college completion. One of their strategic investments was in Credly, a popular technology platform for verifying, sharing, and managing badges (Lumina Foundation, 2016). Lumina Foundation has also invested heavily in several credentialing efforts and projects, including Connecting Credentials and Credential Engine (Fein, 2017). Both efforts are intended to improve credentialing mechanisms and information about credentials in the complex and muddy credentials landscape.

The badge community has its own set of facilitators. Perhaps the most prominent is the Open Badge Community previously described, the origins of which are rooted in Mozilla (Gibson et al., 2013). Other dominant facilitators in the badge space include Acclaim, Credly, Merit Pages, and BadgeOS. Some of these facilitators also issue badges and many, such as Credly, provide the technology platform for badges.

Credential Gatekeepers

The new landscape of credentials includes an important third category of stakeholders that serve as gatekeepers to these credentials. Gatekeepers play an important role in the social and legal space related to credential validation and endorsement. There are two dominant stakeholders in this space: institutions of higher education and the federal government. There are likely more, including employers or other professional organizations, but colleges and the federal government arguably play a more immediate role.

Although they are also credential providers in this new landscape, colleges and universities play important gatekeeper roles, mostly credential/credit acceptance and transfer. For example, as the first MOOCs emerged and individuals received completion certificates from Stanford and MIT, the certificates of completion that students received specifically noted that the MOOCs were not equivalent to standard courses (Friesen & Wihak, 2013). Similarly, other institutions were not accepting MOOCs for transfer credit. Why have colleges and universities been gatekeepers in this space? This likely boils down to two related explanations: quality and competition/revenue.

Quality is one obvious explanation because new credentials emerged that were unfamiliar to many institutions and that had not been vetted through existing quality assurance mechanisms such as accreditation or governments. MOOC completion certificates or digital badges offered in partnership with credible institutions of higher education do not easily align with existing quality assurance frameworks.

Beyond quality assurance mechanisms, these new credentials also do not align with many institutional general education frameworks. As Zemsky (2014) notes, institutional general education philosophies are less about a checklist of courses and competencies than preparing learners for a major, a career, and more broadly for life. Thus, MOOCs, badges, microcredentials, or other short-term credentials that serve as a skill repository are likely disconnected from an institution's larger purpose to provide a high-quality and integrated general education and vocational experience.

The second explanation is competition/revenue. Competition is alive and well within higher education, and new credential providers or frameworks for offering credentials pose a threat to higher education's value proposition. Similarly, given that many institutions rely heavily on tuition revenue, they have little incentive to widely accept new credentials such as MOOCs or badges as substitutes for their own courses and curricula. Indeed, as noted above, MOOCs are already moving to a model that generates profit for institutions and for which standard academic credit is being accrued.

The second critical stakeholder is the federal government. The federal government is the primary gatekeeper for students or individuals accessing federal financial aid for these alternative credentials. That is, because MOOCs, badges, microcredentials, bootcamps, and others are not within the domain of traditional higher education, learners and students do not have access to federal financial aid. In 2016, this changed as the U.S. Department of Education announced a new financial aid experiment called EQUIP: Educational Quality through Innovative Partnerships. Eight partnerships were selected that represented partnerships between a higher education institution, a "non-traditional provider," and a quality assurance entity (U.S. Department of Education, 2016). Existing federal policy requires that at least half of the content and instruction be provided by an institution for a student to receive federal aid, but this experiment allows non-traditional providers to provide more than half of the content and instruction (U.S. Department of Education, 2016). According to the experiment announcement, the quality assurance entity will ensure that student learning outcomes and competencies are met, and institutions must receive the endorsement of their accrediting agency.

IMPLICATIONS FOR HIGHER EDUCATION

So what does all of this mean for the future of higher education access, affordability, equity, and completion? Well, if the short history of MOOCs and early history of badges and microcredentials are any indication, there are a few observations to make.

First, despite the proliferation of new credentials, traditional higher education likely retains the market share of most credentials. Indeed, we have observed an increase in the awarding of certificates among most institutional types in the past several years (U.S.

Department of Education, 2016), which might suggest that higher education's market share is only gaining strength. Given the role of credentialing theory and its purposes in the workforce, a credential in Principles of Game Design from Michigan State University is likely to have more credibility to an employer than a certificate from an unknown or largely unknown private company. Indeed, credentialing theory likely suggests that credentials, badges, or certificates from organizations or entities other than Michigan State University, Stanford, and other public and private elites will never be more valuable because that would disrupt existing social power structures and privileges.

Even though it is likely that higher education retains the market share of credentials, data collection on newer credentials and certificates is not standardized, so this observation should be interpreted with caution. Perhaps the more critical observation is that despite the emergence of new credential providers and facilitators, traditional higher education remains an important stakeholder. It is not as if these new credentials are forcing existing colleges and universities to go out of business. If anything, new credentials are expanding the diversity of credential types and expanding access to learning and subsequent educational and life opportunities. In theory, this is positive for higher education access, equity, and affordability because more people and more types of people have access to learning and the cost is often, but not always, significantly lower than traditional higher education models. In practice, however, we have little evidence on the efficacy of these credentials so it is too early to ascertain their effects.

This first observation relates to a critical second observation: colleges and universities have been and continue to be strategic partners in this new credentials landscape. From certificates that represent partnerships between colleges and employers, to MOOCs that represent partnerships between venture capitalist-backed companies, to the infusion of badges into higher education institutions, many new credentials or credential-based activities include colleges and universities as strategic partners. Because of these strong partnerships, perhaps these credentials do nothing more than to reproduce existing issues related to higher education access, affordability, equity, and success. The jury is still out. However, it is clear based on the development of many existing models that higher education institutions are critical partners in their development and success. Perhaps where unanswered questions are most obvious are questions concerned with quality. That is, what role will higher education play in assuring the quality of new badges, microcredentails, certificates, or MOOCs? How will these new credentials be accepted for transfer credit or will credit be given for prior learning? These questions and others are necessary to answer to understand how these new credentials will impact issues of access, affordability, equity, and success. After all, how valuable are digital badges or microcredentials if they do not align with other credible and valid credentials?

The third observation is that supply and demand for new credentials appears to be extremely robust. What little data that do exist on certificates, badges, microcredentials, and MOOCs suggest that there is a market of students and learners, eager to learn outside traditional systems of higher education. Participation has been relatively robust in many learning environments that lead to credentials, including those connected to and not connected to colleges and universities. Similarly, the expansion of suppliers in this new credentials landscape is robust. Many new providers and facilitators have been eager to invest and develop, suggesting there is no shortage of entities willing to compete with traditional higher education.

A final observation and implication for higher education has to do with the extent to which new certificates and credentials fit within a broader credential framework in U.S. higher education. Who recognizes these new credentials and what value do they provide to individuals? How do they align with existing postsecondary degrees? What is a viable cost structure and does that complement or compete with existing postsecondary degrees? And what are the regulatory and accountability mechanisms to ensure these new credentials are credible and valuable?

This chapter may raise more questions than it does provide answers. The new credentials landscape suggests the need for more research on the configurations, implementation, and impact of new models. Similarly, more research is needed on the roles that colleges and universities play, particularly as it relates to MOOCs, badges, and microcredentials.

QUESTIONS FOR DISCUSSION

1. What are the primary types of credentials in the new credentials landscape?
2. What are the characteristics of certificates, badges and microcredentials, and MOOCs and what differentiates them?
3. Who are the primary stakeholders involved in the new credentialing landscape and what are their motivations?
4. What are the implications of new credentials on higher education access, quality, equity, and affordability?
5. What are the opportunities and challenges associated with certificates, badges and microcredentials, and MOOCs?

REFERENCES

Association for Career and Technical Education. (2017). *What is a credential?* Retrieved from www.acteonline. org/wp-content/uploads/2018/02/What_is_a_Credential_71417.pdf.

Baker, D. P. (2011). Forward and backward, horizontal and vertical: Transformation of occupational credentialing in the schooled society. *Research in Stratification and Mobility, 29*, 5–29.

Bielick, S., Cronen, S., Stone, C., Montaquila, J., & Roth, S. (2013). *The Adult Training and Education Survey (ATES) Pilot study: Technical report (NCES 2013–190).* U.S. Department of Education. Washington, DC: National Center for Education Statistics.

Brooks, D. (2012, May 3). The campus tsunami. *The New York Times.* Retrieved from www.nytimes.com/2012/05/04/opinion/brooks-the-campus-tsunami.html.

Brown, D. K. (2001). The social sources of educational credentialism: Status cultures, labor markets, and organizations. *Sociology of Education, 74*, 19–34.

Brown, D. K., & Bills, D. B. (2011). An overture for the sociology of credentialing: Empirical, theoretical, and moral considerations. *Research in Stratification and Mobility, 29*, 133–138.

Brown, J., & Kurzweil, M. (2017). *The complex universe of alternative postsecondary credentials and pathways.* American Academy of Arts & Sciences. Retrieved from https://amacad.org/multimedia/pdfs/publications/researchpapersmonographs/CFUE_Alternative-Pathways/CFUE_Alternative-Pathways.pdf.

Chronicle of Higher Education. (2013). *Major players in the MOOC universe.* Retrieved from www.chronicle.com/article/Major-Players-in-the-MOOC/138817.

Coursera. (2017). *Master of Business Administration (iMBA).* Retrieved from www.coursera.org/degrees/imba

Cusack, A. (2014, January 10). A handy cheatsheet on MOOCs. *EdSurge.* Retrieved from www.edsurge.com/n/2014-01-10-a-handy-cheatsheet-on-moocs.

Derryberry, A., Everhard, D., & Knights, E. (2016). Badges and competences: New currency for professional credentials. In L. Y. Muilenburg & Z. L. Berge (Eds.), *Digital badges in education: Trends, issues, and cases* (pp. 12–20). New York, NY: Routledge.

Educause. (2012). *7 things you should know about badges.* Retrieved from https://library.educause.edu/~/media/files/library/2012/6/eli7085-pdf.pdf.

EdX. (2017a). *Start your freshman year online and work toward a college degree.* Retrieved from www.edx.org/gfa/courses.

EdX. (2017b). *Micromasters credentials are a pathway to today's jobs.* Retrieved from www.edx.org/micromasters.

Everhart, D., Ganzglass, E., Casilli, C., Hickey, D, & Muramatsu, B. (2016). *Quality dimensions for connected credentials.* Washington, DC: American Council on Education.

Ewert, S., & Kominski, R. (2014). *Measuring alternative educational credentials: 2012: Household economic studies.* Washington, DC: U.S. Department of Commerce, Economics and Statistics Administration, U.S. Census Bureau.

Fein, P. (2017, October 18). A kayak for credentials. *InsideHigherEd.* Retrieved from www.insidehighered.com/news/2017/10/18/credential-engine-seeks-create-database-public-information-all-credentials.

Fong, J., Janzow, P., & Peck, K. (2016). *Demographic shifts in educational demand and the rise of alternative credentials.* Pearson Education and UPCEA. Retrieved from https://upcea.edu/wp-content/uploads/2017/05/Demographic-Shifts-in-Educational-Demand-and-the-Rise-of-Alternative-Credentials.pdf.

Friesen, N., & Wihak, C. (2013). From OER to PLAR: Credentialing for open education. *Open Praxis, 5*(1), 49–58.

Gibson, D., Ostashewski, N., Flintoff, K., Grant, S., & Knight, E. (2013). Digital badges in education. *Education and Information Technologies, 20*(2), 403–410.

Grant, S. L. (2016). History and context of open digital badges. In L. Y. Muilenburg & Z. L. Berge (Eds.), *Digital badges in education: Trends, issues, and cases* (pp. 3–11). New York, NY: Routledge.

Hepler, L. (2013, November 22). Coursera lands $20 million in new funding, despite online education turmoil. *Silicon Valley Business Journal.* Retrieved from www.bizjournals.com/sanjose/news/2013/11/22/coursera-lands-20-million-in-new.html.

Herold, B., & Doran, L. (2015, October 20). MacArthur Foundation launches nonprofit to scale up digital learning. *EdWeek.* Retrieved from www.edweek.org/ew/articles/2015/10/21/macarthur-foundation-launches-nonprofit-to-scale-up.html.

Ho, A. D., Reich, J., Nesterko, S., Seaton, D. T., Mullaney, T., Waldo, J., & Chuang, I. (2014). *Harvard X and MITx: The first year of open online courses* (HarvardX and MITx Working Paper No. 1). Cambridge, MA: Harvard University/MIT.

Indiana Department of Education. (2017). *Paraprofessionals.* Retrieved from www.doe.in.gov/licensing/paraprofessionals.

Kierstead, K., & Roth, L. (2018, April 25). Education Design Lab releases 21st Century Skills Badge Program. *Cision PRWeb.* Retrieved from www.prweb.com/releases/2018/04/prweb15439389.htm.

Koller, D., Ng, A., & Chen, Z. (2013, June 3). Retention and intention in massive open online courses: In depth. *Educause Review.* Retrieved from https://er.educause.edu/articles/2013/6/retention-and-intention-in-massive-open-online-courses-in-depth.

Lumina Foundation. (2016, May 9). *Lumina Foundation announces strategic social investment strategy.* Retrieved from www.luminafoundation.org/news-and-views/2016-05-09-strategic-social-investment-strategy-announcement.

McAuely, A., Stewart, B., Siemens, G., & Cormier, D. (2010). *The MOOC model for digital practice.* Retrieved from https://oerknowledgecloud.org/sites/oerknowledgecloud.org/files/MOOC_Final.pdf.

Mozilla Foundation. (2012). *Open badges for lifelong learning.* Retrieved from https://wiki.mozilla.org/images/5/59/OpenBadges-Working-Paper_012312.pdf.

Open Badges. (2017). *Discover open badges.* Retrieved from https://openbadges.org/.

Perna, L. W., Ruby, A., Boruch, R. F., Wang, N., Scull, J., Ahmad, S., & Evans, C. (2014). Moving through MOOCs: Understanding the progression of users in massive open online courses. *Educational Researchers, 43*(9), 421–432.

Pursel, B. K., Stubbs, C., Choi, G. W., & Tietjen, P. (2016). Digital badges, learning at scale, and big data. In L. Y. Muilenburg & Z. L. Berge (Eds.), *Digital badges in education: Trends, issues, and cases* (pp. 93–101). New York, NY: Routledge.

Shah, D. (2017, July 6). MOOCs find their audience: Professional learners and universities. *EdSurge.* Retrieved from www.edsurge.com/news/2017-07-06-moocs-find-their-audience-professional-learners-and-universities.

Shah, D. (2016, December 25). By the numbers: MOOCs in 2016. *Class-Central.* Retrieved from www.class-central.com/report/mooc-stats-2016/.

U.S. Department of Education, National Center for Education Statistics. (2016). Table 318.40: Number of degrees and certificates conferred by postsecondary institutions and percentage change, by control of institution and level of degree: Academic years 1994–95, 2004–05, and 2014–15. In U.S. Department of Education, National Center for Education Statistics, *Digest of education statistics* (2016 ed.). Retrieved from https://nces.ed.gov/programs/coe/indicator_cts.asp.

U.S. Department of Education. (2017). *Reimagining the role of technology in education: 2017 national education technology plan update.* Washington, DC: Office of Educational Technology.

U.S. Department of Education. (2018). *Degree and nondegree credentials held by labor force participants (NCES 2018-05).* Washington, DC: Institute of Education Sciences, National Center for Education Statistics.

University Learning Store. (2017a). *Partners.* Retrieved from http://universitylearningstore.org/partners/.

University Learning Store. (2017b). *About the University Learning Store.* Retrieved from http://universitylearningstore.org/about/.

Wan, T. (2016, Dec. 26). Ka'Ching! 2016 US edtech funding totals $1 billion. *EdSurge.* Retrieved from www.edsurge.com/news/2016-12-26-ka-ching-2016-us-edtech-funding-totals-1-billion.

Zemsky, R. (2014). With a MOOC MOOC here and a MOOC MOOC there, here a MOOC, there a MOOC, everywhere a MOOC MOOC. *The Journal of General Education, 63*(4), 237–243.

6

VIGOROUS CIVILITY

Aspirations for Free Expression on Campus

FREDERICK M. LAWRENCE

The challenge of free expression on our campuses has never seemed greater. These challenges come in all directions and all contexts: they come from the left and they come from the right. They involve students, they involve faculty, and they involve those outside the campus who affect the community as invited speakers. Given our society's current hyper-polarization, it is perhaps no surprise that this issue presents itself with such urgency on our campuses today—public and private; small liberal arts colleges, and large research universities. At this moment, it is especially important to clarify first principles pertaining to our democracy's core value of free expression as it manifests on campus.

I would articulate two such principles. First, robust free expression and free inquiry are central to the mission of all our colleges and universities. The limits of such expression are far out at the margins of expressive activity, involving behavior that threatens or instills fear in a victim or victims. Hate speech is protected; hate crimes are not. Second, hate speech, although protected, nonetheless causes harm to members of our communities. In an increasingly diverse society, there is a moral imperative for campus leaders to respond vigorously to hateful speech—not to suppress it, but to identify it for what it is and to criticize it.

Each of these principles warrants careful attention and analysis. The issues involved are complex, nuanced, and subtle precisely because they implicate the twin missions of colleges and universities, missions that do not always coexist easily: the pursuit of liberal, rational open learning; and the creation of a true academic community where heterogeneous stakeholders are knitted together in pursuit of this ideal. In short, the challenge is both to protect free expression and to maintain civility. The stakes, for our colleges and universities, could not be higher.

In exploring the contours of free expression on our campuses, we begin with a consideration of the general boundaries of free expression in America, especially in the troubling context of hate speech. This boundary must be expansive: difficult, challenging, and even hateful speech ought to be protected under our tradition of free expression. This view is largely consonant with accepted First Amendment doctrine, but as we are concerned with both public and private institutions, we will consider both First Amendment jurisprudence, which governs all public institutions, and normative principles of free expression that emanate for the very nature of a liberal education and that apply even outside the context of government regulation. Exploring the development of these doctrines where hate speech (as well as hate or bias crimes) is concerned will demonstrate that the division between speech that is protected and behavior that can be punished cannot be drawn along a speech–conduct distinction. It is tempting to do so, but the distinction will not hold up under careful analysis. Instead, the distinction between that which we should protect and that which we may prohibit should be drawn based on the intent of the actor, much as we generally do in the criminal law. When we do so, we see that certain verbal behavior—think of them as verbal assaults—will in fact *not* fall into the category of protected speech but rather into the category of that which may be proscribed and thus punished. This careful distinction is crucial for administrators of higher education to understand as they continue to face unexpected upheavals. Finally, we will return to the category of hateful speech that is in fact protected, and ask what the proper response to such speech ought to be. This will bring us to perhaps the most compelling challenge of all: how can we further both free expression *and* civility on our campuses?

THREE STORIES TO SET THE CONTEXT

I begin with three stories from over the past two decades to set the context. The first took place in the spring of 2001 at University College London (UCL). I was a Senior Research Fellow at UCL, studying racial violence law in the UK, and was presenting a paper about hate speech. A UCL colleague, puzzled at the depth of attention with which I dissected an actor's intent in determining whether expressive conduct could be prohibited, posed the following hypothetical question: would I prohibit a skinhead, who had painted racist slogans on a van, from driving the van into the heart of Brixton, a London neighborhood with a predominant community of African or Caribbean descent? As I began my answer, using the reasoning discussed in more detail below, on the need to ascertain the skinhead's state of mind, or intent, he stopped me: "Why is this so hard for you? We all know it's wrong."

The second story took place took place at Williams College, where I served as a Trustee. A Jewish student complained that a faux eviction notice had been placed on her dorm room door. "If you do not vacate the premises by tomorrow at 6PM, we reserve the right to demolish your premises without delay," the notice read. "We cannot be held responsible for property or persons remaining inside. Charges for demolition will be applied to your student account." The student understandably felt attacked and unsafe. The President's first impulse was to find the offender and dispatch punishment yet he hesitated, realizing the matter was complex. And he called to get my perspective.

The third story is the most recent, in December of 2014, and occurred on the Brandeis University campus, when I was President of the university. It occurred right after the murder of two police officers in "revenge" for the death of Eric Garner and Michael Brown. A prominent student member of the campus Black Lives Matter movement tweeted that she had no sympathy with the police officers and their families. Knowing this student, I believe that what she meant was that she was deeply frustrated and troubled that, in her view, vastly more attention had been paid to the deaths of officers Wenjian Liu and Raphael Ramos in the broader community than was given to the deaths of Garner and Brown. But alas, that is not what she said. And, with "help," if that is the right word, from one of the 60 or so students who received the tweet, who posted it on what can best be described as an extremist website, her tweet went viral to millions of hateful "trollers." I received enormous pressure from all sides. Some urged that the student be thrown out of school or at least lose her financial aid package. Others argued that I should issue a short statement supporting free speech and the right of all members of the community to say what they wished. We will return to the Williams and Brandeis stories below.

FREE EXPRESSION AS A CORE VALUE THAT COVERS HATE SPEECH

The first story, taking place in England, calls for contextualizing the discussion. An analysis of free expression in the United States is fundamentally different from that in most, if not all, other advanced democracies, which punish pure hate speech. Consider the following illustrative examples from statues defining punishable speech:

- Canada – "hatred against any identifiable group where such incitement is likely to lead to a breach of the peace."
- Denmark – statements "by which a group of people are threatened, derided or degraded because of their race, color of skin, national or ethnic background."
- Germany – attacks on "the human dignity of others by insulting, maliciously maligning or defaming segments of the population."
- New Zealand – "threatening abusive or insulting … words likely to excite hostility against or bring into contempt any group of persons … on the ground of their color, race, or ethnic or national or ethnic origins of that group of persons."

- UK – "threatening, abusive or insulting words, or behavior" intended to "stir up racial hatred" or when "having regard to all the circumstances racial hatred is likely to be stirred up thereby."

So, as my interlocutor at University College London put it, "why is this so hard for *us*?"

The context of hate speech, and hate crimes as well, is located at the intersection of three sets of significant individual and societal rights and interests: (1) freedom of expression; (2) personal safety for oneself, one's family, and one's property; and (3) personal dignity. The third right in particular can push up hard against the first. As developed by Waldron (2012) in *The Harm in Hate Speech*, dignity is concerned with a person's basic social standing, and the interest in being recognized as "proper objects of society's protection and concern" (p. 5). If the right to one's safety is inherently individualistic and about liberty, the right to one's dignity is inherently comparative and about equality—to have one's dignity respected is to be accorded the same basic social standing as any other member of the society. As Lyndon Johnson is said to have answered a question concerning the moral necessity for the Civil Rights Act of 1964, "A man has the right not be insulted in front of his children."

When we discuss hate speech and hate crimes in America, we are concerned with legitimate and significant rights on all sides, i.e., for the speaker and the listener. We must proceed with great caution protecting rights where we can, and limiting rights only when we must. The reason that the limitation of expression "is so hard for us" is that free expression is a core value of our system of government and our society. Speech, even hate speech, is presumed to be constitutionally protected. By hate speech I mean that which offends or insults a group along racial, ethnic, national, religious, gender, or sexual identity lines. The definition of the German statute puts it well—attacks on "the human dignity of others by insulting, maliciously maligning or defaming segments of the population"—and allows us to draw on Waldron's idea of dignity.

I ally myself here with the arguments presented by such scholars as the late Professor Edwin Baker and former Yale Law School Dean Robert Post. Baker (2009) based his free expression understanding in a fundamental concept of autonomy. In his essay "Autonomy and Hate Speech," he wrote, "Law's purposeful restrictions on [the speaker's] racist or hate speech violate [that person's] formal autonomy" (p. 143). Post, in his influential 1995 book *Constitutional Domains* and elsewhere has recognized the harm inflicted by hate speech, but argued persuasively that the fundamental societal interests of public discourse will almost always outweigh this harm. In America, Post (2009) writes, "public discourse is an arena for the competition of many distinct communities, each trying to capture the law to impose its own particular norms" (p. 133). Public discourse in our democracy, Post (2009) adds, thus has the "extraordinarily difficult task of ensuring democratic legitimacy in a climate of comparatively severe suspicion and distrust" (p. 137).

I find further foundation for an expansive view of free expression in the jurisprudence of Justice Louis D. Brandeis. Brandeis is often twinned with Justice Oliver Wendell Holmes, Jr., as the two great judicial champions of free speech, through dissents in the early twentieth century that ultimately shaped Supreme Court doctrine through the balance of the century and into the present. It is important for our purposes, however, to distinguish Holmes from Brandeis, which I will do briefly here. Holmes is famous for his "marketplace of ideas" metaphor, borrowed from neoclassical economics. Just as the underlying theory of the market is that a free and unfettered market will produce the most efficient use of goods and services in an economy, the free and unfettered marketplace of ideas allows the best ideas to emerge and aids the search for truth. The worth of expression, therefore, is in the consequences that this expression may be expected to produce.

Brandeis was no stranger to consequentialist argument. In his celebrated opinion in *Whitney v. California* (1927), Brandeis wrote that when faced with *bad speech*, the "remedy to be applied is more speech, not enforced silence," and that the fundamental "freedom to think as you will, and to speak as you think are means indispensable to the discovery and spread of political truth" (p. 375, 377). But Brandeis also saw the value of free speech as fundamental to the very way in which we participate in our society. In his dissenting opinion in *Gilbert v. Minnesota* (1920), Brandeis wrote:

> The right of a citizen of the United States to take part, for his own or the country's benefit, in the making of federal laws and in the conduct of the government, necessarily includes the right to speak or write about them; to endeavor to make his own opinion concerning laws existing or contemplated prevail; and, to this end, to teach the truth as he sees it. (pp. 337–338)

To Brandeis, expressive activity was essential to our very humanity and the way in which we actualize ourselves as social beings.

SIGNIFICANT LEGAL CASES ON EXPANSIVE FREE EXPRESSION RIGHTS

The normative argument of Post, Baker, and others finds deep resonance in American case law where we find that free expression jurisprudence, as a starting point, provides protection for hate speech. This jurisprudence begins with the underlying premise that a state may not punish a person for holding an opinion regardless of how obnoxious the opinion may be to the general public or even how good a predictor it might be for future anti-social conduct. It is striking that in 1950, Chief Justice Fred Vinson, not renowned as a strong advocate of a robust view of the First Amendment, saw no need to provide any support for his assertion that "one may not be imprisoned or executed because he holds particular beliefs" (American Communications, 1950, p. 408).

Consider the context of flag burning, which continues to press the limits of the right to express unpopular views. The Supreme Court, even as it has become more conservative in its approach to numerous areas of the law, has repeatedly upheld the right to burn an American flag. In *Texas v. Johnson* (1989), in which the Texas flag burning prohibition was struck down, the Court held that "if there is a bedrock principle underlying the First Amendment, it is that the government may not prohibit the expression of an idea simply because society finds the idea itself offensive or disagreeable" (p. 414).

Justice Oliver Wendell Holmes, Jr., a towering figure of American free expression jurisprudence, was one of the greatest champions of this "bedrock principle" to which the Court referred in *Texas v. Johnson*. In 1929, he dissented from an opinion in which the Supreme Court upheld the denial of citizenship to Rosika Schwimmer (*United States v. Schwimmer*, 1929). The sole basis on which Ms. Schwimmer's application was denied was her ardent pacifism that led her to state that she would not bear arms in order to defend the United States. In his pointed dissent, Justice Holmes set out his views as to the scope of the First Amendment:

> Some of her answers might excite popular prejudice, but if there is any principle of the Constitution that more imperatively calls for attachment than any other it is the principle of free thought—not free thought for those who agree with us but freedom for the thought that we hate. I think that we should adhere to that principle with regard to admission into, as well as to life within this country. (pp. 654–655)

This dissent became the law 17 years later, when the Supreme Court overruled *Schwimmer*, relying extensively on Justice Holmes. It is thus clear that a racist may not be punished merely for his racist beliefs and, not surprisingly, no law has sought to punish mere racist beliefs. Holding a belief is what Professor Thomas Emerson (1970) called the "first stage in the process of expression" (p. 21).

Regulation of the succeeding stages of expression has occurred, prominently in the context of university speech codes beginning in the 1980s. Concerned over the increase in racial tensions on campuses, many schools adopted policies proscribing the expression of bigotry. None of these codes survived a First Amendment challenge in court. Campus speech codes at public universities have been viewed as unconstitutional prohibitions of speech based solely on the content of that speech. Although sympathetic with the goals of the campus speech codes, the district courts that struck down such regulations as those adopted by the University of Michigan and the University of Wisconsin, for example, ruled that the regulations impermissibly interfered with the First Amendment (Doe, 1989; UWM Post, 1991). This broad protection of speech on campus, both under the First Amendment and under basic principles of free expression and free inquiry as integral to the academic mission, still permits universities, both public and private, to protect students from being threatened and protect classes from being disputed. Where is the line to be drawn?

THE FLAWED "SPEECH VS. CONDUCT" DISTINCTION

It is tempting for university stakeholders to draw the line between speech and conduct: speech is protected and conduct may be regulated or prohibited. Despite substantial scholarly criticism (Ely, 1975, pp. 1494–1496; Lawrence, 1993; Nimmer, 1973), the purported speech–conduct dichotomy and its role as a tool in constitutional analysis has a remarkable sticking quality as it appears pragmatically justified. This is the distinction that a unanimous Supreme Court relied upon in *Wisconsin v. Mitchell* (1993), the case in which the Court upheld a Wisconsin bias crime law, the constitutionality of which had been challenged on the grounds that it punished thought or expression. The Court held that bias crimes are conduct and may therefore be punished, whereas pure hate speech is expression and is thus protected.

The speech–conduct distinction is tempting because it promises a predictable and logical way to draw lines: once we can differentiate speech from conduct, we can effectively protect the former and punish the latter. The promise, however, is ephemeral because the speech–conduct distinction is far too brittle to work. Speech and action are not merely intermingled. They are inextricable. Thus, the dialectic encompassing speech and conduct precludes not only a neat separation of the two, but even efforts to determine whether act or expression is the "predominant element" in certain behavior. Consider two examples: flag burning, which, as already briefly discussed, is constitutionally protected, and draft card burning, which the Supreme Court had held may be punished. The Court upheld the prohibition on destroying a draft card, holding that it "cannot accept the view that an apparently limitless variety of *conduct* [emphasis added] can be labeled '*speech*' [emphasis added] whenever the person engaging in the conduct intends thereby to express an idea" (*United States v. O'Brien*, 1968, p. 376).

The slipperiness of the speech–conduct distinction is apparent. Flag burning is surely an expression of political views, but is it not also an act? And what is the conduct in burning a draft card? The conduct of the very act of burning? It is at least plausible that, both in terms of the actor's own understanding of the card burning and in terms of the government's concern with punishing this behavior, the "conduct" of no longer having a draft card predominates in the act. As Professor John Hart Ely (1975) wrote in his classic article on the draft card burning case:

> …burning a draft card to express opposition to the draft is an undifferentiated whole, 100% action and 100% expression. It involves no conduct that is not at the same time communication, and no communication that does not result from conduct. (p. 1495)

We could say the same of flag burning. And yet one is protected and the other is not.

The point here is that the purported distinction between speech and conduct will not add rigor to any attempt to distinguish protected from proscribable behavior. The flying of a swastika flag or a Confederate flag from one's dorm room or home cannot be objectively described as expression alone. It is action as well. Distinguishing between conduct and expression requires a process that assumes its own conclusions. That which we wish to punish we will term "conduct" with expressive value, and that which we wish to protect we will call "expression" that requires conduct as its means of communication. The critical decision—which behavior may be punished and which should be protected—is wholly extrinsic to this process. If a meaningful distinction exists, we must find it elsewhere and the need to find such a distinction is crucial for understanding campus upheavals and how they should be addressed.

REPLACING SPEECH–CONDUCT WITH FOCUS ON THE ACTOR'S INTENT

The search for a meaningful distinction more profitably begins in basic criminal law doctrine. Crimes require both an act (*actus reus*) and an intent (*mens rea*). This distinction differs from the speech–conduct distinction because an "act" may include physical conduct or verbal activity. Speaking itself is a kind of act. Our focus is on intent—the actor's *mens rea*. Is the actor intending to cause harm to a particular victim, or is the actor intending to communicate views, however unpleasant or even hateful? This is not to suggest that the speaker's act of expressing himself or herself is purely deontological; expression has ramifications. As Oliver Wendell Holmes, Jr., said, "every idea is an incitement" (*Gitlow v. New York*, 1925, p. 673). But the expression that we should protect does not seek to cause injury. Several examples illustrate the point. The first two, drawn from *Virginia v. Black* (2003), involve a Virginia cross-burning statute that was struck down by the Supreme Court. The third example is the case described above that occurred at Williams College.

The Virginia cross-burning statute began by making it a crime for anyone, "with the intent of intimidating any person or group of persons, to burn, or cause to be burned, a cross on the property of another, a highway or other public place" (Va. Code. Ann. §18.2–423). The Court would have upheld this part of the law. Justice Sandra Day O'Connor wrote that "the First Amendment permits Virginia to outlaw cross burnings done with the intent to intimidate because burning a cross is a particularly virulent form of intimidation" (*Virginia v. Black*, 2003, p. 363). The Court struck down the statute because of what followed: "Any such burning of a cross shall be prima facie evidence of an intent to intimidate a person or group of persons" (Va. Code. Ann. §18.2–423).

Not every cross burning is in fact intended to intimidate a victim, and the two cases before the Court in *Virginia v. Black* (2003) made the point. Like textbook examples, the two cases represented the two distinct categories of cross burnings—domestic terrorism and expression of White supremacy. In one case, Barry Black led a Ku Klux Klan rally on private property, at the conclusion of which a 25 to 30-foot cross was burned in expression of the Klan's belief in white supremacy, a position steeped in hatred, but a belief nonetheless. In the other case, Richard Elliott and Jonathan O'Mara were prosecuted for attempting to burn a cross on the lawn of an African American, James Jubilee, who had recently moved next door. Elliott and O'Mara were trying to "'get back'" at Jubilee because, among other things, he had complained when they used their back yard as a firing range (p. 350).

The "prima facie evidence" clause of the cross-burning statute impermissibly blurred the lines between the two meanings of burning a cross. As Justice David Souter wrote in his separate opinion, "its primary effect is to skew jury deliberations toward conviction in cases where the evidence of intent to intimate is relatively weak and arguably consistent with a solely ideological reason for burning" (p. 385). To be constitutional, the statute would have to require proof on an intent to intimidate—proof of a cross burning alone is insufficient.

We may now return to the case at Williams College involving the faux eviction notice that had been placed on a student's dorm room, in imitation of the notices placed on Palestinian homes that are to be demolished by Israeli authorities due to the connection between residents and acts of terrorism. The college president asked what I thought should be done to those responsible for the notice. "This," he said to me, "is not just speech. This is actual conduct. Can we sanction these students?" My answer to him was similar to the answer I have given to many university administrators since: what did the student involved intend—to communicate or to threaten? How could we know the student's intent? In this case, I suggested looking into the way the notices were posted. Were only the leaders of a Jewish student organization targeted? For that matter, were only Jewish students targeted? As it turned out, every student in that dorm, regardless of affiliation, received one. That the complaining student honestly felt intimidated is not the issue. The issue is the actual intent of those who posted the notices—to intimidate and threaten individual Jewish students or, rather, to make a dramatic statement about their views concerning the Israel-Palestine conflict.

VERBAL ASSAULTS

We may apply a similar analysis to cases of pure speech. Under American law, and of particular significance to campus life, words alone can be harmful, and their use can even constitute a crime. Behavior designed to instill serious fear certainly may be criminalized and it does not matter whether it takes the form of spoken words alone, physical conduct alone, or some combination of the two. Many states have some form of assault law that proscribes the creation of fear or terror in a victim (Model Penal Code §211.1(1)(c), §211.3, §250.4(2); Iowa Code §708.1(2); Fla. Stat. §784.011). These laws, variously enacted as "menacing," "intimidation," and "threatening" statutes, may be violated through the defendant's use of words alone (Greenwalt, 1989, pp. 90–104; Greenwalt, 1990, pp. 298–300; Smolla, 1992, pp. 48–50). Reviewing courts have upheld various forms of verbal assault statutes, if sufficiently narrow in focus. Intimidation statutes, which criminalize words used to coerce others through fear of serious harm, are constitutional so long as it is clear that they apply only when the words are purposely or knowingly used by the accused to produce a fear and that the threat is real (Montana Intimidation Statute (<u>Mont. Code Ann</u>. 45-5-203), 1991). Menacing statutes differ from intimidation statutes. Whereas intimidation statutes focus upon coercion, the gravamen of menacing is the specific intent to cause fear (Colorado Menacing Statute (<u>Co. Rev. Stat.</u> §18-3-106)). Finally, "terroristic threatening" statutes are similar to intimidation laws in that they criminalize the use of fear to achieve specific results (Alaska Terroristic Threatening Statute (<u>Alaska Stat.</u> 11.56.810)). In each case, verbal assault statutes make words alone the basis for a criminal charge when those words are used purposely or knowingly to create fear in another.

Even pure speech, therefore, may in some cases, cross the line between protected expression and that which may be sanctioned or punished. But punishment is only appropriate, whether verbal or physical behavior is involved, when the purpose of the behavior is to instill fear of imminent serious harm. A racial epithet, when screamed at another student in a menacing manner, or a Confederate flag, when brandished on the lawn of a Black student fraternity to terrorize them, are no longer protected forms of expression; each has crossed over into that which may be punished by the university, and the offending student would be properly subject to disciplinary sanctions, suspension, or even expulsion from the institution.

RESPONDING TO PROTECTED HATEFUL SPEECH

To say that universities and colleges ought to protect most verbal activity on campus as free expression—even hateful speech—is not the end of the matter. How should institutions of higher learning respond to hateful speech on campus? Robert Hughes (1992), writing about the controversial exhibition of photographs by Robert Mapplethorpe in the early 1990s in Cincinatti, Ohio, provides an instructive approach (pp. 21–27). Hughes observed that the debate over the photographs had become largely constitutionalized, that is, it focused on whether, as a matter of a constitutional right, a museum may exhibit this work, or whether a city may, as Cincinnati did, shut down such an exhibition (Harrison, 1990; Wilkerson, 1990a; 1990b). Hughes wrote that the focus on questions of constitutional limits precluded the discussion of an arguably more important question: as a matter of art criticism and aesthetics, is this art any good?

The constitutional and jurisprudential questions that have occupied us thus far are critically important. But they are best seen as threshold issues, not as the ultimate societal issues. To address those, there must be a context for a moral response to protected hate speech, just as there must be room for aesthetic questions as to the merits of constitutionally protected art. This is especially true of residential campuses, public and private, where the very mission of the institution includes building a community and preparing future citizens.

The required response to hateful speech is to describe it as such and to criticize it directly. Supreme Court Justice Louis D. Brandeis wrote in *Whitney v. California* (1927) that, except in those rare cases in which the harm from speech is real and imminent, the answer to harmful or hateful speech is not "enforced silence" but, rather, "more speech" (p. 377).

This allows us to return to the story from my own campus set out above. Recall the student tweet of "no sympathy" with the murdered New York City police officers. Strictly speaking this is not hate speech, but the case remains relevant. I rejected the idea of expelling the student from the university, or of pursuing any student disciplinary charges or other sanctions, such as terminating financial aid. That would have been to engage in "enforced silence." I believed her tweet to be protected speech. But I also believed that this was a case that called for more than a mere statement confirming her rights. In the same statement that defended her freedom of expression and her academic freedom, I added a criticism of my own, saying that, in my view, her comments were contrary to the highest values of the university and that I found them to be abhorrent. Fundamentally, campus administrators are first and foremost educators; their remarks educate even those who have violated the highest values of the university. The reverberations of such a stance strengthen the fabric of the community as a whole.

Consider now the case that occurred at the University of Oklahoma in March 2015. Members of the Sigma Alpha Epsilon fraternity, on their way to a fraternity "Founders Day" event, engaged in horrific racist chanting that included the use of the n-word and celebrations of violence. Two student leaders of the fraternity were expelled from the university. I am highly sympathetic to the impulse for this expulsion and share in full the sentiment expressed by the university's president, who said in a statement that he was "sickened" by the event. But I question the case for the expulsion. Had the context been different, had this occurred outside of a predominately African American fraternity house, for example, this could have been a case of verbal assault, warranting full punishment. But with the actors chanting on a chartered bus in the presence solely of their own members, this was an instance of protected hate speech—vulgar, disgraceful, and indeed sickening, but also protected. There was no intent to threaten or cause direct harm to anyone. The well-intended impulse to punish the leaders stems, in large part, from a correct sense that this behavior required the strongest possible condemnation, but also from an incorrect assessment of the possible responses. An opportunity, to educate the offending students and advance the difficult community discussion, was lost.

We bind ourselves to an impoverished choice set if we believe that we can either punish speech or validate it. There is a middle position, expressed in Brandeis's dictum of "more speech," that allows us to respond without punishing. In the face of hate speech, the call for more speech is not merely an option; it is a professional or even moral obligation.

When I criticized the student tweet, and on one similar occasion when I protected but criticized a faculty listserv that included vulgar and disgusting language directed at, among others, my predecessor and the State of Israel, I was accused by some of creating a "chilling effect" on their right and ability to express themselves. My response will be surprising to some: not all "chilling effects" are bad. Some are cases of the type of enforced silence of which Justice Brandeis spoke; this is classically what we mean by a chilling effect, and these are pernicious and contrary to our system of free expression and the core mission of a university campus. But then there are those that are cases in which we influence each other for the good, when we are touched, as Lincoln said in his first inaugural address, "by the better angels of our nature." We should seek that effect on each other. Having that kind of effect on each other, especially through the ways in which we discuss and disagree, is at the heart of the academic enterprise, especially residential colleges or universities, so vital to American higher education.

FURTHERING "VIGOROUS CIVILITY" ON OUR CAMPUSES

Campus leaders—students, faculty, administrators and trustees—must search for respectful ways to disagree, whether we debate and discuss in person or virtually. I would advance three principles for respectful disagreement, to promote what I term "vigorous civility." Although I believe these to be of general applicability to liberal democracies, I am particularly concerned here with the application of these principles in the context of colleges and universities. The principles of vigorous civility are:

- Assume the best in each other, and not suspect the motives of those with whom we disagree;
- Disagree without attacking each other personally—dispute, without delegitimizing; and
- Look for common ground even when we disagree and articulate that common ground as part of the discussion.

The first principle—assuming the best and not suspecting motives—is not grounded in a naïve assumption that there are not those whose motives we might well question. Recall the student mentioned above whose motive in posting a fellow student's tweet on an extremist website was likely to expose that individual student, and perhaps the entire university, to ridicule among those who had no connection with the university community whatsoever. The first principle, however, does articulate a critically important starting point in campus debate. If we begin by focusing and questioning the motives of others, we tend to avoid engagement with their ideas and their arguments. Moreover, the very essence of an academic community is based on the idea that the members of that community are engaged in a process of discovering and creating knowledge and in transmitting that knowledge to others. We begin by presuming that those with whom we discuss and debate share a commitment to this idea. To be sure, this is a rebuttable presumption and in some instances, over time, will be shown not to apply in a particular case. But we start by assuming good faith and, to the extent possible, interpret the opposing argument through this lens.

The second principle—disagreeing without delegitimizing—is particularly significant in a time of hyper-polarization. Delegitimization is a process by which we define our opponent out of the community. We do not simply disagree with his or her argument; we deny the very legitimacy of the argument and of the opponent personally or by membership in a group. Social psychologist Chiara Volpato and her co-authors describe delegitimization as "a categorization of groups into extreme negative social categories, which are ultimately excluded from society" (Volpato, Durante, Gabbiadini, Andrighetto, & Mari, 2010, p. 272). As with the concern underlying the first principle, delegitimization avoids engaging with the ideas of the other; we would instead undermine the very right of the other to assert those views. Ultimately, delegitimization goes even further because it seeks to challenge not just another's ideas but his or her very membership in the community. It is thus entirely inconsistent with the notion of an academic community committed to learning, discussing, and debating because instead of contending with another person *within* the community, it defines that person as being *outside* of the community.

The third principle—the search for common ground—may seem simple, but it is nothing of the sort. A personal example illustrates the point. I have long been an advocate of the enhanced punishment of bias-motivated crimes, given the additional and particularized harm that these crimes cause to their victims, to the target community of the crime, and to the greater society (Lawrence, 1999). There are those scholars who have argued that giving any weight to the bias criminal's motivation in determining the appropriate sentence is an impermissible punishment of thought (Jacobs & Potter, 1998). Notable among these was Susan Gellman (1991), who wrote an influential article challenging the premise of increasing the level of punishment for bias crimes. Professor Gellman and I debated each other in print and in person on a number of occasions. Several years after our scholarly debate began, we were each invited to participate in a symposium at Harvard Law School and to submit papers that would be published in the *Harvard Journal of Legislation*. This appeared to be yet another opportunity for us each to articulate our respective positions on these issues. It was at this time that I read an intriguing op-ed piece in *The New York Times* that was co-authored by a pro-life advocate and pro-choice supporter. In that piece, neither author attempted to persuade the other of the ultimate issue of the morality of abortion. Rather, the two authors sought to articulate a set of points on which they could agree, for example, the importance of finding ways to reduce the frequency of unwanted pregnancies. It was a significant search for common ground on an issue that is all-too-often completely polarized.

Inspired by this op-ed article in the *Times*, I proposed that Professor Gellman and I co-author a single article, setting out points of agreement on the question of how bias crimes ought to be treated by the criminal law. The result was an article entitled "Agreeing to Agree: A Proponent and Opponent of Hate Crimes Laws Reach for Common Ground" (Gellman & Lawrence, 2004). In this article, after we each summarized our respective positions as to which we *disagreed*, we set out a series of observations and conclusions that we shared. In fact, we found sufficient common ground to be able to propose a model bias crime statute that, although satisfying neither of us entirely, was sufficiently acceptable to each of us that we were willing to recommend it as a compromise we could each support. We wrote this article both to bridge a divide on a particular issue of deep concern to us both, but also to demonstrate a means by which debate might profitably go forward. In summarizing the goal of the article, we wrote that "[w]e do not intend to compromise that which cannot be compromised, but we do intend at the very least to clarify that which can be clarified. That is, after all, at least one model of the legislative process in a democratic society" (Gellman & Lawrence, 2004, p. 422).

The third principle of vigorous civility proposes that discussions and debates that take place on our campuses include a conscious and expressed search for and articulation of shared points of agreement. In some cases, such as with Professor Gellman and me, this search will in fact lead to a shared set of conclusions. In others, it will be sufficient that there is a shared commitment to the process of intellectual engagement and free inquiry that is the hallmark of liberal and open-minded education. I conclude with an extraordinary example of such a shared commitment between Professors Charles L. Black, Jr. and Alexander Bickel.

Black was a legendary figure in constitutional law at the Yale Law School. He was one of the architects of the legal arguments attacking segregation and an advocate of judicial activism. His colleague, the equally legendary Bickel, argued for judicial restraint. When Bickel passed away, Black (1974) wrote in tribute that they had "agreed in everything but our opinions" (p. 200). It is as powerful a statement of respectful, even loving, disagreement as I know. If on our campuses, we have lost the ability to say to those with whom we disagree that we "agree in everything but our opinions," we have lost something very precious and, perhaps, irreplaceable. But if we can do so, we will be building the most important kind of community there is—and one worthy of the great shared mission held America's colleges and universities.

QUESTIONS FOR DISCUSSION

1. How would you define the mission of a college or university and how does this relate to issues of free expression? Consider, for example, that private colleges and universities are not bound by the First Amendment of the United States Constitution. To what extent should these private institutions of higher education take upon themselves the constitutional protections for expression set out in the

First Amendment? What is the source of these protections on a private college or university campus?

2. What steps should a college or university take to prepare for campus visits by highly controversial speakers, either in general or a particular visit by a speaker? Which groups should be involved in this process and what should their respective roles be?

3. Public universities are bound by the First Amendment of the Constitution. Nonetheless, a public institution may define itself as a "limited public forum" rather than an open public forum that is open to all speakers. To what extent, if any, should a public university limit the scope of speakers who come to campus? For example, should outside speakers require an invitation from a university-based group in order to visit campus? If a public university does define itself as a "limited public forum," how does that affect their academic mission?

4. What steps should a college or university take to prepare new students for discussions that lead to disturbing and difficult conversation both inside the classroom and on campus generally? How does this relate to debates over "trigger warnings" and "safe spaces"?

5. In some cases involving particularly controversial speakers, the financial cost of providing adequate security for the event can be substantial. To what extent are these costs an appropriate factor to take into account in determining the manner of the speaker's appearance on campus? To what extent is it appropriate for the college or university to pass some or all of those costs onto the speaker?

6. Under what circumstances, if any, is it appropriate for a college or university to prohibit a form or content of expression altogether, or to discipline a student or faculty member for engaging in certain expressive activity?

7. Imagine that someone puts a Confederate flag:
   (a) on her dorm room door;
   (b) on everyone's dorm room door;
   (c) only on African American students' doors;
   (d) in a common space.

   How should college administrators act in each case? What principles are at stake in your decisions?

STATUTORY APPENDIX

Alaska Stat. 11.56.810. The Alaska Terroristic Threatening Statute provides that a person commits the crime of terroristic threatening if the person:

(a) knowingly makes a false report that a circumstance
   (1) dangerous to human life exists or is about to exist and
      (A) a person is placed in reasonable fear of physical injury to any person;

(B) causes evacuation of a building, public place or area, business premises, or mode of public transportation;

(C) causes serious public inconvenience; or

(D) the report claims that a bacteriological, biological, chemical, or radiological substance that is capable of causing serious physical injury has been sent or is present in a building, public place or area, business premises, or mode of public transportation.

Alaska Stat. 11.56.810. See, e.g., *Allen v. State*, 759 P. 2d 451 (Alaska Ct. App. 1988) (upholding constitutionality of Alaska Terroristic Threatening Statute); *Thomas v. Commonwealth*, 574 S. W. 2d 903 (Ky. 1978) (upholding constitutionality of Kentucky Terroristic Threatening Statute, Ky. Rev. Stat. §508.080 (Baldwin 1984)).

Co. Rev. Stat. §18-3-206. The Colorado Menacing Statute provides that:

A person commits the crime of menacing if, by any threat or physical action, he or she knowingly places or attempts to place another person in fear of imminent serious bodily injury.

Co. Rev. Stat. §18-3-206. See, e.g., Colorado v. McPherson, 619 P. 2d 38 (Col. 1980) (construing Colorado Menacing Statute); State v. Garcias, 679 P. 2d 1354 (Or. 1984) (upholding Oregon Menacing Statute, Or. Rev. Stat. 163.190(1), against challenge under First Amendment).

Mont. Code Ann. 45-5-203 (1991). The Montana Intimidation Statute provides as follows:

(1) A person commits the offense of intimidation when, with the purpose to cause another to perform or to omit the performance of any act, the person communicates to another, under circumstances which reasonably tend to produce a fear that it will be carried out, a threat to perform without lawful authority any of the following acts:
   (a) inflict physical harm on the person threatened or any other person;
   (b) subject any person to physical confinement or restraint; or
   (c) commit any felony.

(2) A person commits the offense of intimidation if the person knowingly communicates a threat or false report of a pending fire, explosion, or disaster which would endanger life or property.

Mont. Code Ann. 45-5-203 (1991). An earlier version of this statute required only a threat without any requirement that there be a reasonable tendency that the threat would produce fear. This earlier version was held to violate the first amendment in a federal habeas corpus proceeding. See *Wurtz v. Risley*, 719 F. 2d 1438 (9th Cir. 1983). The statute was amended to conform with the court's decision and has not been challenged since. See also *State v. Lance*, 721 P. 2d 1258 (Mont. 1986) (upholding section (1)(b) of the un-amended statute).

Model Penal Code §211.1(1)(c) (Official Draft 1985) ("A person is guilty of assault if he … attempts by physical menace to put another in fear of imminent serious bodily injury."); ibid., §211.3 (one is guilty of a "terroristic" threat if one "threatens to commit any crime of violence with purpose to terrorize another…"); ibid., §250.4(2) (one is guilty of harassment if one taunts another in a manner likely to provoke a violent response). See also, e.g., Iowa Code §708.1(2) (West 1989); Fla. Stat. §784.011 (West 1992).

Va. Code. Ann. §18.2–423 (Michie 1991) (enacted in 1950). The prima facie provision was added to the statute in 1968.

REFERENCES

American Communications Ass'n, C.I.O., et. al. v. Douds, 339 U.S. 382 (1950). Chief Justice Vinson applied the "clear and present danger" standard to permit the prosecution of leaders of the Communist Party in *Dennis v. United States*, 341 U.S. 494 (1951) (Vinson, C.J., plurality opinion).

Baker, C. E. (2009). Autonomy and hate speech. In I. Hare & J. Weinstein (Eds.), *Extreme speech and democracy* (pp. 139–157). New York, NY: Oxford University Press.

Black, C. L. (1974). Alexander Mordecai Bickel. *Yale Law Journal*, *84*(2), 199.

Doe v. Univ. of Mich., 721 F. Supp. 852 (E.D. Mich. 1989) (striking down speech code at University of Michigan as violation of students' first amendment right of free expression).

Ely, J. H. (1975). Flag desecration: A case study in the roles of categorization and balancing in first amendment analysis. *Harvard Law Review*, *88*, 1482–1508.

Emerson, T.I. (1970). *The system of freedom of expression*. New York, NY: Random House, Incorporated.

Gellman, S. (1991). Sticks and stones can put you in jail, but can words increase your sentence? Constitutional and policy dilemmas of ethnic intimidation laws. *UCLA Law Review*, *39*, 333–396.

Gellman, S. B., & Lawrence, F. M. (2004). Agreeing to agree: A proponent and opponent of hate crime laws reach for common ground. *Harvard Journal on Legislation*, *41*, 421–448.

Gilbert v. Minnesota, 254 U.S. 325 (1920).

Gitlow v. New York, 268 U.S. 652 (1925) (Holmes, J., dissenting).

Greenwalt, K. (1989). *Speech, crime, and the uses of language*. New York, NY: Oxford University Press.

Greenwalt, K. (1990). Insults and epithets: Are they protected speech? *Rutgers Law Review*, *42*, 287–308.

Harrison, E. (1990, April 8). Mapplethorpe display brings smut charges. *Los Angeles Times*. Retrieved from http://articles.latimes.com/1990-04-08/news/mn-1692_1_mapplethorpe-photographs.

Hughes, R. (1992, April 23). Art, morals, and politics. *The New York Review of Books*, 21–26.

Jacobs, J. B., & Potter, K. (1998). *Hate crimes: Criminal law & identity politics*. New York, NY: Oxford University Press.

Lawrence, F. M. (1993). Resolving the hate crimes/hate speech paradox: Punishing bias crimes and protecting racist speech. *Notre Dame Law Review*, *68*, 673–721.

Lawrence, F. M. (1999). *Punishing hate: Bias crimes under American law*. Cambridge, MA: Harvard University Press.

Nimmer, M. B. (1973). The meaning of symbolic speech under the first amendment. *UCLA Law Review*, *21*, 29–62.

Post, R. C. (2009). Hate speech. In I. Hare & J. Weinstein (Eds.), *Extreme speech and democracy* (pp. 123–138). New York, NY: Oxford University Press.

Post, R.C. (1995) *Constitutional domains: Democracy, community, management.* Cambridge, MA: Harvard University Press.

Smolla, R. A. (1992). *Free speech in an open society.* New York, NY: A.A. Knopf.

Texas v. Johnson, 491 U.S. 397 (1989).

United States v. O'Brien, 391 U.S. 367 (1968). See also Cox. v. Louisiana, 379 U.S. 536, 555 (1965) ("We emphatically reject the notion … that the [First Amendment] afford[s] the same kind of freedom to those who would communicate ideas by conduct … [as] to those who communicate ideas by pure speech."). See also Cohen v. California, 403 U.S. 15, 27 (1971) (Blackmun, J., dissenting) ("Cohen's absurd and immature antic, in my view, was mainly conduct and little speech.").

United States v. Schwimmer, 279 U.S. 644, 654–655 (1929) (Holmes, J., dissenting), *overruled* by *Girouard v. United States*, 328 U.S. 61 (1946).

UWM Post, Inc. v. Bd. of Regents of Univ. of Wis. Sys., 774 F. Supp. 1163 (E.D. Wis. 1991) (striking down the speech code at University of Wisconsin as violation of students' first amendment right of free expression).

Virginia v. Black, 538 U.S. 343 (2003).

Volpato, C., Durante, F., Gabbiadini, A., Andrighetto, L., & Mari, S. (2010). Picturing the other: Targets of delegitimization across time. *International Journal of Conflict and Violence, 4*(2), 269–287.

Waldron, J. (2012). *The harm in hate speech.* Cambridge, MA: Harvard University Press.

Whitney v. California, 274 U.S. 357 (1927) (Brandeis, J., concurring).

Wilkerson, I. (1990a, April 8). Cincinnati gallery indicted in mapplethorpe furor. *The New York Times.* Retrieved from www.nytimes.com/1990/04/08/us/cincinnati-gallery-indicted-in-mapplethorpe-furor.html.

Wilkerson, I. (1990b, October 6). Cincinnati jury acquits museum in mapplethorpe obscenity case. *The New York Times.* Retrieved from www.nytimes.com/1990/10/06/us/cincinnati-jury-acquits-museum-in-mapplethorpe-obscenity-case.html.

Wisconsin v. Mitchell, 508 U.S. 476 (1993).

PART II

AMPLIFYING THE VISIBILITY
OF SPECIFIC STUDENT POPULATIONS

7

REFUTING CONTEMPORANEITY

Trans* Experiences In, Out, and Beyond Higher Education

CHILDREN OF THE HOUSE OF "PAY IT NO MIND"[1]

Presently, there seem to be various conflicting mis/understandings regarding trans* people and populations. Take, for example, the following two competing narratives about trans* people that appeared in 2014. The first saw Laverne Cox gracing the cover of *TIME* magazine. Dressed in a form-fitting navy dress, Cox gazed directly at the reader, and was positioned next to the cover story's headline, which read, "The Transgender Tipping Point." Using Cox as the symbol of trans* visibility, *TIME*'s announcement posed the arrival and social acceptance of trans* people as axiomatic. Furthermore, by having Cox, a trans* woman of color, be the first openly trans* person to be on the cover of *TIME*, the magazine was also implying that trans* women of color were not only visible, but had achieved acceptance in their own right; a social acceptance that belied the ongoing violence and threat trans* women of color face(d) then and now (Gossett & Dunham, 2015). Such an implication created an imaginary in which all trans* people were united as a monolithic category, and as a result, all trans* people enjoyed the same supposed acceptance and safety on account of our seemingly newfound visibility.

Also in 2014, *TSQ: Transgender Studies Quarterly* came out with their first issue, a double issue containing 86 keywords in the burgeoning field of transgender studies. Far from seeking to solidify understandings of people with trans* identities, experiences, and subjectivities, Stryker and Currah (2014) noted in their introduction to the issue that:

> The term *transgender*, then, carries its own antinomies: Does it help make or undermine gender identities and expressions? Is it a way of being gendered

or a way of doing gender? Is it an identification or a method? A promise or a threat? Although we retain *transgender* in the full, formal title of this journal, we invite you to imagine the *T* in *TSQ* as standing in for whatever version of *trans-* best suits you—and we imagine many of our readers, like us, will move back and forth among several of them. (p. 1)

In the first paragraph, on the first page of the first issue, Stryker and Currah did more than recognize the pluralities across trans* identities, experiences, communities, and subjectivities; they actively welcomed the spillages, seepages, and contradictions that have always already been present when talking about a population that is ethereal by design. For example, even the Latin prefix under which many of us come to identify (i.e., *trans-*) means across. Rather than attempting to "pin down" this across-ness, Stryker and Currah's call marks a desire to welcome incoherency as an integral way by which one comes to know trans* people, experiences, subjectivities, and epistemologies.

These two events call into question not only who we understand to be trans*, but how we come to know the social effects of gender-based discourse for a trans* population with perhaps more differences than similarities. It also should come as no surprise that in the aforementioned examples, those who presented a trans*-as-coherent narrative were not trans* themselves, whereas those seeking more complex, nuanced, and precise understandings are ourselves trans*.

In many ways, then, trans* people are both coherent and incoherent, with our incoherencies often being overlooked by a cisgender public seeking an easy understanding of who we are, how we live, and what is good for us. Here, the desire for simplicity and unified understandings of trans*ness could well be understood as a manifestation of multiple forms of systemic oppression; a thread of thought we explore in greater depth later in this chapter.

Taking this call for *in*coherence seriously, we use this chapter to trace the ways in which trans* college students continue to resist knowability in several ways. First, we discuss affirmative-based and trans*-centered literature published in the past four years in the field of higher education. We focus on this literature as a way to resist research that frames trans* people as deficient and/or as a population unworthy of being the sole focus of research and to center the work for and by trans* scholars published during this period. Next, we discuss the various ways in which trans* people defy normative notions of dominance (e.g., whiteness, compulsory able-bodiedness, colonization and U.S. exceptionalism, the Black–White racial binary). Particularly, we wish to trouble the overwhelming whiteness of research on trans* college students in past and current epochs. That is, despite how these framings have made trans* students normative in higher education literature, we enunciate the antinomies contained therein, particularly the methodological violence resulting in the erasure and construction of certain genders as unknowable impossibilities (i.e., trans* people who are non-binary, disabled, etc). We also problematize how systemic exclusions foreclose college going and persistence as a possibility for many trans* people, and thus, to only focus on trans* students *in* college reifies hegemonic notions of excellence and respectability that are rooted in white supremacy, classism, and ableism.

We close our chapter by questioning what it means for trans* collegians to be included as a "contemporary issue." In other words, we question, given that trans* people have always been present throughout society—and thus, throughout education—why is it that the higher education community is just now giving us attention? Moreover, we ask how such attention-giving may itself be steeped in the normativities we previously problematized, and therefore, reify how we as trans* people are continually unexpected (Jourian, Simmons, & Devaney, 2015) and misunderstood (Stewart, 2017a). This exoticizing of trans* bodies and the resultant press to develop "new" approaches to "work with" this "new" student population obfuscates the pre-existent cisgenderism and patriarchy of the academy. In so doing, we use this chapter to practice a politic in which we simultaneously resist contemporaneity and affirm the ongoing antinomies of trans*/gender/people in the academy and, as a result, proclaim that we as trans* people are not your contemporary issue, but a population with pasts, presents, and futures surpassing categorization, and who demand to be known on our own terms.

MOBILIZING A TRANS* EPISTEMOLOGY

In 2017, Nicolazzo imagined a way of knowing centered in the experiences of trans* people. This imaginary was offered as a form of resistance to illogics of gender binarism pervasive throughout the academy (Catalano & Griffin, 2016). How scholars think about—or how they imagine—what they know informs their practice. Therefore, in this chapter, we intentionally mobilize a way of thinking about reality and knowledge that is anchored in a liberatory ethic that is critical, poststructural, and decolonial. This paradigmatic positioning enables us to enunciate the cisgenderism that clouds scholarship and practice involving trans* students in the academy and recognize that what has been advanced by the mainstream literature about trans*ness is itself steeped in colonized and anti-Black assumptions about gender and gender relationships that serve only to reinforce cis supremacy. Moreover, through this lens, we promote our lived reality of trans*ness as defiant and resistant to categorization, fixity, and compartmentalization within frameworks of time, movements, and scholarship.

Nicolazzo's (2017a) proposed trans* epistemology intentionally relied on polyvocality and process—in other words, on the valuing of many voices and questioning "how" over "what," which also informs the construction of this review of literature. Polyvocality is reflected in our incorporation of both academic and non-academic literature and people as sources of knowledge about trans* collegians. We do not present these so-called non-academic voices as merely illustrative, decorative, or subsumed to academic sources, but rather to convey the depths of knowledge about ourselves that cannot be held by the artifices of academic prose. As such, our chapter reflects the result of "community-based praxis and living" (Nicolazzo, 2017a, p. 7). Our process axiology comes through not in our resistance to answering "what" questions, but rather "how." Particularly, how liberation may be realized through the artifacts documented here.

Three of the six provisional tenets offered by Nicolazzo (2017a) are therefore mobilized in this chapter in the following ways. First, by focusing on affirmative scholarship about trans* people, we reject deficit-based narratives that see trans* people as only "of oppression" instead of being subjected to oppression. Much of this affirmative scholarship has been written by trans* people, though not exclusively. On the other hand, much of the deficit-based literature about trans* people in higher education has been written by cis people, though not exclusively. Higher suicide rates and mental health disabilities, educational attrition, job loss and instability, and survival sex work are the result of cisgender systems of oppression; they are not what it means to be trans* in higher education or in society at large. Therefore, we intentionally focus this review on literature that affirms the potential, possibility, and capacity of trans* people in higher education as more informative and insightful than deficit-based scholarship written to appeal to a cis gaze.

Second, this review is informed by an intersectional politic that recognizes the un/common experience of trans* oppression as lived by trans* people across multiple marginalities. As Crenshaw (1991) and Collins (1998) have noted, singular identity activism fails to speak to those whose lives are caught in the nexus of multiple axes of oppression. Consequently, research about trans* people that uses participant samples that exclude racially minoritized trans* people, two-spirit people, trans* women, non-binary femme trans* people, genderqueer and agender people, and trans* people with disabilities does not reflect the varied ways that racism, settler colonialism, (trans*) misogyny, and ableism each interact with cisgenderism to limit life chances, as well as expand the possibilities of trans* identities.

Third, blending Nicolazzo's (2017a) third and sixth tenets, this review recognizes the tension of being both "in" and "out" of higher education and the possibilities created by being "in" it together. As Nicolazzo wrote, "to be visible as a trans* person means to be increasingly watched, scrutinized, and surveilled. In a sense, we are opting into the panopticon of surveillance…" (p. 17). In a way, this review also represents an opting-in to a surveillance culture in the academy through which staffing and financial resources are only appropriated upon the provision of data documenting the existence of embodied needs. At the same time, this review also uplifts the many ways in which trans* people in higher education resist these forms of surveillance and attempted categorization. Through advancing these narratives, we recognize the power of the counter-story (Solórzano & Yosso, 2002) to "commune and create a world in which possibilities for our gendered pasts/presents/futures are proliferated rather than stifled" (Nicolazzo, 2017a, p. 12).

Our paradigm therefore reflects specific and intentional ontological, epistemological, methodological, and axiological orientations. Ontologically, we seek to make real and to realize the insights of trans* people about trans* people as more substantive than those of cis people through a cis-oppressive gaze. Epistemologically, we use this review to highlight knowledges that provoke, are unruly, and which openly disagree with canonical perspectives. Our methodological practice unabashedly forwards citational politics (Ahmed, 2017) that elevates affirmative approaches and intersectional trans* subjectivities as more instructive and liberatory than those which are not. Finally, we value community and kinship, our (trans)matriarchal heritage, those who exist and resist beyond the borders of higher education, those who are confronted by multiple marginalities, and research as a practice of resistance. We invite you to continue reading this review with this positioning in mind.

THE AFFIRMATIVE TURN IN TRANS* RESEARCH IN HIGHER EDUCATION

Currently, there is a nascent body of literature that is changing the possibilities for trans* studies within higher education. To be sure, there has been some previous literature about trans* students; however, much of that literature was either non-empirical and/ or rooted in deficit logics whereby trans* students were positioned as "not enough" in comparison to their non-trans* peers. Written largely—although not exclusively— by trans* scholars, this new wave of trans* research in higher education is broad in scope, addressing students (Catalano, 2015a, 2015b; Jourian, 2017a; Nicolazzo, 2016, 2017b), faculty (Jaekel & Nicolazzo, 2017; Pitcher, 2017), staff (Jourian et al., 2015; Simmons, 2017), research methods (Catalano, 2017; Jourian & Nicolazzo, 2016), and epistemologies (Nicolazzo, 2017a). In addition, scholars are beginning to expose the ways trans* oppression and gender binary discourse (Nicolazzo, 2017b) mediate the experiences of trans* people within supposedly "safe" spaces (e.g., LGBTQ centers; Marine & Nicolazzo, 2014), as well as for non-binary and genderqueer trans* people (Stewart, 2017a), and trans* students of color (Nicolazzo, 2016). Also, two special issues have been published with a focus on trans* people, pedagogies, curricula, and research (methods) in higher education (Nicolazzo, 2017c; Nicolazzo, Marine, & Galarte, 2015a).

The aforementioned recent turn in trans* scholarship in higher education signals what has been termed "the trans* paradox," or the reality that alongside a rise in visibility and recognition of trans* ways of being and thinking resides a persistent *mis*recognition, *un*knowing, and violent erasure of trans* people (Nicolazzo, 2017b). As Nicolazzo (2017a) stated, "What has become painfully clear to me is that how we [trans* people] are understood socially, and the way we have been focused on throughout much of the current public discourse, has been from the perspective of the gazing cisgender eye" (p. 3). In this sense, then, as soon as trans* scholars(hip) has seemingly "arrived" on the higher education scene as a "contemporary issue," we have simultaneously been erased, written over, and deemed "unexpected" (Jourian et al., 2015).

Mirroring Delgado Bernal's (2001) "pedagogies of the home," we as an authorship assert that "although we may be *from* oppression, we are not *of* oppression" (Nicolazzo, 2017a, p. 9; emphasis in original). In other words, despite the paradoxical asymmetry between the recent boom in affirmative trans* scholarship and the ongoing ways we are un/made as deficient, we will continue to make our own way through the academy—and indeed, the U.S. state—which is deeply invested in trans* oppression (Harris & Nicolazzo, 2017; Nicolazzo, 2017b). We assert the need to do this through our aforementioned trans* affirmative citational practice as well as detailing the ways monolithic understandings of trans*ness have occluded the wild profusions of our communities. It is to the latter concern that we now turn, discussing recent literature both in and beyond the field of higher education that expands through whom and how we come to know trans*.

PROLIFERATING VISIONS OF TRANS*NESS IN, OUT, AND BEYOND HIGHER EDUCATION

Taking Delgado Bernal's (2001) notion of "pedagogies of the home" as our starting point, we use this section to inquire: just whose home(s) are (not) being invoked when we (mis)recognize trans* people in higher education? In addressing this question, we assert there is a compelling need to discuss those trans* people and populations who have been kept at bay from higher education due to generational and systemic oppression. Indeed, we claim the story of trans* people in higher education cannot and should never be told separately from those trans* people who were never invited, encouraged, or expected to take part in higher education in the first place. Thus, we use literature in and beyond higher education to deconstruct how structural oppression has framed how many have come to (not) know trans* populations.

Gender, Anti-Blackness, and (Non-)Being

In the United States, slavery is imagined as a singular event even as it changed over time and even as its duration expands into supposed emancipation and beyond. But slavery was not singular; it was, rather, a singularity … Emancipation did not make free Black Life free; it continues to hold us to that singularity. The brutality was not singular; it was a singularity of antiblackness. (Sharpe, 2016, p. 106)

As Weheliye (2014) stated, "There exists no portion of the modern human that is not subject to racialization, which determines the hierarchical ordering of the Homo sapiens species into humans, not-quite-humans, and nonhumans" (p. 8). Both Patton (2016) and Ahmed (2012) have detailed the applicability of such effects of the omnipresence of racialization in institutions of higher education. Specifically, both have elucidated how racism and anti-Blackness continue to frame the organization of higher education, to say nothing about the life chances of people of color in and beyond the academy. Thus, as the above quotation suggests, anti-Blackness and its concomitant ordering of (non)humanity is a singularity that has always already included higher education in its wake.

The ordering of (non)humanity Weheliye (2014) discussed has various edges, including epistemological concerns of how one comes to (not) know trans* subjects as having racialized identities, experiences, and histories. Far from being a philosophical meditation, how one comes to (not) know particular populations (e.g., trans* people) is intimately tethered to that population's (non)humanity and (lack of) ability to exist in public life. As such, it is telling that at the time of writing this chapter there exists an extreme silence in higher education scholarship focusing on Black trans* people, Indigenous trans* and two-spirit people, Latinx trans* people, and Asian American, Pacific Islander, and Desi trans* people. Of the work that currently exists, Jourian (2017a), Simmons (2017), Stewart (2017a), and Nicolazzo's (2016) studies stand out as among the very few that amplify and/or center trans* populations of color.

Far from being a problem contained within higher education literature, Ellison, Green, Richardson, and Snorton (2017) expressed skepticism about the ongoing institutionalization of transgender studies, particularly as it relates to the field's ongoing failure to honor Black feminism's contributions to the theorizing of gender. This deracializing of gender is, at its core, intimately connected to the ongoing degendering of Blackness and Black people (Sharpe, 2016; Spillers, 1987). These actions work to bolster the ongoing "universalization of whiteness" (Krell, 2017, p. 235) and what Sharpe (2016) described as "antiblackness as total climate" (p. 21).

Such a lack of Black (trans*)feminist theorizing mediates material life chances for Black trans* people. In other words, the inability to think Black trans* people into existence has both theoretical and material effects on the livability of Black trans* life. That is, despite the reality of Black trans* existence, the universalization of whiteness around which (non)humanity congeals poses the existence of Black trans* life as a threat that can only begin to be understood via whiteness (e.g., white standards of beauty; Glover, 2016). This is especially true for Black trans* women (Mock, 2017).

Circling back to the hailing and subsequent interrogation of the "transgender tipping point" we discussed in the introduction to this chapter, we ask: for whom is this sociopolitical moment a tipping point? Green (2017) and Michaelson (2015), among others, have added to the chorus of voices resisting the notion that trans* people of color have seemingly arrived at a moment of social acceptance, and that such supposed acceptance has meant an increase of life chances. Moreover, both Green and Michaelson are part of a broader pantheon of critical (trans*) scholarship (e.g., Ahmed, 2012; Ferguson, 2012; Spade, 2015) that suggests structural diversity (e.g., efforts for greater inclusion of trans* people in the public sphere) will equate to increased life chances for trans* people. In fact, just focusing on a politics of inclusion—as opposed to a politics of transformation and redistribution—elides how that very strategy has been co-opted to further the projects of racism, imperialism, and colonization that hurt, harm, and violently erase trans* people; projects that institutions of higher education are very much invested in and further in conjunction with government organizations (Nicolazzo, Marine, & Galarte, 2015b; Stewart, 2017b). As such, we call on Reinaldo Walcott (2014) as a reminder that "anti-Blackness is not and cannot be merely one among other modes of thought, because only engaging anti-Blackness as [a] foundational limit to our collective livability makes visible the overarching racial capitalist ordering of neo-colonial peoples, [I]ndigenous peoples, and Blacks" (p. 102).

Gender, Colonialism, and Two-Spirit Resistance

Educational spaces have long been a site of imperialism, and have been used to assimilate Native people (Marr, 2004). Native peoples have also faced erasure within higher education research (Shotton, Lowe, & Waterman, 2013), mirroring the ongoing erasure and (lack of) recognition of two-spirit people throughout gender-based research, be it in or outside of higher education as a field (Driskill, 2016). Such erasures, omissions, and misrecognitions extend the aforementioned failures to capture the humanity of Black trans* subjects to Native people and nations. Moreover, because of the linking of colonization and the regulation of gender, as well as the historic investment of institutions of higher education in the ongoing project of colonization, it holds that U.S. higher education is also implicated in the negative impacts of colonization on two-spirit populations.

Invoking the metaphor of the asterisk, Shotton et al. (2013) exposed the ongoing ways Native populations are (re)cast as peripheral to higher education research and practice. Although their use of the asterisk as a signifier is distinct from how it is used alongside trans* populations, the symbol becomes yet another point through which one can understand gender and Indigeneity as always already connected. Pulling on this connection further, Driskill (2010) expressed that "no understanding of sexual and gender oppression on colonized and occupied land can take place without an understanding of the ways colonial projects continually police sexual and gender lines" (p. 73). As such, higher education research must be attentive to undermining settler logics within contemporary discourses of gender and sexuality (Arvin, Tuck, & Morrill, 2013). Connecting this need back to our previous conversation about anti-Black racism in and beyond higher education, it becomes quite clear that the study of trans* students cannot be separated from the study and ongoing effects of anti-Black racism and settler colonialism (Collins, 2000; Driskill, 2016; Ferguson, 2004; Lorde, 1984; Moraga & Anzaldúa, 2015; Muñoz, 1999; Tuck & Yang, 2012).

Disability, Normalization, and State Apparatuses

> The history of freakdom extends far back into western civilization … Freak shows populated the United States and people flocked to the circus, the carnival, the storefront dime museum. They came to gawk at 'freaks,' 'savages,' and 'geeks' … They came to have their ideas of normal and abnormal, superior and inferior, their sense of self, confirmed and strengthened. (Clare, 2015, pp. 85–86)

Disability justice has long been concerned with interrogating and exposing the violences enacted by the furthering of hegemonic notions of normalcy. Mia Mingus (as cited in Yarborough, 2015) described disability justice as "a multi issue political understanding of disability and ableism, moving away from a rights based equality model and beyond just access, to a framework that centers justice and wholeness for all disabled people and communities" (para. 5). As Clare (2015) noted, the coupling of disabled people[2] as "freaks" with the ongoing project of surveillance for the express purpose of confirming and strengthening enabled[3] people's sense of superiority has always already been axiomatic. The focus on disabled people's bodies as "not right" and "abnormal" is similarly intimately linked to the ongoing expansion of the U.S. carceral state as a result of the policing of trans* people, particularly trans* women of color. These linkages appear not only because there are disabled trans* people, but also because the violent projection of normalcy overlaps both trans* and disabled ways of being in the world. It should come as no surprise, then, that the U.S. prison–industrial complex continues to lock up trans*, disabled, and disabled trans* people at alarmingly disproportionate rates (Clare, 2015; Gares, 2016; Mogul, Ritchie, & Whitlock, 2012; Spade, 2015; Stanley & Smith, 2015). Whether due to the pernicious effects of systemic poverty, homelessness, and employment insecurity with which trans* people must contend (Grant et al., 2011) or the ongoing dangers of existing in public spaces that lead to one being arrested for what has been termed "walking while trans*" (Strangio, 2014), it becomes clear that not only have disability and trans* justice always already been entwined, but to talk about college access for trans* populations is insufficient if it does not include a discussion of how *in*access is literally built into the functioning of the U.S. state via the ongoing criminalization of "abnormal" ways of being. In other words, it bears stating that the question of college access for trans* people should not just start with admitting trans* students, but with admitting how trans* people—in conjunction with disabled and multiply marginalized peoples (Annamma, 2018)—are policed out of public life, including the ability to even consider going to college. It is to this question of (in)access that we now turn.

A QUESTION OF COLLEGE (IN)ACCESS

> Access – it sometimes seems as though some people have it and some don't. But what if access is much more than such an individual state of affairs? What if access is much more than a substantial, measurable entity? What if it is more like a way of judging or a way of perceiving? (Titchkosky, 2011, p. 3)

Normative notions of access to postsecondary education focus on bodies in spaces. Specifically, conversations of access focus on *who* has access to *where* and *at what time*. As disability studies scholar Tanya Titchkosky indicated, however, access—or the lack thereof—is more than "an individual state of affairs." In relation to trans* collegians, access is more than a matter of getting more trans* bodies to occupy space on college campuses. In fact, if one is to take seriously the incoherence of trans* populations, then such a "substantial, measurable" vision of access may be wholly unknowable and, as a result, may orient one's attention away from how access as "a way of perceiving" continues to frame college-going possibilities for trans* students.

Framing trans* people's access to college as a matter of perception means interrogating several ways in which trans* people are positioned as epistemologically and existentially impossible. It also means understanding how administrative policies and practices continue to be guided by the aforementioned illogics that deem trans* people to be unruly, deviant, and, in many respects, not who we/they claim to be. Understanding trans* access-as-perception, then, means one needs to be skeptical not only of what questions are asked around how many trans* students there are in the first place, but also how policies related to trans* college admission and matriculation continue to occlude how trans*ness is an ongoing process of becoming rather than a singular point of arrival (Catalano, 2017; Garner, 2014; Nicolazzo, 2017b; Stewart, 2017a).

The Tensions of Quantifying Trans*

As Currah and Stryker (2015) stated, "It is usually the case that people who conceptualize transgender as a fluid state of being resist efforts to quantify it" (p. 4). This resistance is in part based on the numerous violences enacted through the project of quantification. For example, Spade (2010) detailed how not only are "trans people an administrative impossibility in the government and commercial systems that count people for various purposes" (p. 74), but that attempts to count trans* people promotes a static notion of what trans* means that would, by definition, further the violent notion of who is/not "trans* enough" (Catalano, 2015b).

These forms of administrative and categorical violence are framed and furthered by epistemological trans* oppression (Nicolazzo, 2017a), or the ongoing unknowability of trans* people. In other words, systemic cissexism continues to further the ways in which trans* people are perceived as epistemological and existential impossibilities. Such a limited perception leads to administrative violence in that trans* people are uncountable. Moreover, when efforts to count trans* people occur, categorical violence ensues based on the delineation of what trans* means and, as a result, who is "trans* enough" to (be) count(ed).

The Tensions of Admitting Trans*

As Spade (2011) stated, "We each tend to be most expert in the bureaucratic systems and communication norms of the institutions we deal with and work in daily. Those are ideal places for us to start spotting gender norm enforcement and dismantling it" (p. 62). Following Spade's direction, the question of admitting trans* students, and what happens when trans* students are (not) admitted, becomes essential in seeking to understand trans* students' experiences as a form of perception. Additionally, the places where trans* admittance is *not discussed* is also instructive, as it serves as a reminder of how various systems of oppression—most notably racism and sexism—mediate whose trans*ness is (im)possible. For example, Jourian (2017b) pointed toward the lack of single-sex men's institutions to explore and expand definitions of "man" and "male," supposing that such a lack is a vast oversight. Furthermore, when Morehouse became an exception to this institutional exploration and expansion, the resulting policy (i.e., the Appropriate Attire Policy; Patton, 2014) was in many respects a response to the ways white supremacy, sexism, and transmisogyny "police Black masculinity through intra-community forces and present a 'respectable' Morehouse ideal that diminishes [trans*]femininity" (Jourian, 2017b, p. 23).

Taking an administrative perspective, Marine (2017) elucidated three critical junctures at which trans* youth face barriers to accessing higher education: "the high school college guidance process, the college application process, and college matriculation and engagement" (p. 221). Bridging K-12 and postsecondary literatures, Marine articulated how trans* oppression persists to foreclose opportunities for trans* students to even consider postsecondary education, let alone apply, be admitted, and matriculate. Be it in the form of trans* antagonism or ignorance on behalf of high school guidance counselors, administrative violence through the Free Application for Federal Student Aid (FAFSA) and other application-related forms, or ongoing threat and harassment, these junctures expose how, at critical points in the college-going process, "The message to trans* students, particularly nonbinary students [is]: you are not truly welcome here" (Marine, 2017, p. 221).

In essence, then, the individual, institutional, and systemic ways college access is curtailed for trans* youth exposes how all postsecondary institutions of education are "gendered organizations" (Acker, 1990). Although some women's institutions have been perhaps more invested in addressing how gender frames (in)access—be it through institutional desire or external pressure (Nanney & Brunsma, 2017)—it should be understood that even *not* discussing how gender influences institutional decision-making regarding admission belies how gender is always already present as a shaping discourse (Jourian, 2017b; Nicolazzo, 2017b). In other words, the active choice to *not* discuss how gender influences postsecondary access, both at single-gender and co-educational institutions of higher education, is an investment in (re)constructing gender as binary, natural, and not requiring attention. As a result, it would behoove educators to expose and interrogate how gender influences access across K-12 and higher educational contexts, as well as how such institutional (in)access and gender (binary) discourse are mutually reinforcing, often in ways that limit educational, economic, health, employment, and personal life chances for trans* people in the United States.

(IN)CONCLUSION

Although this text is focused on "contemporary" issues in U.S. higher education, we recognize that contemporaneity enacts ontologies which presume emergence or newness is fixed to the recognition of minoritized groups by em/powered others. The language of "transgender" and recognition of gender diversity is a modern invention. Yet, people whose genders defy, resist, and evade binary, biological essentialist, and normative categorization have always already been present. The decision to recognize and address trans* people in U.S. higher education *now* is a reflection of trans* collegians' resistance to the cisnormativity embedded in postsecondary education's history, organization, policy, and practice. Through this review, we seek to advance an understanding of trans* collegians that refutes seeing them as this moment's current trend that can be replaced or put away once something more provocative and intriguing comes along. Instead, we assert that the current moment has allowed for higher education's "compulsory heterogenderism" (Nicolazzo, 2017b) to be interrogated and refuted.

The implications of this review for scholars and practitioners are threefold: One, the invisibility of trans* people in U.S. higher education institutions is a direct result of institutional and societal systems and structures featuring the interaction of settler colonialism, anti-Blackness, trans* oppression, and ableism. These endemic features and patterns of control must be rejected and dismantled. Two, the visibility and success of trans* people in U.S. higher education reflects those who have qualities and characteristics that are valued and valuable by the cisnormative gaze. The invisibility of other trans* identities and bodies is due to oppression and is not a question of their lack of fit. Three, improving life chances for trans* collegians must take an intersectional justice approach that would positively affect the experiences and outcomes of all minoritized groups in higher education. As Spade (2015) asserted in forwarding "trickle-up activism" as a politic, equity and justice begins with grassroots efforts addressing the needs of those who are most marginalized.

We do not presume to conclude this review, but rather recognize that what is known and understood about trans* collegians is perhaps just as inconclusive as it is conclusive, if not more so. The nature of trans*ness defies conclusion while inviting a focus on dynamic process. In a like manner, refuting trans*-antagonisms in higher education is a process of learning, unlearning, and relearning ways of thinking about student access, admission, and success beyond gendered, binarist assumptions. Those most equipped to lead these efforts are trans* people our/themselves in, out, and beyond higher education.

QUESTIONS FOR DISCUSSION

1. How has this chapter helped you expand your understandings of trans* peoples and populations in and beyond higher education?
2. What are strategies you can implement in your research and practice to push beyond merely increasing recognition of people with multiple minoritized identities (e.g., trans* people of color) in higher education?
3. According to the chapter authors, why is interrogating the way one comes to knowledge (i.e., one's epistemology) essential when coming to understand people with multiple marginalized identities in and beyond higher education?
4. What are examples in your own research and practice of how what happens *in* higher education influences what happens *beyond* higher education, and vice versa?
5. In this chapter, the authors have discussed why it is problematic to treat trans* people as a contemporary (new) issue for higher education. What are measures you can take to continue to disrupt such attitudes of contemporaneity for trans* people with multiple minoritized identities (e.g., disabled trans* people, Indigenous trans* people) in and beyond higher education?

AUTHORS' NOTE

Children of the House of "Pay It No Mind" is a collective *nom de plume* chosen to signify our indebtedness to the legendary trans* lineage upon which we draw. This iteration of the collective consists of three trans* scholars in higher education and student affairs, in alpha order: Mx. Romeo Jackson, University of Utah; Dr. Z. Nicolazzo, University of Arizona; and Dr. Dafina-Lazarus Stewart, Colorado State University. The thinking and writing reflected in this chapter was shared equally across this collective. This chapter should be cited as Children of the House of "Pay It No Mind" (2018). Refuting contemporaneity: Trans* experiences in, out, and beyond higher education. In M. Gasman & A. C. Samayoa (Eds.), *Contemporary issues in higher education* (pp. 119–134). New York, NY: Routledge.

NOTES

1   Children of the House of "Pay It No Mind" is a collective of trans* scholars in higher education and student affairs.
2   Despite being viewed as a pejorative term by some, Lewis (2015) stated, "'Disabled person' or 'person with a disability' … gained official status as the preferred terms for standard usage in the mid-1980s" (p. 46). Moreover, some disability rights activists use the term to connote resistant stances to normative notions of disability as something to be distanced from one's personhood. In this sense, then, using the term "disabled person" for some is a way of drawing attention to how one's disability is vital to understandings of self and community.

3   As Clare (2015) wrote, "If I call myself disabled in order to describe how the ableist world treats me as a person with cerebral palsy, then shouldn't I call nondisabled people *enabled?* That word locates the condition of being nondisabled, not in the nondisabled body, but in the world's reaction to that body" (p. 82).

REFERENCES

Acker, J. (1990). Hierarchies, jobs, bodies: A theory of gendered organizations. *Gender & Society*, 4(2), 139–158.

Ahmed, S. (2017). *Living a feminist life.* Durham, NC: Duke University Press.

Ahmed, S. (2012). *On being included: Racism and diversity in institutional life.* Durham, NC: Duke University Press.

Annamma, S. A. (2018). *The pedagogy of pathologization: Dis/abled girls of color in the school-prison nexus.* New York, NY: Routledge.

Arvin, M., Tuck, E., & Morrill A. (2013). Decolonizing feminism: Challenging connections between settler colonialism and heteropatriarchy. *Feminist Formations*, 25(1), 8–34.

Catalano, D. C. J. (2017). Resisting coherence: Trans men's experiences and the use of grounded theory methods. *International Journal of Qualitative Studies in Education*, 30(3), 234–244.

Catalano, D. C. J. (2015a). Beyond virtual equality: Liberatory consciousness as a path to achieve trans* inclusion in higher education. *Equity & Excellence in Education*, 48(3), 418–435.

Catalano, D. C. J. (2015b). "Trans enough?": The pressures trans men negotiate in higher education. *TSQ: Transgender Studies Quarterly*, 2(3), 411–430.

Catalano, D. C. J., & Griffin, P. (2016). Sexism, heterosexism, and trans* oppression: An integrated perspective. In M. Adams, L. A. Bell, D. J. Goodman, & K. Y. Joshi (Eds.), *Teaching for diversity and social justice* (3rd ed.; pp. 183–212). New York, NY: Routledge.

Clare, E. (2015). *Exile and pride: Queerness, disability, and liberation.* Durham, NC: Duke University Press.

Collins, P. H. (1998). It's all in the family: Intersections of gender, race, and nation. *Hypatia*, 13(3), 62–82.

Collins, P. H. (2000). *Black feminist thought: knowledge, consciousness, and the politics of empowerment* (2nd ed.). New York, NY: Routledge.

Crenshaw, K. (1991). Mapping the margins: Intersectionality, identity politics, and violence against women of color. *Stanford Law Review*, 43(6), 1241–1299.

Currah, P., & Stryker, S. (2015). Introduction. *TSQ: Transgender Studies Quarterly*, 2(1), 1–12.

Delgado Bernal, D. (2001). Learning and living pedagogies of the home: The mestiza consciousness of Chicana students. *International Journal of Qualitative Studies in Education*, 14(5), 623–629.

Driskill, Q-L. (2016). *Asegi stories: Cherokee queer and two-spirit memory.* Tucson, AZ: The University of Arizona Press.

Driskill, Q-L. (2010). Doubleweaving two-spirit critiques: Building alliances between native and queer studies. *GLQ: A Journal of Lesbian and Gay Studies*, 16(1–2), 69–92.

Ellison, T., Green, K., Richardson, M., & Snorton, C. R. (Eds.). (2017). We got issues: Toward a Black Trans*/ Studies. *TSQ: Transgender Studies Quarterly*, 4(2), 162–169.

Ferguson, R. A. (2004). *Aberrations in black: Toward a queer of color critique.* Minneapolis, MN: University of Minnesota Press.

Ferguson, R. A. (2012). *The reorder of things: The university and its pedagogies of minority difference.* Minneapolis, MN: University of Minnesota Press.

Gares, J. (Director & Producer). (2016). *Free CeCe!* [Motion picture]. USA: Jac Gares Media, Inc.

Garner, T. (2014). Becoming. *TSQ: Transgender Studies Quarterly*, 1(1/2), 30–32.

Glover, J. K. (2016). Redefining realness?: On Janet Mock, Laverne Cox, TS Madison, and the representation of transgender women of color in media. *Souls*, 18(2–4), 338–357.

Gossett, R., & Dunham, G. (2015, April 6). "What are we defending?": Reina's talk at the INICITE! COV4 conference [Blog post]. Retrieved from www.reinagossett.com/what-are-we-defending-reinas-talk-at-the-incite-cov4-conference/.

Grant, J. M., Mottet, L. A., Tanis, J., Harrison, J., Herman, J. L., & Keisling, M. (2011). *Injustice at every turn: A report of the national transgender discrimination survey*. Washington, DC: National Center for Transgender Equality and National Gay and Lesbian Task Force.

Green, K. (2017). Trans* movement/rans* moment: An afterword. *International Journal of Qualitative Studies in Education, 30*(3), 320–321.

Harris, J. C., & Nicolazzo, Z. (2017). Navigating the academic borderlands as multiracial and trans* faculty members. *Critical Studies in Education*. doi:10.1080/17508487.2017.1356340.

Jaekel, K. S., & Nicolazzo, Z. (2017). Teaching trans*: Strategies and tensions of teaching gender in student affairs preparation programs. *Journal for the Study of Postsecondary and Tertiary Education, 2*, 165–179.

Jourian, T. J. (2017a). Trans*forming college masculinities: Carving out trans*masculine pathways through the threshold of dominance. *International Journal of Qualitative Studies in Education, 30*(3), 245–265.

Jourian, T. J. (2017b). *Transmasculine college students' experiences in trans-inclusive feminist women's colleges*. Unpublished manuscript, Department of Organizational Leadership, Oakland University, Rochester, Michigan.

Jourian, T. J., & Nicolazzo, Z. (2016). Bringing our communities to the research table: The liberatory potential of collaborative methodological practices alongside LGBTQ participants. *Educational Action Research*. Advanced online publication. doi:10.1080/09650792.2016.1203343.

Jourian, T. J., Simmons, S. L., & Devaney, K. C. (2015). "We are not expected": Trans* educators (re)claiming space and voice in higher education and student affairs. *TSQ: Transgender Studies Quarterly, 2*(3), 431–446.

Krell, E. C. (2017). Is transmisogyny killing trans women of color?: Black trans feminisms and the exigencies of white femininity. *TSQ: Transgender Studies Quarterly, 4*(2), 226–242.

Lewis, V. A. (2015). Crip. In R. Adams, B. Reiss, & D. Serlin (Eds.), *Keywords for disability studies* (pp. 46–47). New York, NY: New York University Press.

Lorde, A. (1984). *Sister outsider: Essays and speeches*. Berkeley, CA: Crossing Press.

Marine, S. B. (2017). Changing the frame: Queering access to higher education for trans* students. *International Journal of Qualitative Studies in Education, 30*(3), 217–233.

Marine, S. B., & Nicolazzo, Z. (2014). Names that matter: Exploring the complexities of the experiences of trans* individuals in LGBTQ centers. *Journal of Diversity in Higher Education, 7*(4), 265–281.

Marr, C. J. (2004). *Assimilation through education: Indian boarding schools in the pacific northwest*. Retrieved from http://content.lib.washington.edu/aipnw/marr.html.

Michaelson, J. (2015, August 19). A tale of two trans Americas. *The Daily Beast*. Retrieved from www.thedailybeast.com/a-tale-of-two-trans-americas.

Mock, J. (2017, July 31). Dear men of "the breakfast club": Trans women aren't a prop, ploy, or sexual predators. *Allure*. Retrieved from www.allure.com/story/janet-mock-response-the-breakfast-club-trans-women.

Mogul, J. L., Ritchie, A. J., & Whitlock, K. (2012). *Queer (in)justice: The criminalization of LGBT people in the United States*. Boston, MA: Beacon Press.

Moraga, C., & Anzaldúa, G. (Eds.). (2015). *This bridge called my back: Writings by radical women of color* (4th ed.). Albany, NY: SUNY Press.

Muñoz, J. E. (1999). *Disidentifications queers of color and the performance of politics*. Minneapolis, MN: University of Minnesota Press.

Nanney, M., & Brunsma, D. L. (2017). Moving beyond cis-terhood: Determining gender through transgender admittance policies at U.S. women's colleges. *Gender & Society, 31*(2), 145–170.

Nicolazzo, Z. (2016). 'It's a hard line to walk': Black non-binary trans* collegians' perspectives on passing, realness, and trans*-normativity. *International Journal of Qualitative Studies in Education, 29*(9), 1173–1188.

Nicolazzo, Z. (2017a). Imagining a trans* epistemology: What trans* thinks like in postsecondary education. *Urban Education*. Advanced online publication. doi:10.1177/0042085917697203.

Nicolazzo, Z. (2017b). *Trans* in college: Transgender students' strategies for navigating campus life and the institutional politics of inclusion*. Sterling, VA: Stylus.

Nicolazzo, Z. (Ed.). (2017c). What's transgressive about trans* studies in education now? *International Journal of Qualitative Studies in Education, 30*(3), 211–216.

Nicolazzo, Z., Marine, S. B., & Galarte, F. (Eds.). (2015a). Trans*formational pedagogies. *TSQ: Transgender Studies Quarterly, 2*(3).

Nicolazzo, Z., Marine, S. B., & Galarte, F. (2015b). Introduction. *TSQ: Transgender Studies Quarterly, 2*(3), 367–375. Patton, L. D. (2016). Disrupting postsecondary prose: Toward a critical race theory of higher education. *Urban Education, 51*(3), 315–342.

Patton, L. D. (2014). Preserving respectability or blatant disrespect?: A critical discourse analysis of the Morehouse Appropriate Attire Policy and implications for intersectional approaches to examining campus policies. *International Journal of Qualitative Studies in Education, 27*(6), 724–746.

Pitcher, E. N. (2017). "There's stuff that comes with being an unexpected guest": Experiences of trans* academics with microaggressions. *International Journal of Qualitative Studies in Education, 30*(7), 688–703.

Sharpe, C. E. (2016). *In the wake: On blackness and being.* Durham, NC: Duke University Press.

Shotton, H. J., Lowe, S. C., & Waterman, S. J. (2013). Introduction. In H. J. Shotton, S. C. Lowe, & S. J. Waterman (Eds.), *Beyond the asterisk: Understanding Native students in higher education* (pp. 1–24). Sterling, VA: Stylus.

Simmons, S. L. (2017). A thousand words are worth a picture: A snapshot of trans* postsecondary educators in higher education. *International Journal of Qualitative Studies in Education, 30*(3), 266–284.

Solórzano, D. G., & Yosso, T. J. (2002). Critical race methodology: Counter-storytelling as an analytical framework for educational research. *Qualitative Inquiry, 8*(1), 23–44.

Spade, D. (2010). Be professional! *Harvard Journal of Law & Gender, 33,* 71–84.

Spade, D. (2011). Some very basic tips for making higher education more accessible to trans students and rethinking how we talk about gendered bodies. *Radical Teacher, 92*(Winter 2011), 57–62.

Spade, D. (2015). *Normal life: Critical trans politics, administrative violence, and the limits of law* (2nd ed.). Durham, NC: Duke University Press.

Spillers, H. (1987). Mama's baby, papa's maybe: An American Grammar book. *Diacritics, 17*(2), 65–81.

Stanley, E. A., & Smith, N. (2015). *Captive genders: Trans embodiment and the prison industrial complex* (2nd ed.). Chino, CA: AK Press.

Stewart, D.-L. (2017a). Trans*versing the DMZ: A non-binary autoethnographic exploration of gender and masculinity. *International Journal of Qualitative Studies in Education, 30*(3), 285–304.

Stewart, D.-L. (2017b). Producing "docile bodies": Disciplining citizen-subjects. *International Journal of Qualitative Studies in Education* [Special issue: Scholars Respond to the Trump Regime: Varieties of Critique, Resistance, and Community]. doi:10.1080/09518398.2017.1312598.

Strangio, C. (2014). Arrested for walking while trans: An interview with Monica Jones. *ACLU.* Retrieved from www.aclu.org/blog/arrested-walking-while-trans-interview-monica-jones.

Stryker, S., & Currah, P. (2014). Introduction. *TSQ: Transgender Studies Quarterly, 1*(1–2), 1–18. doi:10.1215/23289252-2398540.

Titchkosky, T. (2011). *The question of access: Disability, space, meaning.* Toronto, ON: University of Toronto Press.

Tuck, E., & Yang K. W., (2012). Decolonization is not a metaphor. *Decolonization: Indigeneity, Education, & Society, 1*(1), 1–40.

Walcott, R. (2014). The problem of the human: Black ontologies and "the coloniality of our being." In S. Broeck & C. Junker (Eds.), *Postcoloniality–Decoloniality–Black critique: Joints and fissures* (pp. 93–105). Chicago, IL: The University of Chicago Press.

Weheliye, A. G. (2014). *Habeas viscus: Racializing assemblages, biopolitics, and black feminist theories of the human.* Durham, NC: Duke University Press.

Yarborough, C. (2015, December 3). What's disability justice, anyway? [Blog post]. Retrieved from http://feministcampus.org/whats-disability-justice-anyway/.

8

UNDERSTANDING ISLAMOPHOBIA ON COLLEGE CAMPUSES

SHAFIQA AHMADI, DARNELL COLE, AND MONICA PRADO

Muslims, individuals who practice Islam, are the fastest growing religious group in the world and will surpass those who identify as Christian by 2035 (Pew Research Center, 2017). In the aggregate, Muslims have also gained in average educational attainment from 3.5 years to 6.7 years of formal education in the span of three generations (Pew Research Center, 2017). Information regarding Muslim college students is limited, both in statistical data and research. Muslim Americans are highly educated, with approximately 40 percent attaining a college degree or higher compared to 29 percent of the general American public that have achieved a college degree or higher (Cole & Ahmadi, 2003; Mir, 2014). Even though gains in educational attainment provide a strong platform for continued educational growth, Muslims only account for 1 percent of college graduates in the United States—at a time when over 20 million students are expected to be enrolled in a higher education institution by Fall 2017 (Cole & Ahmadi, 2003; Pew Research Center, 2017).

Adulthood is a time when discrimination and the overall social climate heavily influence identity formation and the overall health of individuals (Kunst, Tajamal, Sam, & Ulleberg, 2012; Samari, 2016). Over 75 percent of Muslim Americans believe that there is great amount of discrimination against Muslims in the United States and approximately 50 percent of Muslims reported difficulty in identifying as a Muslim in the United States (Pew Research Center, 2017). With the current tense political climate, over 60% of Muslims in the United States reported feelings of concern regarding the current presidency and reported perceptions that American people do not consider Islam to be part of mainstream society (Pew Research Center, 2017). Even with such challenges, 89 percent of Muslims in the United States reported identifying as both Muslim and American (Pew Research Center, 2017). Eighty-two percent of Muslims surveyed expressed concern about extremism in the name of Islam, comparable to 83 percent of non-Muslims expressing the same concern (Pew Research Center, 2017). Despite this major commonality, Islamophobia, or the fear of Islam, continues to distance Muslims and individuals perceived to be Muslim from non-Muslim American society. Muslims experience increased prejudices, stereotypes, and discrimination for being associated with Islam (Halstead, 2013).

This chapter will provide an overview of Islamophobia on college campuses, examining its effects on the Muslim student experience, faculty academic freedom, and the student affairs practice. This will be followed by recommendations for policy and practice in reducing Islamophobia on college campuses.

ISLAMOPHOBIA

Islamophobia, a global phenomenon and a form of xenophobia, is rooted in the fear of the other, the unknown, and an unwillingness to connect with difference (Ahmadi, 2011; Akbarzadeh, 2016; Shahzad, 2014). Following the attacks of September 11, 2001, media outlets helped create a negative image of Muslims, depicting the Muslim community as suspicious and untrustworthy: a threat to national security (Shahzad, 2014). As the fear toward Muslims transformed into anger, Muslims experienced exponential increases in prejudice, discrimination, and hate crimes (Ahmadi, 2011; Shahzad, 2014).

Social Media

The social media platform, although under researched, serves as a platform for anti-Muslim online abuse (Awan, 2014). Investigating Islamophobia and Twitter, Awan (2014), found that over 75 percent of the tweets with #Muslim or # Islam studied had discriminatory language, hateful words, and justification for verbal abuse toward Muslims. Online hate crime is an area where many far-right organizations use anonymity to strengthen Islamophobia, avoiding detection by law enforcement and evading responsibility for the social media posts (Awan, 2014). Awan (2014) suggests that further research should be conducted on the effects of online hate crime on young Muslims as social media use is prevalent among teenagers and young adults in higher education.

History of Islamophobia

Islamophobia has deep historical roots dating to the Middle Ages when Christian crusades persecuted Muslims in the East, resenting the Arab conquest of the Byzantine Empire and the Muslim conquest of parts of southern Europe (Halstead, 2013). Although a higher level of religious tolerance was practiced during the Renaissance, anti-Muslim sentiments of the time depicted a homogenous view of Muslims, grouping Muslims together regardless of the array of ethnicities and races represented in Islam (Halstead, 2013).

At the turn of the 21st century, increased immigration, negative political portrayal of predominantly Muslim countries, and the 9/11 attacks in the United States intensified Islamophobia (Halstead, 2013). The collapse of the Berlin Wall marked a time when the focus of the American antithesis shifted from communism to Islam. Political parties sought the transitions in the American antithesis as an opportunity to exercise the notion that western values were superior to Islam and Muslims regardless of cultural background or country of origin (Halstead, 2013). Many individuals interpreted the 9/11 attacks as a validation of their beliefs that Muslims were reluctant to assimilate into American culture, which correlated with increased hate crimes, prejudice, and discrimination against Muslims and individuals perceived as Muslim (Asfari, Hirschbein, Larkin, & Settles, 2017; Halstead, 2013; Samari, 2016; Sriram, 2016).

Types of Islamophobia

Halstead (2013) presents four different types of Islamophobia: (1) pre-reflective personal, (2) post-reflective personal, (3) institutional, and (4) political (Table 8.1).

In pre-reflective personal Islamophobia, individuals are prejudiced and unreceptive toward Muslims and Islam, lacking an underlying reasoning to their hostile thoughts and feelings (Halstead, 2013). Post-reflective personal Islamophobia justifies prejudice against Islam and those perceived to be Muslim (Halstead, 2013). The justification comes from media portrayal of Muslims as terrorists, negative stereotypes of Islamic doctrine and practices, and beliefs that Muslim-majority countries have an agenda to rise as the dominant nation (Brown, Brown, & Richards, 2014; Halstead, 2013). Post-reflective personal Islamophobia evades an individual's pursuit to find accurate information and can result in unjust generalizations.

Institutional Islamophobia illustrates the situational discrimination many Muslims or individuals perceived to be Muslim face as a minoritized group. Muslims are expected to culturally assimilate in order to be accepted while experiencing systematic disadvantages for identifying as Muslim (Halstead, 2013; Mir, 2009). On the institutional scale, Islam is racialized due to the homogenous view of Muslims as one ethnic or racial group, instead of multiple racial and ethnic groups represented among practitioners of Islam. Thus, institutional Islamophobia can be seen through racism and religious discrimination (Halstead, 2013; Mir, 2009; Samari, 2016).

Political Islamophobia constitutes legislative motions that limit the freedoms of Muslims or those perceived to be Muslim. Examples include the U.S. Patriot Act of 2001, which facilitated the use of racial profiling at airports and increased tension in the overall social climate, and the current Muslim Ban, Muslim Ban 2.0 and Muslim Ban 3.0. Political Islamophobia can also be seen by that passage of the French law that prohibited the use of *hijab* in public, destabilizing the freedom

Table 8.1 Types of Islamophobia

	Definition	Root/Expression	Example
Pre-reflective	Innate feelings of hostility toward Muslims.	Suspicion and dislike of the other leading to feelings of insecurity in the presence of the other. Discrimination toward Muslims or individuals perceived to be Muslim in employment or housing. Bullying, rudeness, aggressions, and verbal abuse toward Muslims or individuals perceived to be Muslim.	Acts of violence such as pulling the veil from Muslim women or setting Mosques on fire.
Post-reflective	Feelings of hostility toward Islam and Muslims that are justified or rationalized.	Inferiority of Islam or wickedness of Islam and its practices. Justification expressed in ill-conceived and negative portrayal that Muslims aim to dominate world.	Burning of Qu'ran at a church in Florida after bizarre scenario where the text was put to trial and found guilty.
Institutional	Societal norms that marginalize Muslims and individuals perceived to be Muslim and put them in a disadvantage in comparison to other social groups.	Places Muslims in a position to act contrary to their faith.	Exams scheduled on Islamic holy days where students are put in predicament to choose between faith or education.
Political	Policies that directly or indirectly affect the well-being and liberties of Muslims and individuals perceived to be Muslim.	National security because Muslims are portrayed, especially by the media, as a threat to society.	Racial profiling and search at airports post 9/11 by the enactment of the Patriot Act.

Source: Halstead (2013).

to practice Islam for Muslim women (Halstead, 2013). The limitation to exercise liberties afforded to everyone stigmatizes religious identity and the dynamic of racial profiling in the absence of a single race or ethnicity alludes to the use of stereotypes and generalization—both prevalent in political Islamophobia.

ISLAMOPHOBIA ON COLLEGE CAMPUSES

Students

For students, the first impact of Islamophobia stems from the media, where Muslims are portrayed as strict, conservative, pre-modern, and susceptible to extremism.

Muslims are stigmatized for such misconceived notions and suffer from the stereotype threat, where non-Muslims perceive Muslims to be dangerous because of stereotypes linked to Islamophobia, which often prove to be false and misrepresentative of the Muslim community (Ali, 2013; Brown et al., 2014; Halstead, 2013; Nasir & Al-Amin, 2006). Negative media portrayal of Muslims results in limited access to education, employment, health and social services, and significantly contributes to increased discrimination, stress, and illnesses among Muslims (Samari, 2016). By disseminating Islamophobia through the media to the general public, political leaders are able to create a sense of social chaos and havoc (Shahzad, 2014). In times of crisis, individuals are more accepting of societal medians that may limit the liberties of other individuals for the sake of security, feeding off fear of the other rather than any rationale toward unfair treatment and hostility (Ahmadi, 2011; Shahzad, 2014).

Within postsecondary education, discrimination and prejudice toward Muslims and individuals perceived to be Muslim is heightened by global tensions between western thought, stereotypes, and inaccurate information spread by the media (Brown & Aktas, 2012; Shammas, 2009). Brown et al. (2014) found that Muslim students living in non-majority Muslims countries experienced mistrust from their surrounding non-Muslim community, physical and verbal abuse, and negative impacts on self-esteem. Muslim students typically found themselves justifying their background, defending their religious identity, and speaking on behalf of their religion and culture to rectify misconceived notions (Brown et al., 2014). Muslim students also felt it was necessary to clarify that being Muslim meant identifying with a religion, and did not mean they belonged to a homogenized group portrayed in the media, highlighting the differences between Islamic practice and extremism (Brown et al., 2014).

The Muslim Student Experience

Muslim students reported that most incidents of Islamophobia occurred during tense political times, when negative images portrayed in the media intensified anti-Muslim sentiments (Berlet, Cash, & Planansky, 2014). Some Muslim students sought incidents of bigotry as opportunities to speak up about the systematic issues of Islamophobia, extending the conversation about its effects beyond the college campus (Berlet et al., 2014).

 In the classroom setting, Muslim students reported doing academically better in courses where they felt welcomed and appreciated by peers (Seggie & Sanford, 2010). Additionally, Muslim students felt more comfortable with their university community and embraced their identity at institutions where diversity was a priority in their mission and values (Seggie & Sanford, 2010).

Muslim college students who are subject to incidents of prejudice and discrimination experience higher levels of discomfort and anxiety due to negative stereotypes, fear of identity disclosure/justification, and fear of verbal or physical abuse, which overall negatively impacts their academic success (Brown et al., 2014; Seggie & Sanford, 2010). Most recently, university communities across the country have experienced increased tension because of Islamophobia and lower university satisfaction among students who identify with a minority religious group (Bowman & Smedley, 2013; Stoltzfus & Wexler, 2015).

Friendships and relationships with peers depend on whether the campus climate was receptive to socially diverse relationships (Seggie & Sanford, 2010). Muslim women reported a limited number of friendships on campus due to prejudice and discrimination and difficulty connecting with peers whose actions or behaviors contradict their religious values (Seggie & Sanford, 2010; Shareef, Dolby, Ciftci, Phillion, & De Olivera, 2013). Although ethnic identity was not found to be a direct indicator of friendship-building in the college experience, perceived discrimination directly influenced students' drive to develop same-ethnic or same-faith friendships (Shammas, 2009). Shammas (2015) found that 75 percent of campus friendships among Arab and Muslim students were both same-ethnic or same-faith relationships and 25 percent of campus friendships were of different ethnicity or religion. This suggests that Muslim and Arab students create their own community within a campus community as a reaction to perceived discrimination.

Stereotypes, Marginalization, and Exclusion

Contrary to popular thought, many Muslim women make the choice to practice *hijab*, or veil (Cole & Ahmadi, 2003; Shareef et al., 2013). On college campuses, *hijab* functions as an identity marker for Muslim women, associating Muslim women with otherness and/or difference, making Muslim women more susceptible to prejudice and discrimination (Shareef et al., 2013). Muslim students who chose to wear the *hijab* on campus reported receiving gazes, questions regarding their Islamic values, and often remove themselves from classroom interaction as a response to suspicion and inquiry from peers (Shareef et al., 2013).

In regard to Islamophobia, non-Muslim peers consider the *hijab* as an identity marker that symbolizes resistance to assimilate into the American culture, strengthening anti-Muslim sentiment (Shareef et al., 2013). *Hijab* is seen as a barrier for social relationships due to ensuing discrimination from anti-Muslim sentiment in the classroom and around college campuses. Muslim women who wore *hijab* were also more susceptible to microaggressions based on negative stereotypes portrayed in the media (Seggie & Sanford, 2010; Shareef et al., 2013). In the classroom, Muslim women who chose to wear *hijab* were perceived to be less intelligent, less motivated to achieve academic success, and less capable of completing the coursework by their non-Muslim counterparts, setting them apart and resulting in limited student interaction (Seggie & Sanford, 2010). According to Seggie and Sanford (2010), female Muslim students reported being defined by their *hijab* rather than their contribution to class, especially when non-Muslim students were afraid to speak to Muslim students, resulting in Muslim students being afraid to speak up in class in fear of judgment.

In order to mediate the effects of negative stereotypes, both female and male Muslim students reported taking the initiative to create a positive image of Islam and Muslims (Seggie & Sanford, 2010). In some instances, the non-Muslim community placed an expectation of representation on Muslim students, especially women who choose to wear *hijab*, to speak on behalf of the Muslim community and Islam (Seggie & Sanford, 2010). Although such an expectation could be deemed a microaggression and unjust, many Muslim students seized the challenge as an opportunity to deconstruct negative preconceived notions about Islam and Muslims (Berlet et al., 2014; Shareef et al., 2013). Regardless of their choice to wear *hijab*, Muslim women expressed a sense of obligation to increase cultural and religious awareness in order to transform the image of Islam from negative to positive (Seggie & Sanford, 2010; Shareef et al., 2013).

Internalized Oppression

Muslim students who felt marginalized and excluded sometimes expressed sentiments related to internalized oppression such as rationalization of discriminatory behavior (Berlet et al., 2014; Shareef et al., 2013; Stubbs & Sallee, 2013). In comparison to their counterparts, Muslim students were more likely to report incidents of bigotry and discrimination (Berlet et al., 2014). Even then, most incidents of overt aggression or verbal abuse remained unreported and Muslim students avoided confronting bigotry because they feared that any tension could be interpreted by the non-Muslim community as a confirmation of negative stereotypes (Berlet et al., 2014; Stubbs & Sallee, 2013). Additionally, Muslim students felt guilty about open acts of defense against bigotry (Seggie & Sanford, 2010; Stubbs & Sallee, 2013).

Identity Development

Cole and Ahmadi (2003) found that the identity development of Muslim women in college is heavily influenced by the political and social climate, where a sense of belonging and acceptance influences religious and/or social commitment. In examining the meanings of being both Muslim and American in college, some of the participants decided to continue *hijab*. Perceived negative campus attitudes were a manageable aspect of their educational journey and *hijab* a religious and social obligation symbolizing modesty, chaste behavior, and an identity as a "good Muslim" (Cole & Ahmadi, 2003). On the other hand, Muslim women in college who stopped wearing *hijab* attributed their decision to increased employability and as a means to avoid the marginalization and experienced isolation from wearing the veil, adding to the notion that Muslim students who experience feelings of isolation and alienation in college usually reevaluted their decision to wear *hijab* (Cole & Ahmadi, 2003). Campus climates impose a dichotomy between being a good Muslim and an effective Muslim in choosing to wear *hijab* (Cole & Ahmadi, 2003). Muslim American women in college are influenced by negative campus attitudes, including stereotypes and a misconception of docility and submissiveness, in their choice not to veil. This alludes to the fact that the choice to veil as a good Muslim stemmed from religious and social practices whereas the choice to remove the veil was an appeal to become an effective Muslim where society was not receptive of the practice of veiling (Cole & Ahmadi, 2003).

Muslim women who transitioned from a private Islamic school to a public university in the United States experienced some levels of cultural incongruity (Shareef et al., 2013). Muslim students who attended liberal institutions felt the environment was more receptive of diversity in the student body, reducing tensions related to Islamophobia. Simultaneously the social climate of the university's late-night parties and alcohol consumption did not align with Islamic values, thus creating a challenge for identity development and campus relationships (Shareef et al., 2013). Muslim students found that the saliency of their identity development depended on their social network, living situation, and social expectations placed on them by family and friends (Lamont & Collet, 2013; Stubbs & Sallee, 2013).

As part of their identity development, Muslim women have had to develop mechanisms to mitigate the marginalization that results from wearing *hijab* while also solidifying the bond with their values and beliefs (Shareef et al., 2013). Mir (2009) coined the term "third space" for Muslim American women in college who developed an identity with minimal cognitive dissonance, where they felt comfortable with elements of both American society and Islamic values. For instance, those who expressed a sense of "third space" may attend nightclubs or college parties and feel comfortable not drinking, in events where alcohol has the effect of invisibility or hyper-visibility (Mir, 2009). Student affairs professionals can incorporate these findings into strategies to encourage Muslim students toward a stable sense of general wellbeing that may include a "third space" (Mir, 2009).

FACULTY

Relationship with Students

Regarding faculty, Muslim students reported that the lack of understanding of Islam and the Muslim community on campus resulted in feelings of exclusion and marginalization (Seggie & Sanford, 2010). The lack of knowledge regarding the Muslim community and Islam among faculty poses a challenge for Muslim women who find it difficult to communicate ideas in a classroom that may be clouded by judgment and stereotypes directed at them, limiting their interaction (Seggie & Sanford, 2010). A diverse faculty with an interdisciplinary curriculum that includes courses about Islam would be beneficial to easing the tension of Islamophobia on college campuses by increasing the knowledge of Islam and the Muslim community while removing stigmas linked to stereotypes (Seggie & Sanford, 2010). For instance, Cole and

Ahmadi (2010) found that welcoming environments may help change the perception of Muslim women who wear *hijab*. In challenging feminine paradigms of matriarchal submissiveness, the classroom environment could be a place of awareness, maturity, and diverse consciousness (Cole & Ahmadi, 2010).

Political Islamophobia

Ahmadi (2011) offers a comprehensive overview of how after 9/11, the Patriot Act negatively impacted Muslims in higher education. Section 217 of the act allowed government authorities to intercept personal communications believed to have some relation or association with terrorists while section 411 of the Patriot Act rescinded visas for Muslims who the government determined could use their power or position to coerce terrorist actions. Both Section 217 and 411 limited the academic freedom of Muslim scholars within higher education in the United States. All scholars, especially scholars who identified as Muslim, were hesitant in undertaking research topics that could potentially be linked to terrorism, even when the intent of the research was purely academic. Moreover, Muslim scholars who either experienced their own visas being revoked, or those of their Muslim colleagues, did not engage in meaningful free exchange of ideas for fear of being labeled a terrorist (Ahmadi, 2011).

Along with the Patriot Act, the U.S. government also instituted the Student & Exchange Visitor Information System (SEVIS) that requires higher education institutions to report private confidential information about international scholars and students (Ahmadi, 2011). Such disclosure of private information intrudes into the personal lives of international scholars and students, removing any space for privacy and making scholarly work in the United States unappealing to international scholars (Ahmadi, 2011). While SEVIS contains personal information on international scholars and students, Section 505 of the Patriot Act gives government officials the power to request and gain access, through National Security Letters (NSL), to information on all university members of a higher education institution, which limits civil liberties guaranteed under the Fourth Amendment of the U.S. Constitution. The Fourth Amendment protects citizens from warrantless search and seizure. With NSLs, the U.S. government could gain access to personal information on U.S. citizens without their permission (Ahmadi, 2011).

The Patriot Act restricted academic freedom for Muslim scholars by compromising free association, inquiry, free speech, and the exchange of ideas (Ahmadi, 2011). Muslim students also feel that the restrictions imposed by the Patriot Act limits their involvement in Muslim student organizations for fear of being associated with terrorism (Ahmadi, 2011). Although the Patriot Act did not specifically target Muslims, the political Islamophobia that ensued had an institutional effect on our educational system (Ahmadi, 2011). NSLs increased search and seizures in higher education while policymaking skewed in the name of national security negatively impacted the Muslim academic community, risking not only the personal well-being and safety of Muslim academics but also their capacity as scholars (Ahmadi, 2011).

THE TRAVEL BAN (MUSLIM BAN)

Executive Order 13769 (Muslim Ban)

On January 27, 2017, Trump issued an executive order 13769 titled "Executive Order: Protecting the Nation from Foreign Terrorist Entry into the United States." This executive order, also referred to as the Muslim Ban, starts with discussing its purpose, where it cites the terrorist attacks of September 11, 2001 (Executive Order No. 13769, 2017; Ahmadi & Cole, forthcoming, 2019). The Muslim Ban then states that the United States must protect its citizens from foreign nationals who want to commit terrorist attacks in the United States (Executive Order No. 13769, 2017). The Muslim Ban does not clearly state which countries were targeted, but the countries were later identified by the Department of Homeland Security (DHS) as seven Muslim-majority countries of Iraq, Syria, Sudan, Iran, Somalia, Libya, and Yemen (Ahmadi & Cole, forthcoming, 2019). While the Muslim Ban cited September 11, 2001 and the following years, what it fails to consider is that no Muslims from these seven countries have killed Americans in almost two decades (Ahmadi & Cole, forthcoming, 2019; Myre, 2017). In fact, the list of countries who have carried out fatal attacks in the United States since September 11, 2001 included an entirely different set of countries and not all were Muslim dominant (Ahmadi & Cole, forthcoming, 2019; Myre, 2017).

Executive Order 13780 (Muslim Ban 2.0)

On March 6, 2017, Trump issued the second executive order 13780, titled "Executive Order Protecting the Nation from Foreign Terrorist Entry into the United States." This new executive order revoked and replaced order 13769 (Executive Order No. 13780, 2017; Ahmadi & Cole, forthcoming, 2019). This new executive order has noticeable differences in language and content and Iraq is not included as one of the countries affected by this order (Executive Order No. 13780, 2017).

While executive order 13769 led to thousands of visas getting revoked, this order specifically mentions that any person whose visa was revoked or canceled can receive a travel document confirming that they can travel to the United States (Executive Order No. 13780, 2017; Ahmadi & Cole, forthcoming, 2019). The major changes include exemption to permanent residents and visa holders as well as changing the indefinite ban on Syrian refugees to a 120-day ban (Executive Order No. 13780, 2017).

Since the issuance of Muslim Ban 2.0, there have been two major legal battles held in the U.S. Court of Appeals. First, on May 25, 2017, the Fourth Circuit's 13-judge panel ruled that *the* Muslim Ban 2.0 should be halted (*International Refugee Assistance Project v. Trump*, 2017). This ruling is significant because it is the first ruling on this issue from a U.S. Court of Appeals.

The chief judge for the Fourth Circuit wrote that the Muslim Ban 2.0 "speaks with vague words of national security, but the context drips with religious intolerance, animus, and discrimination" (*International Refugee Assistance Project v. Trump*, 2017). The majority in this case ruled that Trump's numerous statements while campaigning for President calling for a shutdown of Muslims was proof that this executive order violated the First Amendment that prohibits government establishment of religion (*International Refugee Assistance Project v. Trump*, 2017; Ahmadi & Cole, forthcoming, 2019).

Second, on June 12, 2017, three judges from the Ninth Circuit Appeals Court unanimously upheld Federal District Court Judge Derrick Watson's decision to temporarily block the Muslim Ban 2.0 (Ahmadi & Cole, forthcoming, 2019). Rather than weighing in on the violations of the Establishment clause of the First Amendment as the Fourth Circuit did, the Ninth Circuit judges ruled on the statutory grounds of Trump's immigration order (Ahmadi & Cole, forthcoming, 2019; Liptak, 2017). The panel stated that Trump "exceeded the scope of the authority delegated to him by Congress" and that "the President did not meet the essential precondition to exercising his delegated authority" (*State of Hawaii v. Trump*, 2017).

Specifically, the Court narrowed in on the inadequate evidence by Trump to enact the executive order; the Court stated:

> In short, the order does not provide a rationale explaining why permitting entry of nationals from the six designated countries under current protocols would be detrimental to the interests of the United States. (*State of Hawaii v. Trump*, 2017)

When taking the lawsuit, the Ninth Circuit panel found that Washington and Minnesota have standing to sue Trump, because both states were harmed by the executive orders. The Court specifically cited the harm to the proprietary interest of these states, in that both states' public universities will suffer under the executive order: (1) "prevents nationals of seven countries from entering Washington and Minnesota"; and (2) "some of these people will not enter state universities, some will not join those universities as faculty, some will be prevented from performing research, and some will not be permitted to return if they leave" (*State of Washington v. Trump*, 2017; Ahmadi & Cole, forthcoming, 2019).

After the Fourth Circuit and Ninth Circuit rulings against the Muslim Ban 2.0, the Supreme Court issued an unsigned decision stating that it would revisit this issue in October of 2017 (Ahmadi & Cole, forthcoming, 2019). On June 26, 2017, the Supreme Court justices announced in a 13-page decision that they will allow parts of Trump's Muslim Ban 2.0 that have been on hold since March to go into effect (Rose & Chappel, 2017). The 90-day ban for travel to the United States from six Muslim-majority countries—Iran, Libya, Somalia, Sudan, Syria, and Yemen—went into effect in June 2017 "with respect to foreign nationals who lack any bona fide relationship with a person or entity in the United States" (Rose & Chappel, 2017).

Trump's administration added some clarity as to who is exempt due to a "bona fide relationship," such as education, business, or family (Jarrett & Labott, 2017). Without a bona fide relationship, the travel ban is 90 days from six Muslim-majority countries and 120 days if you are a refugee from any country (Jarrett & Labott, 2017). Hawaii filed an emergency motion on June 29, 2017 asking for more clarity and to issue an order confirming that extended family should not be excluded (Ahmadi & Cole, forthcoming, 2019; Jarrett & Labott, 2017).

Muslim Ban 3.0

In September 2017, the Trump administration updated the Muslim Ban 2.0 to include Venezuela, North Korea, and Chad, i.e. Muslim Ban 3.0 (Seipel, 2017). Muslim Ban 3.0 was supposed to go into effect on October 18, 2017, but on September 25, 2017, the Supreme Court canceled the hearing on Muslim Ban 2.0 (Ahmadi & Cole, forthcoming, 2019). Additionally, on October 17, 2017, U.S. District Judge Derrick K. Watson in Hawaii blocked Muslim Ban 3.0 from going into effect. On October 18, U.S. District Court Judge Theodore Chuang in Maryland granted a nationwide injunction against Muslim Ban 3.0, stating that the administration had "not shown that national security cannot be maintained without an unprecedented eight-country travel ban" (Ahmadi & Cole, forthcoming, 2019; Hesson, 2017).

RECOMMENDATION FOR POLICY AND PRACTICE

Higher education institutions serve as a platform to encourage positive social change with information to combat the negative impact of stereotypes portrayed in the media about Muslims and to increase security and support for the Muslim student population (Will, 2015). One of the most harmful effects of Islamophobia is the separation between "us" and the "other," making Muslims and individuals perceived to be Muslims or associated with Islam as the "outsiders" (Ahmadi, 2011). Normalizing the otherization of Muslims can only be systematically removed through information and education and by empowering educational institutions to provide professional development for their staff and faculty in the following ways: (1) conducting further research on educational satisfaction and engagement of Muslim students; (2) creating and supporting multicultural and identity centers that are supportive of Muslim students; (3) promoting freedom of religion; (4) reporting incidents of prejudice and discrimination; (5) creating a safe space for Muslim students; (6) awareness of Christian privilege; (7) countering Islamophobia; and (8) understanding and addressing Trump and his administration's rhetoric, laws, policies and practices, and the negative impact on Muslim students, international students, and the rest of the campus communities.

Further Research on Educational Satisfaction and Engagement of Muslim Students

Cole and Ahmadi (2010) found that Muslim student academic performance did not differ from their Jewish and Christian counterparts. Although Muslim students experienced less educational satisfaction, they participated in a greater number of diversity-related activities including engagement in ethnically and racially diverse student organizations, socialized more with individuals of different ethnic and racial backgrounds, had a roommate of different ethnicity or race, and attended ethnic/racial awareness workshops. The findings indicate that religious identity, student development, and diversity impact the campus climate of higher education institutions. Further research should be conducted on the extent to which religious diversity impacts campus climate and the inquiry should focus on the indirect relationship between educational satisfaction and increased diversity-related engagement among Muslim college students. As practitioners, student affair professionals and faculty could positively impact the educational outcomes of Muslim students by encouraging and facilitating the development of religious identity; research has shown that helping students to develop a religious identity could have positive educational outcomes (Cole & Ahmadi, 2010).

Multicultural and Identity Centers that Support Muslim Students

Furthermore, institutional support of multicultural and identity centers and student-run organizations has helped to reduce anti-Muslim sentiments on college campuses by reducing stereotypes and increasing contact with students of various backgrounds (Asfari et al., 2017). Multicultural centers allow for students of diverse backgrounds to connect and interact with each other, identifying shared values and commonalities. Contact with diverse students helps individuals to develop respect for differences and produces knowledge, eliminating the perceived element of threat associated with Islamophobia (Asfari et al., 2017).

Multicultural centers serve as a platform for diverse community building where Muslim students have the space to express themselves, share their experiences, and develop campus relationships (Seggie & Sanford, 2010). Research has shown that student participation in intercultural and/or interfaith activities and student groups helped mediate the effects of discrimination and prejudice on college campuses, encouraging higher education institutions to support student-run organizations (Berlet et al., 2014). However, some Muslim students appreciated the work of multicultural centers but did not participate regularly (Seggie & Sanford, 2010).

Promoting Freedom of Religion

Institutions should promote the freedom to practice religion by creating safe spaces for Muslim students to pray (Seggie & Sanford, 2010; Stubbs & Sallee, 2013). Perceived with suspicion and skepticism when looking for a place to pray on campus, Muslim students reported feeling more susceptible to prejudice and discrimination (Nasir & Al-Amin, 2006). Making a space available for Muslim students to openly and freely pray would help alleviate identity management issues, found to be taxing on an academic focus for Muslim students, and will positively impact their educational outcomes (Nasir & Al-Amin, 2006).

Reporting Incidents of Prejudice and Discrimination

Institutions should also focus on the growing need to harbor a safe space where Muslim students can report incidents of prejudice and discrimination (Seggie & Sanford, 2010). The majority of macroaggressions and incidents of bigotry against Muslim students are not reported to university or college officials, signaling a need for higher education institutions to create a policy and processes that include anonymity, where Muslim students feel comfortable reporting such cases (Seggie & Sanford, 2010).

Creating a Safe Space for Muslim Students

Mir (2011a) found that as Muslim students experience marginalization and isolation on college campuses, they are faced with a choice to be invisible or to be outspoken. Muslim women on college campuses who wore *hijab*, which served as an identity marker, opted to speak against discrimination and prejudice. On the other hand, Muslim women who did not wear *hijab* acknowledged the systematic issues of oppression, but preferred to assimilate into American culture, in an effort to combat such issues through silence (Mir, 2011a). It seems that the choice is whether to react or to act. Both scenarios point to the unjust burden put on Muslim women in college and other immigrants alike; they must make a choice that non-Muslim or non-minority students may not have to make (Mir, 2011a). A space and campus climate where Muslim students could feel comfortable voicing their concerns and experiences, outside a multicultural center, are needed in higher education institutions (Berlet et al., 2014; Cole & Ahmadi, 2003, 2010; Mir, 2009; Mir, 2011a; Seggie & Sanford, 2010; Stubbs & Sallee, 2013).

Awareness of Christian Privilege

Furthermore, there should be growing awareness of Christian privilege in higher education institutions (Ahmadi & Cole, 2015). Students who identify as Christian benefit from academic calendars designed around Christian holidays, accessible food options, and a positive image of the Christian religion on college campuses (Ahmadi & Cole, 2015). Unlike religious minority students, Christian students most likely do not experience conflict, and ensuing resolution, between their religious identity and hostility toward their faith on college campuses (Ahmadi & Cole, 2015).

Countering Islamophobia

Over 50 percent of Americans do not know or have not come in contact with a person that identifies as Muslim (McCollum, 2017). In order to counter the effects of Islamophobia, increased exposure and contact with the lives of Muslim Americans through leadership, speakers, conferences, interfaith events, and panels are needed (McCollum, 2017). Islamophobia, steeped in the fear of the other, can cause avoidance, religious intolerance, and disrespect. Therefore, student affairs professionals should focus on transforming that fear into opportunity, and challenge stereotypes through education, information, and intercultural and inter-religious community building (Kunst et al., 2012).

Trump and his Administration's Rhetoric, Laws, Policies, and Practices

The decisions made by the Trump administration continue to mistreat the Muslim community. For the first time in over 20 years, the White House and Trump did not celebrate *Eid al-Fitr*, the Muslim holiday that marks the end of Ramadan (Stark, 2017). Furthermore, Secretary of State Rex Tillerson did not honor the State Department's Office of Religion and Global Affairs to host a reception for the holiday (Stark, 2017). Although this may not seem surprising considering this administration's actions against Muslims and Muslim-majority countries with the *Muslim bans* and overall rhetoric, this adds to the continued strain and negative actions taken against the Muslim community. When comparing his actions in celebrating Muslim holidays to other religious holidays, Trump and the White House did host the annual Easter egg roll in April, and hosted a Passover Seder, although neither he nor his children attended (Stark, 2017). Trump's actions as President of the United States have lasting ramifications and significance in this country and in the world.

There are many reasons to be concerned about the Muslim bans' impact, especially since the United States typically exchanges both domestic and international students and faculty at higher education institutions across the country and world (Ahmadi & Cole, forthcoming, 2019). In 2015–2016, over 12,000 Iranians studied in the United States (Wilhelm, 2017). However, this number is bound to change because of the Muslim bans and general climate toward students and scholars from Iran, and in general toward all Muslim international students. Due to Trump's various statements and actions against globalization, Royall & Company surveyed prospective international students to better understand whether this administration impacts the students' desire to study in the United States (Royall & Dodson, 2017). This survey was conducted between the first and second executive orders or Muslim bans in February, and surveyed over 2,000 international students who had expressed interest in applying to colleges in the United States. The survey found that nearly one in three prospective international students indicated they had less interest in studying in the United States because of the current political climate (Royall & Dodson, 2017). Almost 69 percent of those students stated that one of the factors was because of "concerns about the U.S. presidential administration" (Royall & Dodson, 2017). The other top reasons for less interest in studying in the United States included: worries about travel restrictions, safety concerns, cost, and prejudice or discrimination. It is important to note that this survey was conducted in over 150 countries, meaning it did not just come from students from the six countries directly impacted by the Muslim bans (Royall & Dodson, 2017). In fact, only 16 students surveyed are from one of those six countries, showing that the Muslim bans and overall political climate is influencing many other international students beyond the scope of the executive order (Royall & Dodson, 2017). Moreover, early reporting in April 2017 cited that "students from those six countries alone bring in more than $500 million to the U.S. economy each year" (Carapezza, 2017). While the significance of the Muslim bans has yet to be decided, the implications for policy and practice are significant for higher education administrators, faculty, and students.

QUESTIONS FOR DISCUSSION

1. Given the ever-changing nature of laws and policies such as the current Muslim Ban, Muslim Ban 2.0, and Muslim Ban 3.0, how can institutions of higher education be proactive in supporting their students?
2. The Patriot Act, SEVIS, Muslim Ban, Muslim Ban 2.0, and Muslim Ban 3.0 all directly impact the Muslim community in their own regards. How do these laws intersect to affect Muslim college students?
3. Does your institution have policies that ensure accommodations for Muslim students' faith practices? For example, prayer space, Halal food, religious holidays, etc.
4. When considering international students specifically, what strategies can institutional leaders and agents employ to improve the campus climate?
5. Muslim students reported that the lack of understanding of Islam and the Muslim community on campus resulted in feelings of exclusion and marginalization (Seggie & Sanford, 2010). How can faculty–student interactions be improved on your campus? What training is available, or could be made available, for faculty to better understand Islam and the Muslim community?

REFERENCES

Ahmadi, S. (2011). The erosion of civil rights: Exploring the effects of the PATRIOT Act on Muslims in American higher education. *Rutgers Race and the Law Review, 12*(1), 1–55.

Ahmadi, S. & Cole, D. (forthcoming, 2019). *Muslim students in higher education.* Ann Arbor, MA: University of Michigan Press.

Ahmadi, S., & Cole, C. (2015). Engaging religious minority students. In S. J. Quaye & S. Harper (Ed.), *Student engagement in higher education* (2nd ed.; pp. 171–185). New York, NY: Routledge.

Akbarzadeh, S. (2016). The Muslim question in Australia: Islamophobia and Muslim alienation. *Journal of Muslim Minority Affairs, 36*(3), 323–333. doi:10.1080/13602004.2016.1212493.

Asfari, A., Hirschbein, R., Larkin, G., & Settles, T. (2017). *An empirical assessment of multicultural education programs in reducing Islamophobia on a college campus* (Doctoral dissertation). Retrieved from ProQuest Dissertations and Theses database.

Awan, I. (2014). Islamophobia and Twitter: A typology of online hate against Muslims on social media. *Policy & Internet, 6*(2), 133–150. doi:10.1002/1944-2866.POI364.

Berlet, C., Cash, D., & Planansky, M. (2014). Constructing campus conflict: Antisemitism and Islamophobia on U.S. college campuses, 2007–2011. *Political Research Associates*. Retrieved from www.politicalresearch. org/wp-content/uploads/downloads/2014/06/CCC_May2014.pdf.

Bowman, N. A., & Smedley, C. T. (2013). The forgotten minority: Examining religious affiliation and university satisfaction. *Higher Education*, *65*(6), 745–760. doi:10.1007/s10734-012-9574-8.

Brown, L., & Aktas, G. (2012). Turkish university students' hopes and fears about travel to the west. *Journal of Research in International Education*, *11*(1), 3–18. doi:10.1177/1475240912441445.

Brown, L., Brown, J., & Richards, B. (2014). Media representations of Islam and international Muslim student well-being. *International Journal of Educational Research*, *69*, 50–58. doi:10.1016/j.ijer.2014.10.002.

Carapezza, K. (2017, December 4). Travel ban's 'chilling effect' could cost universities hundreds of millions. *WGBH News*. Retrieved from http://blogs.wgbh.org/on-campus/2017/12/4/presidents-immigration-policies-rhetoric-disrupt-international-college-admissions/.

Cole, D., & Ahmadi, S. (2003). Perspectives and experiences of Muslim women who veil on college campuses. *Journal of College Student Development*, *44*(1), 47–66.

Cole, D., & Ahmadi, S. (2010). Reconsidering campus diversity: An examination of Muslim students' experiences. *Journal of Higher Education*, *81*(2), 121–139.

Exec. Order No. 13769, 3 C.F.R. 8977 (2017).

Halstead, J. (2013). Islamophobia. In R. Schaefer (Ed.), *Encyclopedia of race and racism* (pp. 763–765). New York, NY: Sage Publications.

Hesson, T. (2017, October 18). Second judge halts Trump's latest attempt at travel ban. *Politico*. Retrieved from www.politico.com/story/2017/10/18/trump-travel-ban-maryland-judge-blocks-243901.

International Refugee Assistance Project v. Trump, 857 F. 3d 554 (4th Cir. 2017).

Jarrett, L., & Labott, E. (2017, June 30). Travel ban 2.0 in effect, court challenges begin. *CNN Politics*. Retrieved from www.cnn.com/2017/06/29/politics/revised-travel-ban-thursday/index.html.

Kunst, J. R., Tajamal, H., Sam, D. L., & Ulleberg, P. (2012). Coping with Islamophobia: The effects of religious stigma on Muslim minorities' identity formation. *International Journal of Intercultural Relations*, *36*(4), 518–532. doi:10.1016/j.ijintrel.2011.12.014.

Lamont, S., & Collet, B. (2013). Muslim American university students' perceptions of Islam and democracy: Deconstructing the dichotomy. *Equity & Excellence in Education*, *46*(4), 433–450. doi:10.1080/10665684.2013.838126.

Liptak, A. (2017, October 24). Supreme Court wipes out travel ban appeal. *The New York Times*. Retrieved from www.nytimes.com/2017/10/24/us/politics/supreme-court-travel-ban-appeal-trump.html.

McCollum, S. (2017). Expelling Islamophobia. *Education Digest*, *82*(8), 14–18.

Mir, S. (2009). Not too "college-like," not too normal: American Muslim undergraduate women's gendered discourses. *Anthropology & Education Quarterly*, *40*(3), 237–256.

Mir, S. (2011a). "I didn't want to have that outcast belief about alcohol": Muslim women encounter drinking cultures on campus. In Y. Haddad, F. Senzai, & J. Smith (Eds.), *Educating the Muslims of America* (pp. 209–229). Oxford, UK: Oxford University Press.

Mir, S. (2011b). "Just to make sure people know I was born here": Muslim women constructing American selves. *Discourse: Studies in the Cultural Politics of Education*, *32*(4), 547–563.

Mir, S. (2014). *Muslim women on campus: Undergraduate social life and identity*. Greensboro, NC: University or North Carolina Press.

Myre, G. (2017, January 31). Trumps' executive order on immigration, annotated. *National Public Radio*. Retrieved from www.npr.org/2017/01/31/512439121/trumps-executive-order-on-immigration-annotated?ft=nprml&f=512439121.

Nasir, N. I. S., & Al-Amin, J. (2006). Creating identity-safe spaces on college campuses for Muslim students. *Change: The Magazine of Higher Learning*, *38*(2), 22–27.

Pew Research Center. (2017, April 5). *The changing global religious landscape*. Retrieved from www.pewforum.org/2017/04/05/the-changing-global-religious-landscape/.

Rose, J., & Chappel, B. (2017, June 26). Supreme Court revives parts of Trump's travel ban as it agrees to hear case. *NPR*. Retrieved from www.npr.org/sections/thetwo-way/2017/06/26/533934989/supreme-court-will-hear-cases-on-president-trumps-travel-ban.

Royall, P., & Dodson, A. (2017). Effect of the current political environment on international student enrollment: Insights for U.S. colleges and universities. *EAB Royall & Company*. Retrieved from http://ns.eab.com/International-Student-Survey.

Samari, G. (2016). Islamophobia and public health in the United States. *American Journal of Public Health*, *106*(11), 1920–1925. doi:10.2105/AJPH.2016.303374.

Seggie, F. N., & Sanford, G. (2010). Perceptions of female Muslim students who veil: Campus religious climate. *Race Ethnicity and Education*, *13*(1), 59–82. doi:10.1080/13613320903549701.

Shahzad, F. (2014). The discourse of fear: Effects of the War on Terror on Canadian university students. *American Review of Canadian Studies*, *44*(4), 467–482.

Shammas, D. S. (2009). Post-9/11 Arab and Muslim American community college students: Ethno-religious enclaves and perceived discrimination. *Community College Journal of Research and Practice*, *33*(3–4), 283–308. doi:10.1080/10668920802580507.

Shammas, D. (2015). We are not all the same: Arab and Muslim students forging their own campus communities in a post-9/11 America. *Journal of Muslim Minority Affairs*, *35*(1), 65–88. doi:10.1080/13602004.2015.1019730.

Shareef, A.(2013). *From an Islamic school to American college campuses: The challenges of islamophobia for Hijabi women* (Dissertation). Purdue University. Retrieved from https://docs.lib.purdue.edu/dissertations/AAI1547483/.

Seipel, A. (2017). Trump administration revises travel ban to expand beyond Muslim-majority countries. *NPR*. Retrieved from www.npr.org/2017/09/24/553353302/trump-administration-revises-travel-ban-expands-beyond-muslim-majority-countries.

Sriram, S. K. (2016). A Foucauldian theory of American Islamophobia. *International Journal of Islamic Thought*, *10*, 47–54.

Stark, L. (2017, June 27). What the White House's decision to forgo Ramadan event means for religion and politics under Trump. *CNN Politics*. Retrieved from www.cnn.com/2017/06/27/politics/trump-iftar-white-house/index.html.

State of Hawaii v. Trump, 17-965 585 U.S. (2017).

State of Washington v. Trump, 847 F.3d 1151 (9th Cir. 2017).

Stoltzfus, K., & Wexler, E. (2015). Muslim campus leaders describe 'climate of fear'. *The Chronicle of Higher Education*, *62*(16), A10.

Stubbs, B. B., & Sallee, M. W. (2013). Muslim, too: Navigating multiple identities at an American university. *Equity & Excellence in Education*, *46*(4), 451–467. doi:10.1080/10665684.2013.838129.

Wilhelm, I. (2017, January 31). Why the travel ban probably hits Iranian professors and students the hardest. *The Chronicle of Higher Education*. Retrieved from www.chronicle.com/article/Why-the-Travel-Ban-Probably/239050.

Will, M. (2015, March 11). Across North Carolina, Muslim students take stock of a trying semester. *The Chronicle of Higher Education*. Retrieved from www-chronicle-com/article/Across-North-Carolina-Muslim/228327.

9

STUDENTS EXPERIENCING HOMELESSNESS ON COLLEGE CAMPUSES

JARRETT GUPTON AND JENNIFER TROST

UNDERSTANDING STUDENTS EXPERIENCING HOMELESSNESS ON COLLEGE CAMPUSES

Low-income students experience multiple barriers on their academic journey toward postsecondary education. The various subgroups of low-income students (e.g., homeless youth, youth in foster care, and first-generation college students) share certain commonalities, but they also have distinct educational experiences and needs. Understanding the unique ways in which higher and postsecondary institutions serve each sub-group provides further insight into how to support persistence and degree completion for vulnerable populations. Of these students, homeless and housing vulnerable receive the smallest scrutiny and may be the most marginalized subpopulation in higher education.

Graduates of postsecondary education typically experience more financially and socially stable lives. One of the public benefits of a higher education is that communities with college graduates often have better economic vitality and less poverty. Thus, receiving a postsecondary degree or credential is one pathway toward economic and social stability. One population of students that is most in need of stability is students experiencing homelessness or housing vulnerability. Little research exists on homeless college students or the specific types of supports higher and postsecondary institutions provide for this population. This chapter addresses several questions related to homeless and housing-vulnerable students in higher and postsecondary education. Our review covers how policy and research literature have tried to define the experience of homelessness, the correlates and antecedents related to experiencing homelessness, and the available demographic data related to homeless college students. Also, we discuss what institutional supports are available to postsecondary students experiencing some form of housing instability. Furthermore, the authors suggest ways to enhance college programs and professional practice to improve recognition, retention, and support for students experiencing homelessness. This chapter adds to the conversation related to institutional support for low-income students, college access, and institutional responsibility to promote success for marginalized populations.

HOW IS HOMELESSNESS DEFINED?

No single social policy defines who is homeless with regard to higher and postsecondary education; current policy and available literature provide three varying definitions to help describe individuals that experience homelessness. The first way to define homelessness is through the lens of social policy, which provides broad categories focused on the lack of adequate, safe, and stable nighttime shelter to identify individuals as homeless. For example, the U.S. Department of Housing and Urban Development (HUD) defined four categories of homelessness (Paden, 2012):

1. Individuals and families who lack a fixed, regular, and adequate nighttime residence and includes a subset for a person who is exiting an institution where he or she resided for 90 days or less and who resided in an emergency shelter or a place not meant for human habitation immediately before entering that institution;
2. Individuals and families who will imminently lose their primary nighttime residence;
3. Unaccompanied youth and families with children and young people who are defined as homeless under other federal statutes which do not otherwise qualify as homeless under this definition; or
4. Individuals and families who are fleeing, or are attempting to flee, domestic violence, dating violence, sexual assault, stalking, or other dangerous or life-threatening conditions that relate to violence against the individual or a family member.

The HUD definition is also linked to the McKinney-Vento Homeless Assistance Act, which is the current policy that governs K-12 education's response to homeless youth. The McKinney-Vento Act (1987) identifies four types of situations that warrant the title and supports for homeless (Title X, Part C, of the No Child Left Behind Act):

1. This includes children or youth who reside in a shelter, welfare hotel, transitional living program, trailer parks or camp grounds due to lack of adequate

accommodations, are abandoned in hospitals, or are awaiting foster care placement;

2. Children or youth who are doubled up or share a residence with other persons due to loss of housing or economic hardship;
3. Children or young people who reside in parks, cars, abandoned buildings, bus or train stations;
4. Migratory children who meet any of the three previous conditions.

Whereas individuals under the HUD definition are identified as homeless through various governmental, social services, and other non-profit agencies, under McKinney-Vento students are identified as homeless usually at the time of enrollment in school. Thus, it is possible for a school not to be aware of a student's change in housing situation.

As Ambrose (2016) points out, social policy tends to focus the criteria of homeless on identification of who qualifies for services. In contrast, the research literature defines homelessness in broader terms. For example, one way to identify homeless youth is in relationship to their family. The literature distinguishes between young people who are with their families and the young people who are unaccompanied or not in the care of a parent, family member, or an adult guardian. Family homelessness is one of the fastest-growing segments of the homeless population (Anooshian, 2005). Studies report that an estimated 600,000 families experience homelessness each year (Burt, Aron, Lee, & Valente, 2001). Further, homeless families account for one-third of the total homeless population.

The second category of unaccompanied youth represents youth only. Unaccompanied youth is a "generic term to refer to minors who are outside a family or institutional setting and who are unaccompanied by a parent or legal guardian" (Robertson, 1992, p. 288). Unaccompanied youth fit into three sub-categories: throwaway youth, service disconnected youth or street youth, and systems youth. While many homeless young people endure with their families, others choose to or are asked to leave home for multiple reasons including physical and sexual abuse. Throwaway youth are those who are asked to leave home by a parent or another adult in the household, and are away from home overnight and prevented from returning (Hammer, Finkelhor, & Sedlak, 2002). Street youth reside in high-risk, non-traditional locations, such as under bridges or in abandoned buildings. Street youth may or may not use shelters or other homeless service agencies; however, they spend most nights sleeping outside in inadequate spaces. Systems youth are those who are involved in government systems (e.g., juvenile justice and foster care). While unaccompanied youth (age 16–24) can be found living in all of these types of situations, scholars document that most unaccompanied youth, in particular, spend their nights doubled up, housed with friends or relatives, until they can find a more permanent solution or are no longer welcome (National Center for Homeless Education (NCHE), 2012). The term "highly mobile" is often used in conjunction or instead of the word "homeless." The term highly mobile can more accurately depict the typical experience of a homeless student but removes the stigma of homelessness. As many of these categories are fluid, many homeless individuals choose to live without the support of social service (service disconnected), thus making it:

1. Harder to accurately represent the number of unaccompanied youth experiencing homelessness, resulting in under-representation;
2. Difficult to assist the young people in finding and maintaining a permanent residence (NCHE, 2012; Wilder Research Foundation, 2015).

William Tierney and colleagues (2008) provide a third alternative to think about homeless youth. They identified six categories of homeless youth that combines the location of homeless youth along with their familial relationship (Tierney, Gupton, & Hallett, 2008, p. 8).

1. Those who live with an adult guardian in an unstable, but secure environment (shelter or storage room).
2. Those who live with an adult guardian in a semi-stable, but potentially dangerous environment (hotel, motel).
3. Those who are unaccompanied and live in long-term group homes as a foster care placement, but have a recent history of unstable or inconsistent housing.
4. Those who live, or have lived for a significant period of time, with or without a guardian on the street and may be in the care of a shelter or agency.
5. Those who are doubled up with a parent or guardian in another person's home for an extended period of time.
6. Those who "couch surf," moving from home to home (nightly, weekly, or monthly) to find any space to sleep, without an adult.

The typology offered by Tierney et al. (2008) provides a more nuanced understanding of the individual and their connection to home and family. Another example of nuanced definitions is Hallett and Crutchfield's Higher Education Housing Continuum (2017). The continuum features four interrelated categories of housing insecurity. Moving from the least secure to secure forms of housing, they list individuals who identify as *homeless*, followed by those that are in *unstable housing* situations (e.g., couch surfing or doubled up). Next the continuum shifts to those with *recent experience of housing instability* (within three years of previous housing insecurity), and finally *housing secure* individuals. The continuum recognizes that each category overlaps with the adjacent categories, and begins to capture the fluidity that is associated with homelessness and housing insecurity. The issue of defining who is homeless is problematic. On the one hand, social policy reduces the experience of homelessness to categorical descriptions that denote what services might be neces-sary. On the other hand, academics describe the nuanced and fluid dynamics of experiencing housing instability. As Hopper and Baumohl (1996) wrote, "it seems that homelessness is at best an odd-job word, pressed into service to impose order on a hodgepodge of social dislocation, extreme poverty, seasonal or itinerant work, and unconventional ways of life" (p. 3). The definitions presented help in understanding who may be considered homeless, but as no particular policy governs documenta-tion of homeless youth in higher education, it is difficult to determine the numbers of homeless college students.

WHAT CAUSES HOMELESSNESS?

While experiencing homelessness can be thought of and defined as the absence of a stable, safe, and adequate nighttime residence, several studies suggest that the experi-ence of homelessness is the intersection of multiple forms of marginality within systems of inequity (Gupton, 2013, 2014, 2017; Hallett, 2010; Hallett & Westland, 2015; Masten et al., 2012; Tierney & Hallett, 2012).

Research on homelessness identifies three correlated patterns (Gupton, 2013, 2014, 2017). Poverty is primarily linked to homelessness. Bassuk and Rosenberg (1988) found that the experience of homelessness exacerbates the experience of poverty. Individuals and families in poverty are at greater risk of losing their housing if their income is disrupted (e.g., loss of employment or other unexpected costs). Once an individual or family enters into homelessness, it becomes increasingly difficult to return to a place of economic stability. The lack of financial resources means homeless students can find themselves stuck in a cycle of poverty in which they cannot gain economic mobility or personal security.

Next, individuals experiencing homelessness have a greater likelihood of experi-encing familial conflict or separation from their immediate family (Greenblatt & Robertson, 1993; Robertson, 1989). Multiple studies have focused on the increased levels of family conflict, mental or physical trauma, and other educational or develop-mental issues for homeless students (Buckner, 2008; Cutuli et al., 2013; Herbers et al., 2012; Masten et al., 2012; Obradović et al., 2009; Samuels, Shinn, & Buckner, 2010). Separation from immediate family, whether by choice or force, breaks important ties of social support and makes it difficult for young people to build new trusting relationships. Lastly, homelessness is highly associated with residential mobility and other multiple risk factors that lead to grade retention and dropout (Wolff, 2000). The increased frequency of residential mobility in homeless youth and families may be distinct from other low-income students (Ziesemer, Marcoux, & Marwell, 1994). When youth do not expect to remain in a school for an appreciable time, making friends or investing in homework can seem like a pointless endeavor (Cauce, 2000; Julianelle & Foscarinis, 2003).

Despite the chaos of homelessness, many homeless students aspire to achieve a postsecondary degree or credential at similar rates compared to their non-homeless peers; they still experience lower rates of degree attainment (McMillen, Auslander, Elze, White, & Thompson, 2003; Reilly, 2003). From an economic and social justice standpoint, increasing the educational success of homeless and housing-vulnerable students is imperative.

WHO EXPERIENCES HOMELESSNESS?

Homeless and highly mobile youth represent a highly diverse population. Gender, race/ethnicity, experience, educational ability, support systems, and family structure run the gamut for students experiencing homelessness. While it is a challenging population to identify, a few numbers exist. The Office of Juvenile Justice and Delinquency Prevention reports nationally that 68 percent are 15 to 17 years old, and 57 percent of homeless youth identify as White, 27 percent identify as Black or African American, and 3 percent identify as Native American or Alaskan Native (Hammer et al., 2002). Furthermore, individual experiences with homelessness can be cyclical, resulting in repeated periods of instability and disenfranchisement at different points in a person's life (Thompson, Pollio, Eyrich, Bradbury, & North, 2004). Therefore, college students with prior experience of homelessness may be at risk for additional bouts of homelessness.

While gender, family background, race, and income may vary, some individuals experiencing homelessness report previous contact with the "system" (e.g., juvenile justice, foster care, disability services, etc.) before the homeless period. Owen and Decker Gerrard (2013) found that 58 percent of respondents experienced at least one placement in a foster home, group home, or home for those with emotional and behavior disorders. This finding bolsters the research highlighting the link between former foster care youth and homelessness (Barth, 1990; Brandford & English, 2004; Merdinger, 2005; Pecora et al., 2003; Reilly, 2003). Merdinger (2005) found that former foster students, successful in enrolling and persisting in college, experienced homelessness with a mean of 75.12 nights and a median of 30 nights per year. Often former foster youth lack a stable home and an adult in their world to help make the transition from system life to independent living easier; thus, former foster care youth are considered particularly vulnerable to homelessness (NCHE, 2012).

HOW MANY COLLEGE STUDENTS ARE HOMELESS?

In the United States, an estimated 1.7 million youth, younger than 18 years, experience homelessness each year (National Coalition for the Homeless, 2008). In the last few years, federal policies made it possible for institutions to track the number of homeless students applying for financial aid. This change in policy revealed a small but significant number of homeless students applying for financial aid. In 2012, of the number of students who identified as independents on their Free Application for Federal Student Aid (FAFSA), 58,000 identified as homeless according to the National Association for the Education of Homeless Children and Youth (NAEHCY) (Gross, 2013). While FAFSA data provides a number, there are multiple reasons why that number is not an accurate reflection of the homeless student population. First, the U.S. Department of Education utilizes a different definition of "youth," than social service providers. For financial aid purposes "youth" includes individuals under the age of 21. By contrast, people under the age of 24 are considered "youth" by social service agencies and policy. This confusion in terms means that homeless individuals between the ages of 22 and 23 cannot be considered "independent" from their families for financial aid. The second issue is that FAFSA data does not disaggregate homelessness based on any particular category and thus cannot be used to help determine what services might be appropriate to better support homeless students on campus. Lastly, the process for youth to verify their homeless status for financial aid purposes is cumbersome for both the individual and the university. While the FAFSA data provide some indication of how many homeless students participate in higher education, colleges and universities are still not required to keep track of homeless students at the institution, suggesting that the homeless student population may be larger than reflected in FAFSA data.

Community colleges are one sector of higher education where recent scholarship has grown. A nationwide study of community college students by Goldrick-Rab, Richardson, and Hernandez (2017) found that of the over 33,00 students surveyed roughly 14 percent identified as homeless. Further, their study found that nearly 30 percent of former foster youth identified as homeless. In the state of California, a survey carried out by the U.S. Department of Agriculture on the Los Angeles Community College District (230,000 students) found that roughly 19 percent of students were homeless (Holland, 2017). Beyond these few studies, very little data is available about the homeless college student population. Many institutions simply do not track this population and have not set up institutional structures to monitor and support this community.

WHAT BARRIERS TO COLLEGE EXIST FOR HOMELESS STUDENTS?

Regardless of the makeup of the homeless and highly mobile population, striking similarities emerge in educational outcomes. Homeless and highly mobile youth aspire to achieve a postsecondary credential at the same rate as their non-homeless peers, yet they reach that goal at much lower rates (McMillen et al., 2003; Reilly, 2003). While youth may want to attend postsecondary education, the immediate challenges of homelessness often force young people to put their educational plans on hold (Hagedorn & Fogel, 2002; McDonough, 1997). Therefore, homeless high school graduates often encounter multiple barriers as they attempt to transition to college.

One of the barriers to postsecondary enrollment stems from a lack of information and resources. Homeless youth estranged from their families will not be able to use their parents as a resource, both emotionally and financially, when applying to college. Tierney and Auerbach (2004) point out that family play a crucial role in serving as a support network for students preparing for college. Without help from their families, homeless youth must look for alternative forms of support. Youth residing in shelters may turn to shelter staff members to help them navigate the process of applying to college, although shelter staff members are rarely trained to provide educational support in the area of college applications and financial aid. Lacking clear guidance makes it difficult for homeless individuals to navigate the complex system on their own or seek external mentors. Additionally, young people in shelters have a difficult time building a sense of self-efficacy in regard to academic performance and the college application process (Hagedorn & Fogel, 2002; McDonough, 1997). Thus, this creates a situation where students make choices on their own with little support, guidance, or knowledge.

Former foster youth often graduate from high schools with a weak college-going culture, which includes low expectations by the adults, lack critical knowledge of college options, and see overwhelming financial barriers to success (Wolanin, 2005). Thus, homeless students enroll in college uneducated about campus supports, unprepared for the rigor and demands of the college classroom, with little knowledge of the campus environment, and overall limited experience with the institution (Wolanin, 2005). Furthermore, college students experiencing homelessness often go undetected upon enrollment and then do not reach graduation (Merdinger, 2005). The lack of tracking creates a situation in which homeless students are at "especially high risk of not completing their educational goals, resulting in [increased] debt load and no new marketable skills" (Minnesota Interagency Council on Homelessness, 2013, p. 21).

WHAT DO WE KNOW ABOUT HOMELESS COLLEGE STUDENTS?

As homelessness in college is a developing area of the literature, a small body of research exists on homeless students' experiences in college. This area of study highlights several areas of convergence among the experiences of homeless college students. Within this area of research, the first major distinction is between students that experience homelessness before college (Gupton, 2009, 2017; Hallett, 2010) and students that first experience homelessness while in college (Ambrose, 2016; Paden, 2012). For students that experience homelessness before entering college, the research emphasizes the importance of attending to basic needs for homeless students during the college transition process (Ambrose, 2016; Gupton, 2013, 2014; Hallett, 2010). As Paden (2012) notes:

> Students may have initially had support from home, scholarships, financial aid, etc. that allowed them to decide to pursue their college degree. Once enrolled, a number of factors could result in loss of a permanent place to live. (p. 670)

College students often enter into homelessness in similar ways to homeless families or unaccompanied youth: the loss of familial support, lack of employment, leaving violent or otherwise unsafe housing situations. Research suggests that for students that first experience homelessness in college, the major issue is identifying the student as homeless, and then providing a contact person and resources (Paden, 2012). While this distinction is informal, it acknowledges that different supports are necessary for students experiencing homelessness for the first time.

Regarding student experiences, research identifies three overlapping experiences for homeless students. First, homeless college students report feelings of isolation and invisibility (Crutchfield, 2012; Gupton, 2017). As institutions do not track homeless students, faculty and student service personnel are not aware of their presence on campus. Coupled with the fact that it can be difficult for students to disclose their housing situation, this creates an invisible and isolated student population. In Crutchfield's study of homeless college students, she found that "Almost all of the youth spoke about feeling alone in college and often in the world as a whole" (2012, p. 114). The feelings of isolation and invisibility make it difficult for homeless students to build support networks on campus, participate in campus activities, or find resources to remedy their housing instability.

Beyond invisibility and isolation, students experiencing homelessness also report increased levels of stress and difficulty meeting their basic needs (Ambrose, 2016; Crutchfield, 2012, Crutchfield, Chambers, & Duffield 2016). Based on the literature, inability to meet basic needs (e.g., hunger, safety, or shelter) overlaps with increased mental or emotional stress, which can exacerbate feelings of invisibility and isolation on campus.

While much of the literature presents the negative consequences of being a homeless college student, the research also identifies that many homeless students also view higher education as a source of hope of social mobility (Ambrose, 2016; Crutchfield, 2012; Geis, 2015; Gupton, 2009). Crutchfield writes: "Despite the challenges that impact their experiences in college, most of the youth felt that staying in college is the way to make it out of poverty" (2012, p. 126). Gupton (2009) refers to "educational shelter" to denote that homeless students view education as a source of stability and support. The question that looms large is whether that sentiment of hope holds out against feelings of alienation and struggles to meet basic needs.

WHAT CAN HIGHER EDUCATION DO TO SUPPORT HOMELESS STUDENTS?

How do colleges and universities best support a population that is difficult to define, count, and provide with adequate services? Given the literature that we have presented, we address several ways that colleges and universities can support homeless students.

Meeting Basic Needs

Supports for homeless and highly mobile youth seeking higher education come in multiple forms from federal regulations, scholarship opportunities, shelters, and non-profit programs. In particular, federal regulations have created an environment supportive of homeless youth reaching postsecondary attainment. First, the Higher Education Act incorporates the McKinney-Vento definitions of homelessness to legally identify supports and rights for homeless youth. One of the key benefits of this Act is allowing college-bound students to identify as independents, creating a financial aid boost (Morones, 2013). However, Crutchfield, Chambers, and Duffield (2016) suggest that homeless students still experience multiple burdens in verifying their homeless status. They recommend more support for financial aid administrators, social workers, and district liaisons to eliminate the barriers.

The second congressional bill is the College Cost Reduction and Access Act (CCRAA). Enacted in 2007, CCRAA seeks to implement two protections for vulnerable students. First, CCRAA protects students from taking on too much debt upon graduation. Second, CCRAA attempts to make college more attainable and affordable for all. One of the avenues for reducing costs for college access is waiving the fees for Advanced Placement exams, application fees, and college entrance exams for those eligible students. Fee-waivers are helpful for students experiencing homelessness who may experience significant financial challenges in accessing postsecondary degrees.

One state-level program, the Minnesota Education, and Training Voucher Program (ETV), provides funding, up to $5,000, to assist current and former foster care and adoptive youth to attend colleges, universities, vocational or technical programs. This program, created by the Chafee Foster Care Independence Act, provides eligible students with funds to pay for tuition, fees, books, housing, transportation, and other school-related costs and living expenses. ETV, described as a "gap program," intends to complement whatever funds students have raised/earned to attend postsecondary education (Minnesota Department of Human Services, n.d.). Ideally, students accessing the ETV program could hold off homelessness.

Third, institutions should look to create an economic crisis office that can help students locate financial and housing assistance if necessary. Gupton (2013) cites the need for an economic distress student support network office that would provide resources and support for students who are or become homeless during the academic year. Students need one place to visit on campus to assist with the economic challenges. Spreading services out to multiple people or offices challenges students' ability to successfully navigate.

For campuses that offer on-campus housing, we suggest giving homeless students priority in the selection of on-campus housing and allowing access to year-round residential options. One of the best ways to help homeless students is to provide them with a non-cost prohibitive, stable, and safe place to stay. Living in a residence hall could help homeless students battle feelings of isolation and invisibility in college. Further, students would have direct access to built-in on-campus support services. The institution should ensure that students may stay on campus in a residence hall during extended school breaks (i.e., winter and summer holidays). Homeless students may not have an adequate place to go if they are forced to leave their residence during school breaks. In some cases, students return to a shelter or group home over the break.

Beyond housing, we suggest that campuses also provide resource centers and food pantries to help students meet basic needs. Sara Goldrick-Rab and colleagues have addressed the issue of food and housing insecurity on campus (Goldrick-Rab, Broton, & Eisenberg, 2015; Goldrick-Rab, Richardson, & Kinsley, 2017). They recommend that campuses establish food shelves and resource centers on campus to ensure that students have ways of meeting their basic needs. Campuses that do not have the resources to sustain their own food pantry or resource center should look to partner with community organizations that can provide resources to meet students' basic needs.

Educational and Social Needs

We suggest two areas where colleges and universities could expand services to be more supportive of homeless students. First, they could create programs designed to support the specific academic, psychosocial, and mental health needs of highly mobile and homeless students (Gupton, 2017). Such programs should include outreach to local non-profits that work with homeless individuals. As homeless and highly mobile students are often unfamiliar with or mistrusting of on-campus support structures, this would involve working to build relationships with the student, case workers, or community agencies. Individuals that experience homelessness often do not receive complete or adequate information about higher education. The information is often filtered through a caseworker, mentor, or employee at a group home, so it is important to provide a connection to the college or university. Providing support from both the K-12 and postsecondary ends helps them transition to college, particularly since many homeless adolescents are estranged from their families and cannot go to them for any support.

Second, beyond creating a student support and outreach program, community colleges should incorporate homeless students into existing institutional-level efforts to improve academic success. The use of summer bridge programs and other student success programs are vital to helping homeless students thrive in their transition to college. It remains, however, to be seen if academic success programs will be inclusive of students from residentially unstable backgrounds. Multiple forms of institutional and personal support that help students foster academic resilience would be useful in meeting the diverse challenges of college life.

Reduce Isolation

For many homeless students, invisibility can be beneficial; they could attend class and not feel stigmatized because of their living situation. Being able to blend in with other students helps to relieve some of the stressors of homelessness. Invisibility on campus also allows students a space to explore their own identities and interests. The down-side of invisibility is that when homeless students do need assistance (e.g., usually about financial aid), they do not have a definite place or person they can contact. While university staff members are knowledgeable, they receive little to no training on policies, opportunities, or scholarships related to homeless students.

In helping with issues of isolation, college campuses serve as sources of stability and provide opportunities for homeless students to build supportive networks. We suggest that colleges and universities develop systems for identifying and supporting homeless students. Although many of the campuses have created food banks to address issues of hunger, more needs to be done to create tangible and accessible support services for homeless and housing-vulnerable students. The creation of a homeless student support and outreach coordinator would go a long way in begin-ning to build transparent support structures on campus. Next, colleges and univer-sities should consider providing training for faculty and staff on how to incorporate a strength-based perspective into the curriculum and campus culture. Creating an institutional climate built around the assets and abilities that students have will con-tribute to creating a more inclusive and supportive campus environment. This is an approach that supports all marginalized communities, not simply students struggling with homelessness.

SO WHAT'S NEXT FOR THE STUDY OF COLLEGE STUDENTS EXPERIENCING HOMELESSNESS?

Postsecondary institutions often exhibit dismay or surprise when asked about the homeless student population. As illustrated in this review of the literature, the assumption that homeless and highly mobile students do not attend higher educa-tion is false. Youth experiencing homelessness do enroll in postsecondary institutions, and while the reported numbers remain small, they are still an important student population. In this chapter, we have tried to stress that the experience of homeless-ness is a unique experience that is not reducible to a singular solution. Addressing issues of housing instability in college students is a matter of systemic and personal responsibility. Next steps related to this area of inquiry should focus on improving institutional capacity to identify and support students experiencing homelessness. Further, more work that focuses on community colleges as well as adult (over the age of 25) homeless students would provide greater nuance and completeness to the experience of homelessness in higher education. The study of higher education will not be complete until we address issues of access and success for those most on the margins, focusing on how higher and postsecondary institutions might better serve their diverse student populations.

QUESTIONS FOR DISCUSSION

1. Gupton and Trost highlight researchers' struggle to identify the number of students experiencing homelessness. How can higher education professionals address a problem if they do not know the scale of the issue? Working in teams, identify potential solutions to the documentation or tracking of housing-vulnerable students. How might these solutions be implemented? What barriers do you foresee? What issues may arise with creating a formalized tracking of students experiencing homelessness or housing insecurity?

2. In this chapter, the authors suggest establishing a Student Support Distress Network Office. In small groups, determine how you might design this office? Within which functional unit would you house it at your home institution? How might you make the case to other colleagues about its need and sustainability?

3. Gupton and Trost suggest that institutions must consider "providing training for faculty and staff on how to incorporate a strength-based perspective into the curriculum and campus culture." In pairs, develop the questions that a training of this type should address. How would you ensure that the program is developed through an asset-based perspective?

4. The authors suggest that a key solution for homeless college students is for higher education institutions to provide priority and preference in residence hall placement. What options exist for students enrolled at non-residential campuses? Also, what role should commuter colleges take to provide opportunities for students to access safe and stable housing? Generate some potential resources and practices that commuter colleges could offer to support housing-vulnerable students.

5. Non-profit agencies, cities, counties, and regional governments all work to provide access to safe and secure housing for their residents. Furthermore, many agencies also provide services and supports to meet basic human needs. Is it imperative, as the authors suggest, for postsecondary institutions to also engage and partner in this work? List some examples of potential community and university partnerships. How does this expand universities' mission? What might be the social or economic implications of this work?

REFERENCES

Ambrose, V. K. (2016). *"It's like a mountain": The lived experience of homeless college students* (Doctoral dissertation). University of Tennessee. Retrieved from https://trace.tennessee.edu/utk_graddiss/3887/.

Anooshian, L. (2005). Violence and aggression in the lives of homeless children: A review. *Aggression and Violent Behavior, 10*(2), 129–152.

Barth, R. P. (1990). On their own: The experiences of youth after foster care. *Child and Adolescent Social Work, 7*(5), 419–441.

Bassuk, E. L., & Rosenberg, L. (1988). Why does family homelessness occur? A case-control study. *American Journal of Public Health, 78*(7), 783–788.

Brandford, C., & English, D. (2004). *Foster youth transition to independence study* (Final report). Seattle, WA: Office of Children's Administration Research, Washington State Department of Social and Health Services. Retrieved from www.dshs.wa.gov/pdf/ca/FYTfinal2004.pdf.

Buckner, J. C. (2008). Understanding the impact of homelessness on children: Challenges and future research directions. *American Behavioral Scientist, 51*, 721–736.

Burt, M., Aron, L., Lee, E., & Valente, J. (2001). *Helping America's homeless: Emergency shelter or affordable housing?* Washington, DC: The Urban Institute.

Cauce, A. (2000). The characteristics and mental health of homeless adolescents: Age and gender differences. *Journal of Emotional and Behavioral Disorders, 8*, 230–239.

Crutchfield, R. M. (2012). *"If I don't fight for it, I have nothing": Experiences of homeless youth scaling the collegiate mountain* (Doctoral dissertation). Retrieved from ProQuest Dissertations and Theses database (UMI No. 3530671).

Crutchfield, R. M., Chambers, R. M., & Duffield, B. (2016). Jumping through the hoops to get financial aid for college students who are homeless: Policy analysis of the College Cost Reduction and Access Act of 2007. *Families in Society: The Journal of Contemporary Social Services, 97*(3), 191–199.

Cutuli, J. J., Desjardins, C. D., Herbers, J. E., Long, J. D., Heistad, D., Chan, C. K., ... Masten, A. S. (2013). Academic achievement trajectories of homeless and highly mobile students: Resilience in the context of chronic and acute risk. *Child Development, 84*, 841–857.

Geis, Q. D. (2015). *Exploring the academic and social experiences of homeless college students.* (Master's thesis). Retrieved from http://digitalcommons.unl.edu/cehsedaddiss/234/.

Goldrick-Rab, S., Broton, K., & Eisenberg, D. (2015). Hungry to learn: Addressing food & housing insecurity among undergraduates. *Wisconsin HOPE Lab,* 1–25. Retrieved from http://wihopelab.com/publications/Wisconsin_hope_lab_hungry_to_learn.pdf.

Goldrick-Rab, S., Richardson, J., & Hernandez, A. (2017). Hungry and homeless in college: Results from a national study of basic needs insecurity in higher education. *Wisconsin HOPE Lab,* 1–32. Retrieved from www.wihopelab.com/publications/Hungry-and-Homeless-in-College-Report.pdf.

Goldrick-Rab, S., Richardson, J., & Kinsley, P. (2017). Guide to assessing basic needs insecurity in higher education. *Wisconsin HOPE Lab,* 1–29. Retrieved from www.wihopelab.com/publications/Basic-Needs-Insecurity-College-Students.pdf.

Greenblatt, M., & Robertson, M. J. (1993). Homeless adolescents: Lifestyle, survival strategies and sexual behaviors. *Hospital and Community Psychiatry, 44*, 1177–1180.

Gross, L. (2013, October 21). College campuses see rise in homeless students. *USA Today.* Retrieved from www.usatoday.com/story/news/nation/2013/10/21/homeless-students-american-colleges/3144383/.

Gupton, J. T. (2009). *Pathways to college for homeless adolescents* (Doctoral dissertation). Retrieved from ProQuest Dissertations and Theses database. (UMI No. AAI3368700).

Gupton, J. T. (2013). Marginalized but resilient: Homeless youth and urban education. *National Journal of Urban Education and Practice, 7*, 44–57.

Gupton, J. T. (2014). Homeless youth in college. In S. R. Harper & S. J. Quaye (Eds.), *Student engagement in higher education: Theoretical perspectives and practical approaches for diverse populations* (2nd ed.; pp. 221–236). New York, NY: Routledge.

Gupton, J. T. (2017). Campus of opportunity: A qualitative analysis of homeless students in community college. *Community College Review, 45*(3), 190–214. doi:10.1177/0091552117700475.

Hagedorn, L. S., & Fogel, S. F. (2002). Making school to college programs work: Academics, goals, and aspirations. In W. G. Tierney & L. S. Hagedorn (Eds.), *Increasing access to college: Extending possibilities for all students* (pp 169–193). Albany, NY: SUNY Press.

Hallett, R. E. (2010). Homeless: How residential instability complicates students' lives. *About Campus*, *15*(3), 11–16.

Hallett, R. E., & Crutchfield, R. (2017). Homelessness and housing insecurity in higher education: A trauma-informed approach to research, policy, and practice. *ASHE Higher Education Report*, *43*(6), 7–118.

Hallett, R. E., & Westland, M. A. (2015). Foster youth: Supporting invisible students through visibility. *About Campus*, *20*(3), 15–21.

Hammer, H., Finkelhor, D., & Sedlak, A. J. (2002). *Runaway/thrown away children: National estimates and characteristics* (Juvenile Justice Bulletin No. NCJ196469). Washington, DC: Office of Juvenile Justice and Delinquency Prevention.

Herbers, J. E., Cutuli, J. J., Supkoff, L. M., Heistad, D., Chan, C.-K., Hinz, E., & Masten, A. S. (2012). Early reading skills and academic achievement trajectories of students facing poverty, homelessness, and high residential mobility. *Educational Researcher*, *41*, 366–374.

Holland, G.(2017, June 29). 1 in 5 L.A. community college students is homeless, survey finds. *Los Angeles Times*. Retrieved from www.latimes.com/local/lanow/la-me-ln-homeless-community-college-20170628-story.html.

Hopper, K., & Baumohl, J. (1996). Redefining the cursed word: A historical interpretation of American homelessness. In J. Baumohl, (Ed.), *Homelessness in America* (pp. 3–14). Phoenix, AZ: Oryx Press.

Julianelle, P., & Foscarinis, M. (2003). Responding to the school mobility of children and youth experiencing homelessness: The McKinney-Vento Act and beyond. *Journal of Negro Education*, *72*, 39–54.

Masten, A. S., Herbers, J. E., Desjardins, C. D., McCormick, C. M., Sapienza, J. K., Long, J. D., … Zelanzo, P. D. (2012). Executive function skills and school success in young children. *Educational Researcher*, *41*, 375–384.

McDonough, P. (1997). *Choosing colleges: How social class and schools structure opportunity*. Albany, NY: State University of New York.

McKinney-Vento Homelessness Assistance Act, Pub. L. No. 100–77, § 11301, 101 Stat. 482 (1987).

McMillen, C., Auslander, W., Elze, D., White, T., & Thompson, R. (2003). Educational experiences and aspirations of older youth in foster care. *Child Welfare*, *82*(4), 475–495.

Merdinger, J. M. (2005). Pathways to college for former foster youth: Understanding factors that contribute to educational success. *Child Welfare*, *84*(6), 867–896.

Minnesota Department of Health and Human Services. (n.d.). Education and Training Voucher Program ETV. Retrieved from https://mn.gov/dhs/people-we-serve/children-and-families/services/adolescent-services/programs-services/education-and-training-voucher.jsp.

Minnesota Interagency Council on Homelessness (2013). *Heading home: Minnesota's plan to prevent and end homelessness*. Retrieved from www.leg.state.mn.us/docs/2015/other/150346.pdf.

Morones, S. M. (2013). Resource relationship characteristics of homeless youth accessing higher education opportunities. *Resource Relationships and Homeless Youth*, *3*(2), 1–23.

National Center for Homeless Education (NCHE) (2012). *Increasing access to higher education for unaccompanied homeless youth: Information for colleges and universities*. Retrieved from https://nche.ed.gov/downloads/briefs/higher_ed.pdf.

National Coalition for the Homeless. (2008). *NCH fact sheet. Homeless youth* (NCH Fact Sheet #13). Washington, DC. Retrieved from https://rhyclearinghouse.acf.hhs.gov/library/2008/homeless-youth-nch-fact-sheet-13.

Obradović, J., Long, J. D., Cutuli, J. J., Chang, C., Hinz, E., Heistad, D., & Masten, A. (2009). Academic achievement of homeless and highly mobile children in an urban school district: Longitudinal evidence on risk, growth, and resilience. *Development and Psychopathology*, *21*, 493–518.

Owen, G., & Decker Gerrard, M. (2013, October 8). Start by knowing way: 5 reasons people are homeless in Minnesota. [Blog post]. Retrieved from www.mncompass.org/trends/insights/2013-10-08-5-things-about-homelessness-in-minnesota.

Paden, N. (2012, February). *Homeless students? Not at my university: The reality of homeless college students*. Paper presented at the American Society of Business and Behavioral Sciences Annual Conference, Las Vegas, NV.

Pecora, P., Williams, J., Kessler, R., Downs, A., O'Brien, K., Hiripi, E., & Morello, S. (2003). *Assessing the effects of foster care: Early results from the Casey National Alumni Study*. Seattle, WA: Casey Family Programs.

Reilly, T. (2003). Transition from care: Status and outcomes of youth who age out of foster care. *Child Welfare, 82*, 727–746.

Robertson, J. (1992). Homeless and runaway youth: A review of the literature. In M. Robertson & M. Greenblatt (Eds.), *Homelessness: A national perspective* (pp. 287–297). New York, NY: Plenum Press.

Robertson, M. J. (1989). *Homeless youth in Hollywood: Patterns of alcohol use—Report to the national institute on alcohol abuse & alcoholism*. Berkeley, CA: Alcohol Research Group.

Samuels, J., Shinn, M., & Buckner, J. C. (2010). *Homeless children: Update on research, policy, programs, and opportunities*. Washington, DC: U.S. Department of Health and Human Services, Office of the Assistant Secretary for Planning and Evaluation.

The National Center for Family Homelessness. (2008). *The characteristics of and needs of families experiencing homelessness*. Retrieved from http://community.familyhomelessness.org/sites/default/files/NCFH%20 Fact%20Sheet%204–08.pdf.

Thompson, S. J., Pollio, D. E., Eyrich, K., Bradbury, E., & North, C. S. (2004). Successfully exiting homelessness: Experiences of formerly homeless mentally ill individuals. *Evaluation and Program Planning, 27*(4), 423–431.

Tierney, W. G., & Auerbach, S. (2004). Toward developing an untapped resource: The role of families in college preparation. In W. G. Tierney, J. Colyar, & Z. B. Corwin (Eds.), *Preparing for college: Nine elements of effective outreach* (pp. 29–48). Albany, NY: SUNY Press.

Tierney, W. G., Gupton, J. T., & Hallett, R. E. (2008). *Transitions to adulthood for homeless adolescents: Education and public policy*. Los Angeles, CA: Center for Higher Education Policy Analysis.

Tierney, W. G., & Hallett, R. E. (2012). Social capital and homeless youth: Influence of residential instability on college access. *Metropolitan Universities Journal, 22*(3), 46–62.

Wilder Research Foundation (2015). *Homeless in Minnesota: Youth on their own. Findings from the 2012 statewide study of homelessness*. St. Paul, MN: Amherst H. Wilder Research Foundation.

Wolff, B. (2000). *Residential and academic instability: A comprehensive model linking youth homelessness to poor academics*. Retrieved from www.ctvoices.org/sites/default/files/well00homeless03.pdf.

Wolanin, T. R. (2005). *Higher education opportunities for foster youth: A primer for policymakers*. Washington, DC: Institute for Higher Education Policy.

Ziesemer, C., Marcoux, L., & Marwell, B. E. (1994). Homeless children: Are they different from other low-income children? *Social Work, 39*, 658–668.

10

CURRENTLY AND FORMERLY INCARCERATED STUDENTS

DEBBIE MUKAMAL AND REBECCA SILBERT

Although the United States still holds the dubious honor of incarcerating more of its citizens than other industrialized nations, we are seeing a growing national recognition that mass incarceration must end. As part of this movement, states are acknowledging and seeking to repair the immense damage that mass incarceration has caused to families, communities, and economies. Solutions are complicated—mass incarceration has always been intertwined with racial inequity, poverty, and lack of access to housing and adequate health care, among other things. Solutions, therefore, must likewise come from multiple sectors, from housing to employment to public health, and, indeed, states and localities throughout the nation are looking to these systems for answers. Often overlooked, however, is the public higher education system.

And yet, higher education is a proven way to reduce recidivism, build social mobility, and increase job prospects. Students in prison who participate in correctional education have 43 percent lower odds of recidivating after release than those who do not (Davis, Bozick, Steele, Saunders & Miles, 2013), and the numbers improve even more for college courses: incarcerated students in college programs have 51 percent lower odds of recidivating as compared to those in other education (Davis et al., 2013). Perhaps more importantly, students in prison who receive an education are more likely to find employment upon release, transforming them from "offenders" into contributors and community leaders (Davis et al., 2013). Recognizing this, California has spent the past few years enlisting its public higher education system in the effort to address mass incarceration. These efforts are particularly critical here because, like many other states, California faces a looming shortage of college-educated workers

(Public Policy Institute of California, 2017). As a state and as a nation, we cannot over-look these potential graduates.[1]

California's efforts are remarkable not because currently and formerly incarcerated men and women in California have access to college: there have been individual high-quality programs for justice-involved students here as elsewhere, for many years. But California is systematically folding these students by the thousands into the fabric of the state's existing public higher education system. In this, the state is at the forefront of a movement that has the potential to bring enormous benefit to students, their families and communities, and the state as a whole.

Engaging public higher education to address mass incarceration is not easy. Reaching a new generation of students, particularly those who carry a social stigma, requires intention, thought, and a lot of good will. In focus groups and in interviews, these new students use language that recalls the struggles of the gay rights movement: "I was in the shadows," "I spent my days in class terrified that someone would find out," "I felt like I had a neon sign on my head that said 'he doesn't belong,'" "If I saw someone I knew from parole, I was terrified that they would out me," and "I thought that, if people found out, they wouldn't want me to be in the class." Students share stories of walking onto campus, only to give up and go home after being met with a hostile or unhelpful financial aid or enrollment counselor. For students who are unfamiliar with technology because they lost years to incarceration, the challenges can be even greater. Online enrollment, open source textbooks, and a digital learning management system like Canvas can be overwhelming. Add to the mix an unsupportive parole agent or probation officer, and the hurdles can outweigh even the most dedicated of potential students.

Yet across the state, public colleges and universities are welcoming the challenge. There is certainly more work to be done. But growth in enrollment has been exponential since 2014. Colleges and universities have often struggled to implement strong support strategies, but the doors have opened, and students are coming. Students are speaking up and they are publicly identifying themselves. They are demanding the same opportunity to benefit from higher education that is available to all other Californians, and the system is embracing them.

PUBLIC EDUCATION CAN SCALE A PROVEN SOLUTION

The benefits of higher education are neither new nor unknown. High-quality programs for currently and formerly incarcerated students exist throughout the country and have existed for some time.[2] But these programs are largely privately funded and have not been scaled to sustainably serve the thousands of men and women who have been affected by mass incarceration and could benefit from a college education. The public education system, in contrast, has an already existing structure that can reach the entire state. To truly reach the individuals and communities that have been impacted by mass incarceration, therefore, we must call upon public higher education.

California is particularly well situated to do this, as both the criminal justice and the public higher education systems are immense. There are now 115 community colleges serving over 2 million students every semester (www.cccco.edu). There are 23 California State University (CSU) campuses, and 10 University of California (UC) campuses, serving 478,000 and 217,000 undergraduates, respectively.[3] The state operates under the 1960 Master Plan for Higher Education, which defined the roles of each of the three interconnected segments.[4] Pursuant to the Master Plan, the community colleges are open access to meet the goal of broad access for all. Originally, the state's public college and universities were tuition free. That had changed by the 1980s but in 1984, in response to the implementation of a state-mandated enrollment fee, the Board of Governors for the California Community Colleges created a tuition fee waiver to maintain access for underrepresented and low-income students.[5] The waiver is, and always has been, available to any low-income student in the state, including those who are or who have been incarcerated. Critically, California does not have undergraduate admissions barriers in its public higher education system. None of the three segments—the community colleges, CSU, and UC—ask undergraduate applicants if they have a prior conviction.

On the criminal justice side, it is estimated that 8 million Californians living in the community have a prior arrest or conviction record.[6] The state has 35 prisons holding an average of 120,000 men and woman on any given day.[7] Each of the 58 counties also has a jail system; collectively they incarcerate another 80,000 people on a daily basis (Board of State and Community Corrections, 2017).[8] The state's prison system—run by the California Department of Corrections (CDCR)—is statutorily mandated to provide adult basic education and GED.[9] It also provides career technical education (CTE). Most people released from state prison are placed on a three-year term of community supervision; approximately 50,000 men and women are currently on parole in California.[10] Each county also has many men and women who are being supervised by the county probation department. Although the exact count is unknown, it is estimated that approximately 400,000 people are on probation at any given time.[11] Most counties impose three-year terms of probation, although a few rely on a five-year term.

In 2011, in response to the United States Supreme Court ruling that California must downsize its state prison population,[12] the state passed the Public Safety Realignment Act or AB 109. Among other things, Realignment required that individuals who commit certain low-level crimes must serve their sentences locally in the jail and/or on probation, rather than in state prison. The law lifted the requirement (still common in most states) that jail sentences be no more than one year. As a result, more individuals are serving longer sentences in their local county jails. From an education perspective, the changed landscape created by Realignment means that we cannot think about higher education and criminal justice as solely an issue for the state's prisons; we must also consider the thousands of men and women cycling through the 58 county jails.

The two systems are not only enormous; they are also set up to work together and benefit one another. For the state prisons, there is at least one community college close to every state prison, which means that community college faculty and staff can provide the face-to-face teaching, counseling, advising, and student support services that are critical to student success. For the county jails, 90 percent of the state's jail inmates are less than ten miles from a community college, which further enables effective partnership.[13] Moreover, the two systems work within similar constraints, such as union agreements, state employee requirements, and statutory and regulatory requirements. Although these external considerations can render both systems cumbersome, the fact that their leaders and employees labor under similar bureaucracies has fostered understanding of the constraints within which they both operate.

Challenges exist, of course. But we cannot afford financially or morally to simply sit back and leave millions of people uneducated. And if we want to reach everyone, it means looking to the public higher education system, flaws and all.

THE GREAT LEAP: 2014 TO 2017

Higher education options for incarcerated students were limited prior to 2015. Although the CTE options in prison were robust, only one state prison had a face-to-face college degree program, run through a private university. A single community college was offering a cohort-based degree program inside a women's prison, through a combination of recorded lectures and in-person student support. As a result of Realignment, a handful of jails were starting to offer educational programming, but it was limited to basic education or GED pathways.

Students in prison or jail who sought to expand their education were almost entirely limited to low-quality, non-interactive correspondence education. Packets were mailed from the college to the student, the student completed the packet on his or her own, and the student mailed the packet back to the college. Students endured long delays, they received little to no feedback or educational guidance, there was no tutoring or educational support, and there were rampant reports of cheating.

The options for formerly incarcerated students on campus were not much better. Student groups and clubs targeting these students were virtually nonexistent. Only a handful of community colleges had on-campus programs for formerly incarcerated students, and only one CSU campus hosted a formal program. That program—Project Rebound—has been in existence for 50 years at San Francisco State. Staffed by a formerly incarcerated program manager, Project Rebound is a special admissions program that helps formerly incarcerated students matriculate into SF State. Once enrolled, students in the program receive counseling, tutoring, and stipends for transportation, campus meals, and textbooks. In the UC system, the student support program at UC Berkeley—Underground Scholars—was in its first year of existence and was largely unknown in the rest of the state. In essence, formerly incarcerated students, although they were enrolled in the state's college and universities because of open access and the lack of undergraduate admissions barriers, were largely invisible.

In just three years, the state has transformed the criminal justice and public higher education relationship, and opened pathways to thousands of incarcerated and formerly incarcerated students. The greatest change in California has been inside the state's prisons. Community colleges now teach face-to-face transferrable, degree-building college courses in 32 of the state's 35 prisons. Face-to-face community college unique enrollment inside CDCR rose from zero in 2014 to almost 4,500 in 2017—more than any other state, more than the number enrolled in the federal Second Chance Pell Initiative across the nation,[14] and almost as many as are enrolled in Yale's entire undergraduate class.[15] Bakersfield College, for example, is now providing face-to-face college courses in 10 prisons and jails, serving over almost 800 unique students with an enrollment over 1,000. Students can enroll in classes ranging from Japanese language to Sociology to Communications, with the same syllabi and same professors as students on the nearby campus. Students are subject to the same statewide requirements and degree patterns as those on campus. As far as the college is concerned, students are students, whether they return to a cell or to their neighborhood after class.

These face-to-face courses are offered by the state's community colleges in both men's and women's prisons, in every type of yard at every security level from minimum to maximum. Classes are not limited to low-risk or low-security students, or those being released within a few years. Community colleges teaching the face-to-face classes report waiting lists and growing demand in every prison. In addition to the community colleges, one CSU is now offering a bachelor's program inside a men's facility. The program is cohort-based and recruits from eligible students who have already earned an associate's degree.

Notably, correspondence education enrollment has dropped over the past four semesters, from 8,400 to 7,377. Moreover, some of the correspondence colleges have expanded their programs to include in-person counseling and educational guidance, increasing the quality and bringing correspondence closer to the benefits offered by face to face. The goal, of course, is high-quality, face-to-face, full-credit transferrable courses in every prison, available to every potential student. The state is moving in that direction and, given the achievements in the past three years, continued progress will be made. While that is happening, it is vital to fill the gaps with the highest possible quality alternatives. This means that, at a minimum, all distance education courses must be fully transferrable to the CSU and UC systems; the colleges offering the courses must offer in-person comprehensive educational guidance and counseling; and the colleges cannot rely on the students or their families to cover the high cost of textbooks.

The state's jails have also expanded their offerings, with several of the state's 58 jail systems partnering with their local community colleges. Despite the challenges of lack of programming space and shorter sentences, many colleges are providing academic and CTE courses to students at the jails. To do so, they have implemented a range of solutions, including offering shorter-term classes of six to eight weeks and overcoming the enrollment requirements by offering non-credit classes and for-credit classes comprised of a mix of on-campus and jail students. Key to these efforts is ensuring a warm hand-off for students when they leave jail so that they can continue their studies and rely on the college as a pro-social structure to facilitate their reentry success.

For on-campus students, Project Rebound has expanded from one to nine CSU campuses and more campuses seek to replicate the program. The Underground Scholars Initiative has expanded to two additional University of California campuses (one of which uses a different name). Student groups and on-campus programs similar to Project Rebound and Underground Scholars have proliferated at community colleges across the state with support from Presidents and CEOs, faculty, staff, and administrators—a recent survey showed that a third of all the community colleges in the state either have an existing program or student group, or they are trying to start one. Many of these community college programs adhere to the Project Rebound model, although it has been challenging for them to secure the resources to support a dedicated staff person.

Much work remains to be accomplished, and it is critical that the quality of instruction and programs be monitored to avoid a retreat to the poor practices of the past. Still, progress is being forged. The goal is a series of networks and pathways away from criminal justice and toward higher education, with supports in place so that students around the state are able to attain a certificate or degree. California is not there yet, but the foundation is in place.

KEYS TO SUCCESS

California has benefited from several legislative and policy-building blocks, all of which can be replicated in other states.

Foundation

Three foundational elements have been critical to the expansion. First, Senate Bill 1391 (2014) waived the open-access requirements, thus allowing community colleges to teach face to face and collect their regular student apportionment for students enrolled in prison, just as they can for students on campus.[16] This legislation provided an avenue for expansion and fiscal sustainability, and was the key driver of change after 2014. Although the legislative change applied only to students in state prison, the resulting momentum and visibility contributed greatly to the political will for broader change in jails and on college campuses.

Second, the California College Promise Grant (formerly the Board of Governors Fee Waiver) waives community college enrollment fees for eligible California residents with financial need. Students who are or who have been incarcerated are not excluded. In other states, tuition has been the largest hurdle for states looking to scale their prison–college programs, partly because Pell Grants have been unavailable to students incarcerated in prison. The Promise Grant meant that California did not have to find a new solution to this common problem, because the solution was one that had been created for all low-income students in 1984. Having the Promise Grant also avoided the "free college for felons" counter-argument that has stymied progress in other states, because the waiver is available to all low-income students equally.

And third, the lack of undergraduate admissions barriers at California's public higher education institutions has enabled students who have been in the criminal justice system to attend a UC, CSU, and community college just as any other student in the state. If they are academically ready to succeed, they are eligible to attend a public college or university.

Without these three foundational elements (apportionment, tuition waiver, and open admission), California would have been unable to reach as many incarcerated and formerly incarcerated college students as it has.

Landscape

The state has also benefited from a number of other timely and fortuitous developments that changed the landscape and allowed these programs to flourish. Perhaps most importantly, the state has supportive leadership in both corrections and higher education, from a Governor who said "Aren't redemption and forgiveness what it's all about?"[17] to a Secretary of Corrections who said "Over 90 percent of these inmates will complete their sentence and they'll come back out into the communities. Do you want somebody with no hope, that's involved themselves in criminal activities, doing dope, stabbing people, or would you want a guy that comes out that has an AA degree?"[18] Although change does not materialize solely from a top–down directive, having the open and vocal support of senior leadership has fueled the implementation success of the partnerships.

California has also experienced this change during an era of larger criminal justice reforms and while national attention is focused on the adverse consequences and potential solutions to mass incarceration. Among other things, this momentum has been seen in a number of voter-initiated propositions to reform criminal justice in California. Public Safety Realignment, for example, passed in 2011, represented a drastic shift away from longer-term prison sentences and toward alternative sentences and alternative means by which to achieve public safety. Proposition 57, passed in 2016, likewise reflects statewide support for reform. Proposition 57 had a direct impact on the emerging college programs throughout the state, as it incentivized participation in rehabilitative programs for men and women inside prison, including participation in college courses. Another reflection of the statewide momentum has been the amplification of the voice of those directly involved, including formerly incarcerated students and graduates, staff, faculty, and community advocates. The development of student leaders has been particularly crucial, as there is no stronger voice in support of higher education opportunities than the students themselves.

Also critical has been the fact that California's economy has remained strong since 2014, which means that the community colleges have been incentivized to reach new students over the past few years. By itself this would not be sufficient: it is difficult to build a college–prison partnership, and colleges simply looking to increase enrollment by enrolling incarcerated students are rarely successful. The amount of work required is generally not worth the effort if the college is not otherwise committed to these new students. However, the fact that the colleges were seeking to grow enrollment meant that advocates within the faculty and staff were better able to gain approval and support from senior leadership or from departments that otherwise might have been less supportive.

California's community colleges have also been receiving increased state Equity Funds since 2014. These funds, which are allocated locally, can be used for a broad range of purposes including serving currently and formerly incarcerated students. Colleges are not restricted to spending the funds within traditional race-based definitions. As with the incentive to increase enrollment, increased Equity Fund availability on its own would not have been sufficient to cause colleges to prioritize these students. But, as with the desire to increase enrollment, the availability of these funds provided an avenue for those faculty and staff who were committed to the work to advocate for and obtain funding.

Lastly, because California's Department of Corrections and Rehabilitation (CDCR) has been providing CTE in prison for decades, local community colleges had the ability to focus on full-credit transferrable degree-granting courses for incarcerated students. The colleges did not first have to prioritize short-term job training, which has been an issue faced in other states. Instead, they faced a gap and a demand for transfer-track academic pathways, and it was a gap that they were prepared to fill.

These changes in the landscape—statewide leadership, political momentum, strong economy, flexible funding, and a gap in courses offered—could not, on their own, have created the immense change that we have seen over the past three years. Each in its own way, however, was a vital piece of the puzzle.

Implementation

Finally, a number of smaller decisions made by the state and stakeholders contributed to the growth over the past three years.

First, CDCR and the community colleges view each other as partners, with separate spheres of control. The colleges don't interfere with the security obligations of the institution, and the institutions don't interfere with the education processes of the college. This ensures that educators, rather than corrections officers, are the guardians of educational quality.

Second, for formerly incarcerated students on campus, neither the colleges nor the criminal justice agencies (such as Probation and Parole) funnel the students into special off-campus programs or separate them from the rest of the student population. This allows students to truly develop a transformative student identity.

Finally, both the higher education and criminal justice systems have prioritized solutions that align with existing initiatives. This allows the solutions for incarcerated and formerly incarcerated students to become part of the larger system, thus stabilizing long-term success. For example, the state is implementing Guided Pathways to focus student choices and course scheduling into a smaller number of more valuable options. Just as on campus, community college students inside prison and jail have not been served by a "cafeteria-style" education, with too many credits being accumulated that don't build to a degree. The solution for outside students—Guided Pathways—mirrors the solution for inside students. Likewise, more than half of California's community college students do not initially assess as college-ready in English and math. The state has been focusing on better assessment practices and proven strategies in accelerated learning—again, the same solutions that can and should apply to the many students inside custody who struggle with college readiness. Formerly incarcerated students on campus similarly face many of the same challenges that exist for all community college students, meaning that, again, similar approaches can be adopted. Innovative solutions in transportation (making bus passes available for all enrolled students), food insecurity (having a campus-based food pantry), tutoring (building an on-campus tutoring center), and work–school balance (keeping tutoring centers and student services open late at night and on weekends) assist all community college students to succeed and persist, whether or not they have been involved with the justice system.

Combined, the foundational elements, the background policy changes, and the implementation decisions have helped California build a wave of support for incarcerated and formerly incarcerated college students over the past three years. Success in the moment, however, is not the same as success over the long term.

TURNING A CRITICAL EYE

It would not be fair to trumpet success without an honest assessment of the work that needs to be done to ensure long-term sustainability of high-quality college programs that lead to certificate and degree. Too often, policymakers and advocates announce that a problem has been solved, when in reality the solutions unravel over the long term. For currently and formerly incarcerated college students, we will have achieved success only when we can demonstrate a long-term commitment to quality and completion that mirrors the current commitment to access.

For students inside prison and jail, two key concerns exist. First, there will always be systemic pressure to replace face-to-face education with online or video education, because it is less expensive and easier to provide in a correctional facility. But to truly change lives, these students need face-to-face instruction. Moreover, research affirms that online education doesn't work across the board. Indeed, "online courses can improve access, yet they also are challenging, especially for the least well-prepared students. These students consistently perform worse in an online setting than they do in face-to-face classrooms; taking online courses increases their likelihood of dropping out and otherwise impedes progress through college" (Bettinger & Loeb, 2017, p. 2). Currently and formerly incarcerated students, in general, are among the least prepared in the system.

Second, although many full-credit transferrable classes are being offered to incarcerated students, the vast majority of students are not yet on a structured degree pathway. Among other challenges, students move between institutions or are released prior to degree completion, so they are interacting with multiple college providers over a long period of time. In California the community colleges are highly decentralized, with separate academic senates, separate definitions and strategies for college readiness, and separate degree pathways. Guided Pathways is the statewide answer, but implementing Guided Pathways in one institution is already a challenge. Doing so across multiple institutions is daunting. But creating a Guided Pathway for incarcerated students is critical despite the fact that the students are in multiple institutions and being served by multiple colleges. It is an issue that the state must address.

Colleges teaching inside prisons and jails also face two critical challenges. First, textbooks continue to be a formidable hurdle. The colleges, appropriately, do not want to charge incarcerated students or their families for expensive textbooks. Eventually, it is the goal that incarcerated students will have access to open-source textbooks. But for now the colleges are relying on private funds, textbook sharing, and similar low-cost labor-intensive options. These options are not sustainable over the long term. Second, the California community colleges are funded through per-student apportionment, and they have caps beyond which they cannot collect apportionment. The colleges have been below cap for many years so all students have been welcomed, but at some point the economy will decline and caps may be lowered. When this happens, college administrators will be looking for ways to reduce demand. One obvious way would be to cease teaching inside prisons and jails, and it is this potential future crisis that we must work to avoid. In addition, while one CSU is teaching inside prison now, the funding to cover those students' CSU tuition is being borne by private foundations and the Second Chance Pell Initiative, as the tuition fee waiver available to incarcerated community college students is not available to incarcerated CSU students. To increase and sustain bachelor's-level programs, CSU tuition will need to be addressed.

For all of the colleges, whether they are teaching inside or supporting formerly incarcerated students on the outside, finding funds for dedicated staff is a challenge. And yet, a dedicated staff member is vital. For these partnerships to work, a correctional institution or a probation or parole department needs a singular point of contact.

Particularly for the colleges teaching inside, someone needs to be available to manage the numerous issues that arise each day with getting faculty and materials into the facility. Equally important if not more so, students arriving on campus need a point of contact. For students who feel stigmatized and who may be deeply unfamiliar with the college campus, having an empathic point of contact, preferably someone who themselves has experience with the justice system, can make the difference between persisting to degree and dropping out.

A continuing focus on the balance between quality and quantity is also crucial. Every student deserves the highest-quality individually targeted college education with the full panoply of educational and social supports. But public higher education must reach everyone with limited resources. That is both its strength and its challenge. Although standards are high, California, like the rest of the country, has a diverse set of colleges and universities, particularly in the community college system. Some faculty are outstanding, others less so. Some colleges have strong and visionary leaders, others struggle. All California students have an incredible amount of access to college, particularly through the community college system, but that access comes with uneven quality. The variability is a problem for our incarcerated and formerly incarcerated students, just as it is for all students. But incarcerated students in particular are more vulnerable; they have fewer options and they cannot make choices as an on-campus student can. Does this mean that they should be guaranteed a higher standard, higher than the on-campus students enrolled in the same college? Or perhaps the question is, are these students the same or are they different? Even if different, are they so different that they shouldn't become part of the system, warts and all? Or maybe, even if the students are different, is there a value to having them become college students, just like everyone else?

Finally, as students are becoming more educated and their career aspirations grow, they are ironically facing more structural barriers to employment arising from their criminal records. For example, many formerly incarcerated students who complete their higher education degrees seek careers in social work or law and other professions that require a state occupational license. Yet just as they are demonstrating that they have changed their lives by completing the educational requirements for these careers, the state imposes licensing restrictions arising from a criminal record. As college opportunities are created, attention needs to be placed on ensuring that graduates have a reasonable opportunity through expungement and other means to achieve their professional goals despite their earlier justice involvement.

CONCLUSION

As the nation struggles to change course and tackle mass incarceration, solutions like that being tested in California will become increasingly critical. We haven't achieved perfection; among other things, gaps still exist where students are not being reached and in what the colleges provide, and the state continues to struggle with quality. But the state is prioritizing the problem-solving and network-building that comes from working together and using a student-centered approach, and in so doing the state is taking the steps necessary to build a new vision for currently and formerly incarcerated students. It is not easy, and we cannot expect a quick solution. We cannot expect our public colleges and universities to fix mass incarceration on their own. We can, however, build a system that broadly and systemically recognizes and reaches out to incarcerated and formerly incarcerated potential students, welcomes those students, and supports them through to credential, degree, transfer, and employment. If we achieve this, we will all be better for it.

QUESTIONS FOR DISCUSSION

1. Much of the expansion in California over the past three years has been an expansion of access, with work to be done on degree completion. What is the balance between quantity and quality? Is there a point at which access should be sacrificed to ensure quality?

2. Some have argued that incarcerated students are vulnerable, and should be protected from the weaknesses or inconsistencies inherent in the public higher education system. Are these students more vulnerable, and, regardless, should they be treated differently than other public higher education students?

3. There are some very high-quality prison–college programs nationally that are based in private universities with strict admissions criteria. California has turned instead to its public higher education system and especially its community colleges, which operate under an "open-access" policy. To what extent do the disputes about different kinds of prison education mirror values disputes about private universities versus community colleges? Are there inherent flaws or values in community colleges that should or should not be replicated in prison–college partnerships?

4. Should there be a statewide "gatekeeper" to monitor quality? If so, what is the appropriate entity and what would be its charge and set of responsibilities? Should it be the prison system? Are there models from other systems that we can mirror?

5. What if a state does not have an existing tuition waiver, as California does? Is it fair or politically feasible to create a tuition waiver just for students in prison? What about struggling low-income students in the community? Should they receive more benefits than students who have committed crimes?

6. With limited resources, should we prioritize certain incarcerated students or certain courses of study? Should we limit participation to those convicted of certain crimes or those within a certain number of years of release? Should we offer more vocationally driven college programs rather than traditional academic ones? If higher education is a right and not a privilege, how do we make decisions when we can't serve everyone?

NOTES

1 It is estimated that by 2030 California will be 1.1 million workers short of demand for workers with a bachelor's degree.

2 Prior to 1994, many public and private higher education institutions offered college courses inside state correctional facilities but the passage of the Violent Crime Control and Law Enforcement Act prohibited students incarcerated in state prison from receiving Pell Grants, thus shutting off the financial avenue to enrollment.

3 www2.calstate.edu/csu-system/about-the-csu/facts-about-the-csu/enrollment/Pages/default.aspx; www.universityofcalifornia.edu/uc-system

4 www.ucop.edu/acadinit/mastplan/MasterPlan1960.pdf

5 http://californiacommunitycolleges.cccco.edu/Portals/0/Reports/2016-CCCCO-BOG-FeeWaiver-Report-final.pdf

6 Degrees of Freedom, fn 32. https://law.stanford.edu/publications/degrees-of-freedom-expanding-college-opportunities-for-currently-and-formerly-incarcerated-californians

7 See, for instance, www.cdcr.ca.gov/Reports_Research/Offender_Information_Services_Branch/Monthly/TPOP1A/TPOP1Ad1712.pdf

8 Board of State and Community Corrections data dashboard, accessed January 2018. Most recent average daily population count was 74,948 as of March 2017. https://public.tableau.com/profile/kstevens#!/vizhome/ACJROctober2013/ADPRatedCapacity; see also www.bscc.ca.gov/s_datadashboard.php

9 California Penal Code section 2053; California Penal Code section 2053.1.

10 Parole issues monthly population reports. The most recent report, as of April 30, 2017, shows 49,393 people on parole. http://cdcr.ca.gov/Reports_Research/Offender_Information_Services_Branch/Monthly/Parole/Paroled1704.pdf

11 Degrees of Freedom, page 26. https://law.stanford.edu/publications/degrees-of-freedom-expanding-college-opportunities-for-currently-and-formerly-incarcerated-californians

12 *Brown v. Plata* 563 U.S. 493 (2011).

13 Degrees of Freedom, page 34. https://law.stanford.edu/publications/degrees-of-freedom-expanding-college-opportunities-for-currently-and-formerly-incarcerated-californians

14 Email correspondence on December 19, 2017 with Margaret diZerega, Program Director at Vera Institute of Justice, the entity providing technical assistance to the Second Chance Pell Initiative.

15 Yale has 5,453 undergraduate students enrolled in the 2017–18 year. www.yale.edu/about-yale/yale-facts

16 http://leginfo.legislature.ca.gov/faces/billNavClient.xhtml?bill_id=201320140SB1391

17 www.mercurynews.com/2016/10/07/jerry-brown-on-prop-57

18 www.cbsnews.com/news/reforming-solitary-confinement-at-infamous-california-prison

REFERENCES

Bettinger, E., & Loeb, S. (2017). Promises and pitfalls of online education. *Economic Studies at Brookings; Evidence Speaks Reports*, 2(15). Retrieved from www.brookings.edu/research/promises-and-pitfalls-of-online-education/.

Davis, L. M., Bozick, R., Steele, J. Saunders, J., & Miles, J. (2013). *Evaluating the effectiveness of correctional education: A meta-analysis of programs that provide education to incarcerated adults*. Santa Monica, CA: RAND Corporation. Retrieved from www.rand.org/pubs/research_reports/RR266.html.

Public Policy Institute of California (2017). *Higher education in California: Addressing California's skills gap*. Retrieved from www.ppic.org/publication/higher-education-in-california-addressing-californias-skills-gap/.

11

UNDOCUTRENDS IN HIGHER EDUCATION

SUSANA M. MUÑOZ AND YURI HERNÁNDEZ OSORIO

YURI'S TESTIMONIO PART I

I am part of the roughly 750,000 Deferred Action for Childhood Arrivals (DACA) recipients that reside in the United States (Krogstad, 2017). I, like many under this temporary work permit, was brought to the United States at a young age. I was three years old when my family and I immigrated to the States and have called this country home ever since. My story only paints an accurate picture of my experience as an undocumented student in the United States. This is my story, but this experience reaches so many others and they have their own stories to tell. Growing up undocumented, I always lived in fear and worry and even kept my status a secret until I went to college. The road to college was not easy by any means—I had to overcome financial barriers and racism that my peers did not. When I started my college application process, tuition equity policies did not exist, which meant I could only attend private universities which required me to pay an astronomical price tag for my private school education. I attended college through private funds and private scholarships. However, I was unable to work lawfully so I had to heavily rely on my family to subsidize the cost of living and attending school. In my sophomore year of college, DACA was announced by President Barack Obama, which allowed dreamers the opportunity to come out of the shadows and obtain a work permit. I remember being skeptical of this program and I feared applying. It was not until others like me applied and spoke of the freedom the work permit gave them and how many doors it opened. That is when I made the move to apply. I went through the vetting process and met the eligibility requirements to obtain the work permit. This was not an "easy" process by any means; I had to bring forward 16 years' worth of proof to the U.S. government and declare my "worthiness" for this permit. This allowed me to work for the remaining time I had on campus, which shaped my life greatly. I was able to ease the financial burden on my family, I had the ability to obtain a driver's license and drive, and through all of this I took on research and travel opportunities at my college. Without DACA, I could not engage in paid research and national conference opportunities, and these opportunities were key in my success to get into graduate school.

I have always aspired to achieve an advanced higher education degree. While in college, I saw the need to continue my schooling in order to achieve my professional goals and dreams. I also carry the burden of knowing that not everyone that is in a similar situation like mine has the ability to attend higher education. Knowing that I take up space in a setting that is not meant for me further motivates me to work hard, and go as far as I can with my education. I want to always remember where I came from, and my dream is to improve access to higher education for undocumented students. I applied to graduate programs to earn my master's degree and was accepted into the top school for my program, Social Work. I decided to attend the University of Michigan, but the transition was not easy. I was an out-of-state student and that meant paying out-of-state tuition. Michigan is one of the states that does not have a tuition equity policy in place so the decision falls on each institutional system to determine whether to admit undocumented students. Luckily for me, the University of Michigan had made that decision to accept undocumented students a few years before my arrival.

The hardest part aside from the master's program demands was the social–political climate at the university and the state of Michigan. I started the program right before the 2016 presidential election and the rise of racially targeted attacks spiked on campus. I remember seeing "report illegals" fliers on campus and knowing I was not safe on campus. It was hard as a student to focus on my school work when I was constantly worried about my safety and the fear of seeing my loved ones deported. Since I was an out-of-state student, I also did not have the "normal support system" I was accustomed to like having my family nearby. I was still trying to navigate the large institution, find mentors, and establish a social network. As I wrapped up my master's program, I felt more established and felt more equipped to navigate the hostile climate of the Midwest. However, that constant fear of deportation and losing DACA status is something that kept me awake at night. The fear paralyzed me to an extraordinary level—there were days when I felt discouraged to continue my program and wanted to "throw in the towel."

INTRODUCTION

For many undocumented and DACAmented students, navigating higher education can be a tedious and tumultuous experience. Yuri's testimonio reflects the tension between both hope and fear as a person living without legal status as her livelihood hinges on an executive order, which can easily be erased with one stroke of a pen. Yet, the educational plight of undocumented students is not a new trend in higher educa-tion. Since the Development, Relief, and Education for Alien Minors (DREAM) Act was filibustered by the U.S. Senate in 2010, colleges and universities have struggled with how to include undocumented students into their policies and practices. Yuri's testimonio offers a glimpse into her lived experiences as an undocumented Latinx female, which is shaped by the sociopolitical contexts. This chapter provides an over-view of undocumented immigrants within the U.S. context and how immigration enforcement as well as the lack of federal directives on comprehensive immigration reform has impacted how undocumented and DACAmented students navigate higher education.

UNDOCUMENTED POPULATION OVERVIEW AND PROFILE

It is estimated that approximately 11 million undocumented people reside in the United States. Of the undocumented population in the United States, Latinx[1] make up the largest ethnic representation. The largest country of origin is Mexico followed by Guatemala, El Salvador, and Honduras. It is important to note a developing ethnic shift within the undocumented population. While the majority of the people are from Latinx countries, the fifth largest country represented within the undocumented com-munity is China[2] (Migration Policy Institute, 2014). This change alters the current narrative that undocumented people are Latinx. Undocumented issues are more accurately presented as multidimensional and intersectional.

The undocumented population is a young one, with the majority of undocumented people being 25–34 years of age[3] (Migration Policy Institute, 2014). Given the youth-fulness of the undocumented population, many individuals have educational goals and aspirations. These young people spent the majority of their lives residing in the United States, averaging 10–14 years.[4] Of those aged 25 and older, the majority hold a high school diploma or GED (Migration Policy Institute, 2014). However, 13 per-cent have an educational attainment of grades 0–5. On the opposite side of the spec-trum, only 13 percent hold a bachelor's, graduate, or professional degree. Almost all undocumented persons aged 3–7 are enrolled in school (92 percent), those aged 13–17 are at a 94 percent enrollment rate, and those aged 18–24 are only at a 29 percent enrollment rate, making 71 percent not enrolled in school (Migration Policy Institute, 2014). A subcategory within the undocumented community emerged in 2012 with the implantation of Deferred Action for Childhood Arrivals (DACA) under the Obama administration.

DACA allows a temporary renewable status for undocumented persons that meet certain requirements to apply for a work permit. In theory, DACA allows eligible candidates to remain in the country, work lawfully, continue their education or join the armed services, and have protection from deportation for that period of time (U.S. Department of Homeland Security, 2017).[5] However, DACA does not allow a pathway to citizenship and is a presidential executive action; its existence is solely dependent on the President, leaving DACA recipients in a limbo status.

FEDERAL AID AND STATE POLICY IMPACT

The 1982 Supreme Court Case *Plyer v. Doe* (457 U.S. 202) set the precedent for undocumented students' access to education in the United States. In *Plyer v. Doe*, undocumented students were given the right to attend a free public K-12 education. However, postsecondary education was not included. Federal law[6] has created conditions where undocumented students are considered out-of-state, nonresidents, usually classified as international students in higher education institutions. Due to this classification, undocumented students are required to pay international tuition rates which are usually significantly higher than in-state tuition rates. Due to the undocumented status students hold, they are ineligible for federal financial aid[7] (Yates, 2004).

Despite federal laws, there have been significant gains in regard to state tuition regulations and procedures in recent years. Some states have been leading the way by establishing policies of inclusion for undocumented students. While outliers still exist, barring undocumented students from accessing higher education, some higher education intuitions have shifted from restrictive to open. Figure 11.1 provides a

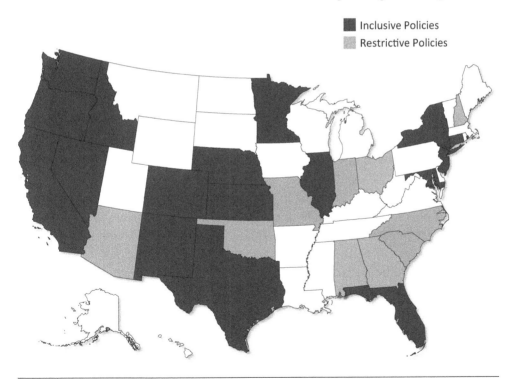

Inclusive Policies
Restrictive Policies

Figure 11.1 Current state policy environments regarding undocumented students, 2017
Source: University Leaders for Educational Access and Diversity, retrieved from https://uleadnet.org/.

current overview of state policies for undocumented students accessing higher education.

In a recent report (Gonzales & Bautista Chavez, 2014), a national survey collected by the National UnDACAmented Research Project retrieved responses from 2,684 DACA-eligible young adults, the largest data sample of this particular population. Key findings indicated that DACA recipients found opportunities through new employment, internships, and the ability to obtain driver's licenses, open bank accounts, and secure credit cards and health care. While the majority of the public takes these amenities for granted, DACAmented individuals are obtaining these opportunities and basic rights at a relatively older age compared with most individuals residing in the United States. The greatest benefactors of DACA are undocumented individuals who have already obtained a bachelor's degree. DACA applicants were 1.5 times more likely to increase their earning capacity, using their college degree as an additional credential, than DACA applicants without a college degree. The report also highlights various reasons DACA-eligible individuals are not applying for the program. The subsample of 244 respondents cite the $465 application fee,[8] lack of knowledge about community resources, missing paperwork, or other legal factors as reasons for not applying for DACA. The respondents also mentioned the lack of trust in the federal government concerning the confidentiality of their personal information and awaiting better options for themselves as additional reasons.

The following are recommendations from the Gonzales and Bautista Chavez (2014) report with regard to how to support undocumented students through DACA:

1. Include expanding resources to serve the needs of DACA-eligible applicants who have not applied to the program because they may not have access to community resources or are unable to pay the application fee.
2. Make access to postsecondary education more seamless and obtainable by charging in-state tuition while opening federal and state financial aid to DACA recipients.
3. Create an intentional partnership with the existing workforce in order to provide job training, skills enhancement, and internship opportunities for community college-level DACA recipients, or those who have yet to access postsecondary education.
4. DACA should be viewed as a temporary solution to the greater issue: the legalization of 12 million undocumented individuals and relief for their family members.

COLLEGE ACCESS AND IDENTITY DEVELOPMENT

It is common knowledge by now that Latinx currently comprise the nation's largest minority group. As illuminated by Gándara (2017), "One in four K-12 students in the

United States is Latino or Latina [Latinx]" (para. 1). High school push-out rates for Mexican native-born students in states without an in-state tuition policy for undocumented students in K-12 is higher than the average (Potochnick, 2014). In states where undocumented students are able to attend higher education through an in-state tuition policy, stop-out rates throughout their higher education trajectory are higher than their native-born or permanent-resident counterparts (Terriquez, 2015). One reason may be the difficulty in paying tuition out of pocket due to the lack of a financial aid policy (Muñoz, 2013; Terriquez, 2015). Sanyal & Johnstone (2011) posit that one of the gatekeepers to higher education are finances as tuition rates continue to increase, and that college access and success are dependent on socioeconomic class. Considering that the majority of undocumented families live below the poverty line due to low-wage and unstable jobs (Diaz-Strong, Gómez, Luna-Duarte, & Meiners, 2011; Terriquez, 2015), college access and success is already challenging. Combined with a lack of comprehensive financial aid policy, the dreams of completing a degree become much slimmer.

Without access to financial aid, entering and completing higher education continues to be a challenge, and institutional barriers continue to serve as gatekeepers for undocumented/DACAmented students (Diaz-Strong et al., 2011). While 20 states have passed in-state tuition policies for undocumented students who meet the qualifications, studies show that in-state tuition is still relatively expensive for low-income students to afford, especially without any form of aid (Diaz-Strong et al., 2011; Flores, 2010;). Therefore, many students who are undocumented or DACAmented do not enter higher education, or often work multiple jobs in order to pay for school (Diaz-Strong et al., 2011; Terriquez, 2015). Many students are drawn to community colleges due to their affordability levels (Diaz-Strong et al., 2011; Teranishi, Suárez-Orozco, & Suárez-Orozco, 2011; Terriquez, 2015). Although community colleges are great options, students should feel like they have a choice in what type of institution they would like to attend. Community colleges can serve as gateways to four-year universities, yet structural barriers within community systems can result in low transfer rates and/or graduation rates (Teranishi et al., 2011; Terriquez, 2015). Aside from the financial barriers and accessibility to a higher education, many undocumented/DACAmented students must also consider the political climate as well as the increase in deportations. These factors may create more fear and isolation for students and their families. Undocumented and DACAmented students may experience added mental health stress, which can be detrimental to enrollment status, retention, and graduation rates.

Social Activism and Self-Identity

The failed DREAM Act legislation ignited a nationwide wave of community organizing and demonstrations by undocumented youth and allies. Youth involved within immigrant-advocacy organizations found refuge and a sense of solitary among other undocumented and unafraid youth who shared similar realities and struggles (Nicholls, 2013; Seif, 2011). Coming out of the shadows and creating a space within the political sphere caught the attention of the national public and became an act of resistance. As Nicholls (2013) states, "Their messages, talking points, and emotional stories stress the most strategic qualities of the group, silencing those other aspects that may distort their central messaging" (p. 11). These undocumented student activists continue to contemplate their future in the midst of anti-immigration policies. They use their experiences to speak out against injustices to their communities and interrogate mainstream views as well as discourse surrounding immigrants in the United States. The push for immigration reform transcends their own needs and explicitly acknowledges the desire for a pathway for citizenship for all 11 million undocumented immigrants, not just the college educated.

Disclosure of Immigration Status

The choice to disclose legal status is dependent on prior experiences and context. Some undocumented students choose to be "undocumented and unafraid" about their immigration status, while others find it difficult to share for various reasons (e.g., social context, stigma, personal trauma, or campus climate). Muñoz's (2013) research reveals that lying and avoidance is a common strategy employed when interacting with school personnel and administrators. While these coping skills are applied to their college-going experiences, they can lead to high levels of stress and anxiety. Research on undocumented youth activists, however, suggests that disclosure of legal status can be an empowering asset and an educational tool for students—one that is usually facilitated through peer solidarity groups (Muñoz, 2015, 2016; Nicholls, 2013; Seif, 2011). On occasion, undocumented students are able to connect with at least one institutional staff member whom they trust and who can help them throughout their academic trajectories (Cervantes, Minero, & Brito, 2015).

State, local, and institutional contexts can play a crucial role in whether a student chooses to disclose. For undocumented students, if disclosing their legal status to a campus entity or person is met with ambivalence or the person lacks the knowledge to support undocumented students, they may be less likely to return to that particular office or person. The lack of institutionalized awareness of undocumented students contributes to their hesitation to disclose their legal status. Colleges and universities should consider ways to build solidarity groups among undocumented students—not only as a mechanism to gain and exchange knowledge among fellow peers but also as a way to establish a supportive presence on college campuses. Institutions can visibly show support and solidarity for undocumented students by participating in United We Dream's national coming-out day (United We Dream, 2015). It is important to note that not all undocumented students will be comfortable talking about their legal status, but college and universities need to provide space for those dialogues to transpire.

DEPORTATIONS AND RESISTANCE DURING
AN ERA OF UNCERTAINTY

Daniel Medina was brought to the United States at the age of seven and grew up in the United States. Daniel is part of the undocumented youth population and when DACA was created he was among the eligible youth to obtain the temporary work permit. Daniel is quoted saying: "The day that I was approved for DACA was one of the happiest days of my life. I felt that I could stop being afraid and fully participate in the incredible opportunities this country has to offer…" (Medina, 2017, para. 5). Daniel, like the other DACA recipients, thought the days of worrying about deportation were a thing of the past. However, he became the first DREAMer to be detained with an active DACA status. Daniel was detained in his Seattle home while Immigration and Customs Enforcement (ICE) agents were there on orders to pick up his father. They took Daniel into custody after an accusation of gang affiliation arose. He was then brought to the Tacoma detention center on February 10, 2017. ICE agents saw a tattoo and made the claim that Daniel was a gang member despite Daniel communicating otherwise. Daniel stated that he was a DACA recipient: "I'm not a gang member. Like all dreamers, I gave all my personal information and fingerprints to the government to qualify for DACA" (Medina, 2017, para. 8).

Daniel was unfortunately not the only DACA recipient that was detained by ICE agents. Shortly after Daniel's arrest, news broke of other DACA recipients being arrested. Emmanuel Ayala Frutos (Portland, OR), Francisco J. Rodriguez Dominguez (Portland, OR), and Daniela Vargas (Jackson, Mississippi) were all arrested by ICE in their homes. The majority were released and are fighting their immigration case by suing the United States government for their arrest. Despite the release of the DACA recipients, the shock of having dreamers deported still remains in the undocumented community. Now DACA recipients' statuses are being revoked and they are being deported at much larger rates than under the Obama administration: "More than 670 former dreamers currently face removal proceedings, with 90 detained in custody … [w]hile a total of 365 were deported during the four plus years the DACA program was carried out under Obama" (Jarvie, 2017, para. 15). At the time of this writing, the Trump administration has announced a plan to rescind the DACA program, which has the potential to uproot the lives of 800,000 DACA recipients.

Heightened Anti-Immigration

Dreamers have been fearful since Trump's inauguration. It seems as if every other day there is media coverage of a DACAmented or undocumented students being detained and deported or immigration agents waiting in courtrooms to apprehend undocumented peoples. DACA recipients continue to be worried about the future of the program. In June 2017, Texas Attorney General Ken Paxton and nine other state Republican attorneys threatened to sue the Trump administration if they do not end the

DACA program (Redden, 2017). A similar tactic was used when the Obama administration introduced Deferred Action for Parents of Americans (DAPA); the lawsuit was successful in stalling and preventing the implementation of DAPA. However, 20 other states' attorney generals have asked the current administration to refute the threat to DACA and reminded the President, "You said Dreamers should rest easy" (Becerra et al., 2017, para. 11).

In Texas, the passage of SB 4 burdens local officials with the task of full cooperation with immigration agents. Any elected or appointed officials who are in violation of this bill can be removed from office and fined $1,000 to $1,500 for the first violation and $25,000 to $25,500 for each one after that. Local officials and law enforcement could also face misdemeanor charges if they do not comply with the law. This bill is a tactic to not only deter localities from becoming sanctuary places but it implicitly relies on local authorities and enforcement to carry out the immigration positions of the current administration (Hing, 2017).

Immigrant activists and experts continue to protest, fight, and yet warn DACA recipients to be prepared for the worst if SB 4 goes into play. While the threat to DACA is real, bi-partisan lawmakers Sens. Dick Durbin (D-Ill.) and Lindsey Graham (R-S.C.) reintroduced the DREAM ACT bill to counter the anti-immigrant attacks. This "new" DREAM ACT is the strongest version to be introduced. If passed, this would provide a pathway to legal status for millions of undocumented immigrant youth, and DACA recipients would be immediately protected (Martinez, 2017).

#SanctuaryCampus

The aftermath of the presidential elections spawned a new type of student movement around making college campuses sanctuary spaces for undocumented immigrants. The American Association of University Professors (AAUP, n.d., para 1.) issued a statement stating:

> Of special importance is the status of those among our students who are undocumented, many of whom have been in this country since early childhood. Concern for the welfare of these students has already prompted a rash of petitions calling on colleges and universities to become "sanctuary campuses." We support the movement for sanctuary campuses.

To some, a sanctuary designation means that a university will protect its undocumented students from federal deportation measures at all costs, much like how sanctuary cities protect undocumented immigrants. Others think a sanctuary campus is more of an unofficial "safe space" for students to learn without fear of xenophobia. Others view the label as too broad and say colleges can protect students without being a "sanctuary" by publishing a list of initiatives and policies to protect undocumented students from deportation (Preston, 2017). Universities like the California

State University system, Rutgers University, and the University of Massachusetts have implemented such policies without publicly declaring themselves sanctuary campuses (Funke, 2016).

Activist organizations, like *Movimento Cosecha*, want colleges and universities to protect undocumented immigrants from ICE (U.S. Customs and Border Protection) by all means necessary, including prohibiting collaboration with campus police. Since sanctuary campuses are relatively new, legal scholars question the legal definition for sanctuary campuses and the legal challenges that colleges and universities may face in court (Dockray, 2016). According to Dockray, 28 institutions of higher education have self-declared themselves to be sanctuaries.

Republican lawmakers in the federal government and in many states have voiced their opposition to sanctuary campuses, with several proposing legislation aimed at preventing colleges and universities from declaring themselves "sanctuary campuses." Governor Gregg Abbott has publicly stated that he would defund any public universities in the state of Texas that declared themselves sanctuary campuses (Funke, 2016). Similar sentiments are felt in Georgia where state lawmakers are currently crafting legislation to punish any colleges or universities that become sanctuaries (Preston, 2017). The move came after students at Emory University, a private school in Atlanta, started a petition to become a sanctuary campus, which they later decided against.

CONCLUSION

On September 5, 2017, Attorney General Jeff Sessions announced that the DACA program would be rescinded, leaving thousands of college students questioning their educational pathways. DACA recipients were given one month to file for renewal as well as garner the $495 fee if their work permit expired before March 5. Witnessing the outpour of public concern from college presidents expressing their disagreement with the administration's decisions was reassuring as many pledged their continued support for DACA students. However, many undocumented students questioned how the supportive rhetoric would be translated into action and change. From our vantage point, colleges and universities should be gravely concerned about the impact of the DACA announcement on the mental health and financial wellness of undocumented college students. A glimmer of hope potentially lies on the bi-partisan legislation, the DREAM Act of 2017, which would give eligible undocumented immigrants a pathway to citizenship. It is imperative that colleges and universities issue pressure regarding their legislative contacts on this matter, but more importantly, cultivate campus climates for undocumented students which include institutionalizing support systems and policies for their success. Let us also remember that college success also includes the safety and wellness of families and communities.

As a new professional and a DACA recipient, Yuri details her challenges, hopes, and call to action as she reflects upon the looming end of DACA.

YURI'S TESTIMONIO PART II

I will never forget the day when the announcement of terminating DACA came out. I had to go to work because my job is to respond to and tackle inclusion issues on my campus. While I was meeting with students impacted by the announcement I too was struggling and processing the decision myself. Supporting my students and reassuring them was extremely difficult when I did not even know what my next step was. My only response in the moment was to remind them (and myself) that there was a time without DACA and whatever will come we will continue to resist. I organized a DACA vigil on campus in response to the announcement and it was a beautiful moment when those impacted and the campus community came together in solidarity. I know the work I do is important and I know I hold a blessing and curse as a result of my legal status. The blessing is that I can relate to students, really understand the issue, and can respond appropriately; they have someone within the administration who has lived experiences and who will continue to fight/advocate for their needs. The curse is that I myself am impacted and I have to navigate the institution from my administrative role with little to nonexistent institutional support as a professional without legal status.

Today more than ever, the reality of losing my DACA work permit is frightening to the point where I struggle to see a light at the end of the tunnel. I am angry that my community and I continue to be political pawns and a platform for politicians to swing voters one direction or another. The current narrative surrounding saving the DACA and dreamers also criminalizes my parents and the parents of people like me. If it were not for the brave and courage acts of my parents, I would not be the person I am today. They deserve the credit for being the original dreamers; giving up their life so I can have a chance at one. It seems like every day I wake up to a new news headliner: "DACA recipients told to prepare for the worst," "DREAM Act expected to pass in Congress"; it is hard to have your life and livelihood dangled before your eyes and have absolutely no power or say in the matter. How can I possibly live my life and plan for a future knowing that if Congress does not act … the life I have known for the past 21 years can be ripped away from me? My parents continue to reassure me to "ten fe algo bueno va salir" (keep faith something good will come).

I hope by sharing a little of my story, my struggles, and my experience that my fellow higher education colleagues can walk away with knowledge to better their own universities and colleges. My recommendations are the following: (1) listen and let those impacted lead the change and voice their needs. (2) Do your due diligence and educate yourself on the issue; read the literature and research; do not put that burden on the students impacted to educate you. (3) Go beyond allyship—now is the time to put words into action and turn out for this population. Yes, that means using your personal time to lobby, march, and demand policymakers to act. We are past the time of gathering discussion and talking; it is now time for action! (4) Step down, check your privilege, and empower those around you; what do I mean by this? We (dreamers) need to be occupying spaces where decisions are made and power is held. Do your part in ensuring that we have an equitable pathway to accomplish this; help create that space. (5) The very least you can do is meet the basic needs like safety and security. Make sure ICE does not have a presence on your campus (includes information sharing and reporting). Provide culturally competent mental health services for students impacted, and make sure students have funding and the ability to continue their studies. I say these are basics because you cannot guarantee our safety but it sure does help to know ICE will not detain students while they are in class, that if students are struggling with anxiety and depression because of the current political climate they can ask for help without the fear of re-traumatization, and that they do not have to worry about how tuition bills will get paid. Ultimately, remember that dreamers and people like me call the United States home despite it not claiming us back. I am more than my status; we are more than our status. I am enough; we are enough. This is my home. We are here to stay.

QUESTIONS FOR DISCUSSION

1. In what ways did UndocuTrends challenge the way you see the United States' immigration system and its impact on higher education?
2. Discuss the role higher education could play in the lives of dreamers. Should it take a role? In what way?
3. In what ways is your campus responding to the needs of undocumented students?
4. What resources and funding are available for undocumented students in your community and on campus?
5. After reading Yuri's testimony, how can the field of higher education better support professionals like her and others? In what way do the testimonies add to your understanding of dreamers?
6. What are the most significant barriers/challenges that dreamers face? How does the possibility of losing DACA heighten these barriers?

NOTES

1 A person of Latin American origin or decent (used as a gender-neutral or non-binary alternative to Latino or Latina) (Oxford University Press, 2017).
2 268,000 undocumented persons are from China, or 2 percent (Migration Policy Institute, 2014).
3 Around 28 percent are aged 25–34 years of age, constituting 3,084,000 of the grand total of 11,009,000 (Migration Policy Institute, 2014).
4 Years of U.S. residency: less than 5 years 18 percent, 5–9 years 23 percent, 15–19 years 16 percent, and 20 or more years 15 percent (Migration Policy Institute, 2014).
5 On June 15, 2012, the Secretary of Homeland Security announced that certain people who came to the United States as children and meet several guidelines may request consideration of deferred action for a period of two years, subject to renewal.
6 The Illegal Immigration Reform and Immigration Responsibility Act of 1996 (IIRIRA) prohibits states from offering the same in-state tuition rates U.S. citizens receive to non-citizen, undocumented students (Yates, 2004).

7   The Personal Responsibility and Work Opportunity Reconciliation Act of 1996 (PRWORA) bars undocumented students from qualifying for federal financial aid or student loans (Yates, 2004).
8   Now a $495 application fee (U.S. Department of Homeland Security, 2017)

REFERENCES

American Association of University Professors (AAUP) (n.d). *Sanctuary campus movement*. Retrieved from www.aaup.org/issues/sanctuary-campus-movement.

Becerra, X., Jepsen, G., Denn, M., Racine, K. A., Chin, D. S., Madigna, L., ... Ferguson, B. (2017, July 21). RE: June 29, 2017 letter from Ken Paxton re Texas, et al., v. United States, et al., Case No. 1:14-cv-00254 (S.D. Tex.) Retrieved from https://oag.ca.gov/system/files/attachments/press_releases/7-21-17%20%20 Letter%20from%20State%20AGs%20to%20President%20Trump%20re%20DACA.final_.pdf.

Cervantes, J. M., Minero, L. P., & Brito, E. (2015). Tales of survival 101 for undocumented Latina/o immigrant university students: Commentary and recommendations from qualitative interviews. *Journal of Latina/o Psychology*, 3(4), 1–15.

Diaz-Strong, D., Gómez C., Luna-Duarte M. E., & Meiners E. R. (2011). Purged: Undocumented students, financial aid policies, and access to higher education. *Journal of Hispanic Higher Education*, 10, 107–119.

Dockray, H. (2016, December 13). While undocumented students fight to create sanctuary campuses, many colleges still refuse. *Yahoo News*. Retrieved from www.yahoo.com/news/while-undocumented-students-fight-create-164816718.html.

Flores, S. M. (2010). State dream acts: The effect of in-state resident tuition policies and undocumented Latino students. *The Review of Higher Education*, 33(2), 239–283.

Funke, D. (2016, December 19). Here's where the sanctuary campus movement stands. *USA Today – Campus Beat*. Retrieved from http://college.usatoday.com/2016/12/19/heres-where-the-sanctuary-campus-movement-stands/.

Gándara, P. (2017, March). *The potential and promise of Latino students*. American Federation of Teachers. Retrieved from www.aft.org/ae/spring2017/gandara.

Gonzales, R. G., & Bautista-Chavez, A. M. (2014). *Two years and counting: Assessing the growing power of DACA*. American Immigration Council. Retrieved from www.americanimmigrationcouncil.org/sites/default/files/research/two_years_and_counting_assessing_the_growing_power_of_daca_final.pdf.

Hing, J. (2017, August 8). Texas's SB 4 is the most dramatic state crackdown yet on sanctuary cities. *The Nation*. Retrieved from www.thenation.com/article/texass-sb-4-dramatic-state-crackdown-yet-sanctuary-cities/.

Jarvie, J. (2017, April 19). Deportations of Dreamers who've lost protected status have surged under Trump. *Los Angeles Times*. Retrieved from www.latimes.com/nation/la-na-daca-deportations-20170419-story.html.

Krogstad, J. M. (2017, September 1). *DACA has shielded nearly 790,000 young unauthorized immigrants from deportation*. Pew Research Center. Retrieved from www.pewresearch.org/fact-tank/2017/09/01/unauthorized-immigrants-covered-by-daca-face-uncertain-future/.

Martinez, G. (2017, July 20). Lawmakers just introduced a Dream Act Bill. What does it mean for you? *Medium*. Retrieved https://medium.com/@UNITEDWEDREAM/lawmakers-just-introduced-a-dream-act-bill-what-does-it-means-for-you-4aa09e193b6f.

Medina, D. R. (2017, March 13). Daniel Ramirez Medina: I'm a 'dreamer,' but immigration agents detained me anyway. *Washington Post*. Retrieved from www.washingtonpost.com/posteverything/wp/2017/03/13/im-a-dreamer-immigration-agents-detained-me-anyway/?utm_term=.6781596555d8.

Migration Policy Institute. (2014). *Profile of the unauthorized population: United States*. Retrieved from www.migrationpolicy.org/data/unauthorized-immigrant-population/state/US.

Muñoz, S. M. (2013). "I just can't stand being like this anymore": Dilemmas, stressors, and motivators for undocumented Mexican women in higher education. *Journal of Student Affairs Research and Practice*, 50(3), 223–249.

Muñoz, S. M. (2015). *Identity, social activism, and the pursuit of higher education: The journey of undocumented and unafraid community activists*. New York, NY: Peter Lang Publishing.

Muñoz, S. M. (2016). Undocumented and unafraid: Understanding the disclosure management process for undocumented college students and graduates. *Journal of College Student Development, 57*(6), 715–729.

Nicholls, W. J. (2013). *The DREAMers: How the undocumented youth movement transformed the immigration rights debate.* Stanford, CA: Stanford University Press.

Oxford University Press. (2017). Definition of Latinx. *Oxford Dictionaries.* Retrieved from https://en.oxforddictionaries.com/definition/Latinx.

Potochnik, S. How states can reduce the dropout rate for undocumented immigrant youth: The effects of in-state resident tuition policies. *Social Science Research, 45,* 18–32. Retrieved from www.ncbi.nlm.nih.gov/pmc/articles/PMC4752170/.

Preston, J. (2017, January 26). Campuses wary of offering sanctuary to undocumented students. *The New York Times.* Retrieved from www.nytimes.com/2017/01/26/education/edlife/sanctuary-for-undocumented-students.html?mcubz=0.

Redden, E. (2017, June 30). State officials make legal threat against DACA. *Inside Higher Ed.* Retrieved from www.insidehighered.com/quicktakes/2017/06/30/state-officials-make-legal-threat-against-daca.

Sanyal, B. C., & Johnstone, D. B. (2011). International trends in the public and private financing of higher education. *Prospects, 41*(1), 157–175.

Seif, H. (2011). "Unapologetic and unafraid": Immigration youth come out of the shadows. In C. A. Flanagan & B. D. Christens (Eds.), *Youth civic development: Work at the cutting edge; new directions for child and adolescent development* (pp. 59–75). Hoboken, NJ: Wiley.

Teranishi, R. T., Suárez-Orozco, C., & Suárez-Orozco, M. (2011). Immigrants in community college: Toward greater knowledge and awareness. *The Future of Children, 21*(1), 153–169.

Terriquez, V. (2015). Dreams delayed: Barriers to degree completion among undocumented Latino community college students. *Journal of Ethnic and Migration Studies, 41* (8), 1302–1323.

United We Dream. (2015, November 13). United we dream marks third annual 'national educators coming out day'. *United We Dream.* Retrieved from https://unitedwedream.org/2015/11/united-we-dream-marks-third-annual-national-educators-coming-out-day/.

U.S. Department of Homeland Security. (2017, September 5). *Consideration of Deferred Action for Childhood Arrivals (DACA).* U.S. Citizenship and Immigration Services. Retrieved from www.uscis.gov/humanitarian/consideration-deferred-action-childhood-arrivals-daca.

Yates, L. S. (2004). Plyer v. Doe and the rights of undocumented immigrants to higher education: Should undocumneted students be eligible for in-state college tuition rates? *Washington University Law Review, 82*(2), 585–609.

12

UNDERSTANDING SINGLE MOTHERS IN COLLEGE

Strategies for Greater Support

CYNTHIA HESS, LINDSEY REICHLIN CRUSE,
BARBARA GAULT, AND MARY ANN DEMARIO

College degrees are a reliable route to long-term economic security for single mothers and their families. Enrolling in and completing college can be challenging for single parents, however, due to the time demands of balancing school, parenting, and work. Along with extra financial challenges, these obstacles make single mothers who enroll in college considerably less likely than married mothers and women without children to complete their degree programs.

Increasing degree attainment rates among single mothers would improve the well-being of individuals, society, and the nation as a whole. Higher education is increasingly necessary to secure high-quality jobs, making postsecondary education critical to helping individuals and families achieve economic security and build wealth. For the nation overall, postsecondary education is essential to ensuring the development of a skilled workforce that can meet the demand for jobs. In addition, because Black, Latina, and Native American women are much more likely than others to be raising children on their own while in college, investing in single mothers' education is critical to progress toward racial/ethnic and economic equity in college access and success.

This chapter describes the single-mother population in higher education, the financial and time-related obstacles they face to persisting in college, the importance of affordable child care on single mothers' ability to remain enrolled and graduate, and how postsecondary credentials affect their labor market experiences. It also highlights findings from a recent Institute for Women's Policy Research study on the costs and benefits of single mothers' achievement of college degrees. The chapter concludes by discussing strategies that institutional leaders and state and federal policymakers can use to promote single mothers' educational attainment.

SINGLE MOTHERS IN COLLEGE: DEMOGRAPHIC CHARACTERISTICS

As of 2012, nearly 2.1 million undergraduate students in the United States were single mothers of dependent children, comprising about 11 percent of the undergraduate student population (Figure 12.1). Both the number and share of student mothers increased substantially between 1999 and 2012; over this time period, the growth in single mothers in college was more than twice the rate of growth seen among the overall undergraduate student population (Kruvelis, Reichlin Cruse, and Gault, 2017).

The share of women college students who are single mothers varies considerably by race and ethnicity. Black women in college are the most likely to be raising a child without the support of a spouse or partner (37 percent), while Asian or Pacific Islander women are the least likely (7 percent; Figure 12.2).

Single mothers in college are most likely to enroll at community colleges (44 percent) and least likely to enroll at public or private four-year colleges (19 percent; Kruvelis et al., 2017). Thirty percent of single mothers in college attend for-profit institutions, making them more than three times as likely to attend for-profit colleges as women students without children (Figure 12.3). Research indicates that for-profit schools specifically recruit and enroll single parents, people of color, and low-income students who are often unable to afford college (Cottom, 2017). Given that tuition at for-profits is much higher than at public institutions and that students at for-profit schools are more likely to take out loans than those at public two- and four-year institutions, enrolling at for-profit schools increases single mothers' financial risk.

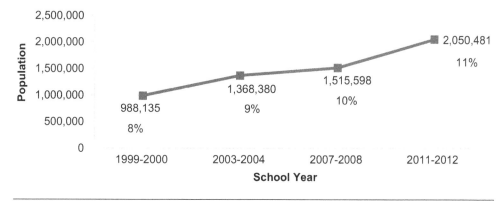

Figure 12.1 Number and share of undergraduate students who are single mothers, 1999–2012
Source: Kruvelis et al. (2017).

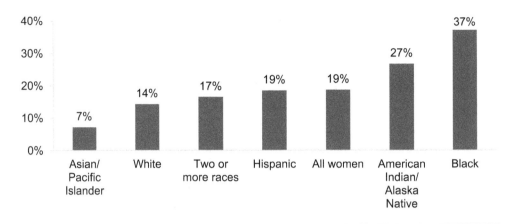

Figure 12.2 Share of women undergraduate students who are single mothers, by race/ethnicity, 2011–2012
Source: IWPR analysis of data from the U.S. Department of Education, National Center for Education Statistics, 2012 Integrated Postsecondary Education Data System (IPEDS) and the 2011–12 National Postsecondary Student Aid Study (NPSAS:12).

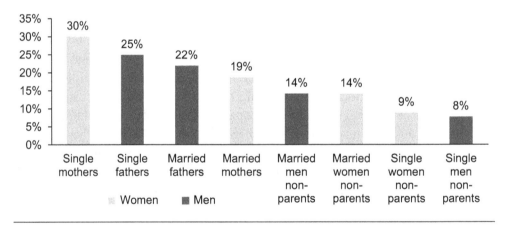

Figure 12.3 Share of undergraduate students enrolled in private, for-profit educational institutions by parent and marital status, 2011–2012
Source: Kruvelis et al. (2017).

SINGLE MOTHERS IN HIGHER EDUCATION FACE FINANCIAL AND TIME CHALLENGES THAT CAN HINDER COMPLETION

Financial Insecurity among Single Mothers in College

Single mothers in college often experience substantial financial challenges that make it difficult to persist to graduation. Nearly nine in ten (89 percent) live with low incomes, with nearly two-thirds (63 percent) at or below the federal poverty level (Kruvelis et al., 2017). Many student parents have difficulty meeting their basic daily needs: one survey of more than 33,000 community college students nationwide found that students with children were more likely than those without children to experience housing and food insecurity. Sixty-three percent reported experiencing housing insecurity, and the same share described their food security as low or very low (Goldrick-Rab, Richardson, & Hernandez, 2017). Among nonparent students, 45 percent faced housing insecurity and 53 percent had low or very low food security.

A large majority of single mothers in college are unable to help pay for the costs of their education. Eighty-one percent have an Expected Family Contribution of $0, which means they have no income of their own or from their families to cover college-related expenses (Kruvelis et al., 2017). Unmet need among single mothers—the amount of college expenses a student is responsible for covering after family contributions, grants, and need-based aid are accounted for—is also quite high. The average unmet need for single mothers in 2012 was over $6,600—about $1,700 more than the unmet need of women without children and $2,000 more than the unmet need of married mothers (Kruvelis et al., 2017).

Among single mothers, unmet need varies across racial/ethnic groups and institution types. Single mothers at for-profit institutions have, on average, $10,402 in unmet need, which is considerably higher than the average unmet need among single mothers at two-year ($4,267) and four-year colleges ($6,023; Kruvelis et al., 2017). Across all institution types, single mothers who are Black, Hispanic, Asian, and Native Hawaiian/other Pacific Islander have an average of nearly $600 more unmet need than their White counterparts (Kruvelis et al., 2017).

The higher unmet need among single mothers compared with other student populations reflects the considerable financial pressures that mothers in college face. Child care, for example, represents a significant expense that student parents incur—the cost for full-time, center-based care for an infant ranged in 2016 from $5,178 in Mississippi to $20,125 in Massachusetts (Child Care Aware of America, 2017a). In Massachusetts, the least affordable state, the cost for the care of an infant in a center is 71 percent of median income for a single parent (Child Care Aware of America, 2017b).

The substantial expenses and limited financial resources of many single mothers in college contribute to high levels of student debt upon graduation. Single student mothers take out more federal loans to pay for college and associated costs than their female peers who are married or do not have children at every institution type. Single mothers at public and private four-year institutions borrow an average of $18,025 for their undergraduate education, $9,000 more than their nonparent counterparts (Figure 12.4). Single-mother student loan debt for those attending for-profit institutions amounts to nearly $16,000, $3,000 more than single women who are not mothers (Figure 12.4). One year after graduation, single mothers who earned a bachelor's degree from a four-year institution who took out loans to pay for college owed an average of $29,064, which is nearly $5,000 higher than the average debt among women without children (Kruvelis et al., 2017). High levels of debt contribute

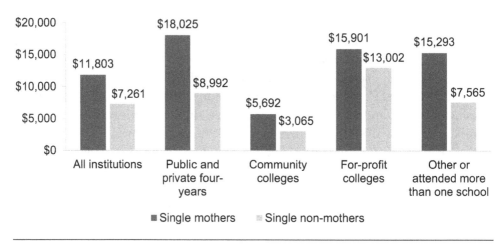

Figure 12.4 Average federal loans borrowed by single women for undergraduate education as of July 30, 2012, by parent status and institution type
Source: IWPR analysis of data from the U.S. Department of Education, National Center for Education Statistics, 2011–12 National Postsecondary Student Aid Study (NPSAS:12).

to economic insecurity for years to come, affecting homeownership, wealth accumulation, and retirement savings (Cooper & Wang, 2014; Miller, 2017).

The process of paying back student debt can be difficult for many students, particularly those who left college without a credential or degree or who attended a for-profit institution, which is less likely to grant a degree that leads to a living wage job (Deming, Goldin, & Katz, 2012; Miller, 2017). Some borrowers end up in default; one recent study found that the percentage of college graduates in loan default four years after college is nearly three times higher for single parents than for students who are not single parents (8.0 percent compared with 2.7 percent; Miller, 2017).

TIME DEMANDS FACING STUDENT MOTHERS

Caregiving Demands Reduce Time for Studying, Sleep, and Exercise

Single mothers in college face significant time demands that can hinder persistence to graduation. More than 60 percent of single student mothers report spending at least 30 hours per week caring for children (Miller, Gault, & Thorman, 2011). IWPR analysis of data from the American Time Use Survey suggests these caregiving responsibilities leave single student mothers with less time for studying and self-care than their nonparent peers. On average, single student mothers report spending nearly two hours (110 minutes) more per day than their nonparent peers on care work, 30 minutes per day more on housework, and 10 minutes per day more on paid work. They spend about 32 minutes less per day on sleep, 24 minutes less per day on homework, and 10 minutes less per day on socializing and exercise than women students

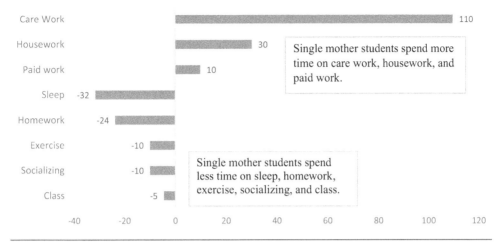

Figure 12.5 Differences in time (minutes per day) spent on activities: Single-mother students compared with women nonparent students, 2003–2016
Source: IWPR analysis of data from the American Time Use Survey available at www.bls.gov/tus/.

who do not have children (Figure 12.5). These time use patterns have implications for single mothers' ability to perform at their full capacity in school, and to maintain good health and well-being, which could relate to lower levels of persistence and completion.

Affordable, quality child care can help student mothers balance their caregiving responsibilities with schoolwork, but this care can be difficult for students to find. Campus child care centers typically have a much higher demand than they can meet; a 2016 survey of nearly 100 campus children's center leaders conducted by IWPR found that 95 percent of centers at two- and four-year schools across the country maintained a waiting list with an average of 82 children (Eckerson et al., 2016). Despite this high demand, the number of campus child care centers across the country has been dwindling. In 2015, only 49 percent of four-year public colleges provided campus child care, down from 55 percent in 2003–2005. The share of community colleges with a campus child care center decreased more sharply, from 53 percent in 2003–2004 to 44 percent in 2015 (Eckerson et al., 2016).

For many student mothers, affordable child care alternatives are in short supply. An IWPR survey of 544 women community college students in Mississippi found that nearly half of respondents (47 percent) with children aged 10 and under said they cannot get the kind of quality child care they want because it is too expensive, and 53 percent said that paying for child care or afterschool care is somewhat or very difficult for them (Hess, Krohn, Reichlin, Roman, & Gault, 2014). As a result, many rely on child care from grandparents or other relatives, neighbors and friends, the children's older siblings, or simply have the children take care of themselves (Hess et al., 2014). Having access to affordable, quality child care would make a difference in their educational outcomes: 59 percent of the student mothers surveyed with children aged 10 and under who report having taken time off from school or having dropped out completely say that having more stable or affordable child care would have helped them stay in college (Hess et al., 2014). IWPR analysis of data from the Community College Survey of Student Engagement at the University of Texas at Austin found that 43 percent of women at two-year colleges who live with dependents say they are likely or very likely to drop out of school due to their dependent care obligations (CCSSE, 2016).

Paid Work

Many single mothers also work in addition to going to school and caring for children, which can further complicate their efforts to persist to graduation. IWPR analysis of data from the 2011–2012 National Postsecondary Student Aid Study indicates that more than one in three (35 percent) single mothers in college work full time while in school, and more than one in four (29 percent) work part-time. While working during college may be necessary for single mothers to make ends meet, research indicates that for students with children, having a paid job is associated with declines in degree completion (IWPR, 2017a; King, 2002; Kuh, Kinzie, Cruce, Shoup, & Gonyea, 2007). The negative effects of paid work on educational outcomes are greater for student parents than for other students: research shows that among nonparents, small amounts of paid work (less than 15 hours per week) are not associated with diminished college completion, whereas *any* paid work at all is associated with declines in completion for student parents (IWPR, 2017a).

Single Mothers are Less Likely to Complete College than their Married and Nonparent Peers, but Child Care Helps

The financial and time-related pressures experienced by single student mothers can affect their ability to persist in school: just 28 percent of single mothers who entered college between 2003 and 2009 earned a degree or certificate within six years, compared with 40 percent of married mothers and 57 percent of women students who were not parents (Figure 12.6). As of 2015, 31 percent of single mothers aged 25 and older in the United States held at least a bachelor's degree, compared with 54 percent of married mothers and 40 percent of all women in this same age range (IWPR, 2017b). Among the largest racial and ethnic groups, the share of single mothers with at least a bachelor's degree varies considerably. Asian/Pacific Islander single mothers are the most likely to have a four-year college degree (24 percent), and Hispanic and Native American single mothers are the least likely (8 percent; IWPR, 2017c).

Greater access to child care could dramatically improve student parents' ability to persist to graduation. Monroe Community College analysis of data on 10,000 student parents with children under six years who were enrolled at the college between Fall 2006 and Fall 2014 found that those who used the campus child care center had a fall-to-fall

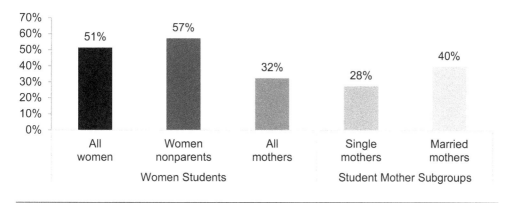

Figure 12.6 Share of female undergraduate students who attained a degree or certificate at all institutions within six years of enrollment, by parent and marital status, 2003–2009
Source: Kruvelis et al. (2017).

persistence rate that was considerably higher than those who did not use the center. More than seven in ten student parents (71 percent) who used the campus child care center persisted to the next fall, compared with slightly more than four in ten student parents (42 percent) who did not use it. In addition, student parents who used the center had an on-time graduation rate that was more than three times higher than those who did not use campus child care (28 percent compared with 8 percent; DeMario, 2017).

INCREASING SINGLE MOTHER'S COMPLETION RATES BENEFITS SINGLE MOTHERS, FAMILIES, AND THE NATION AS A WHOLE

Higher Education and Single Mothers' Economic Security

Completing postsecondary education has a substantial positive impact on the earnings and economic security of single mothers. IWPR analysis of 2015 American Community Survey data indicate that among single mothers aged 25 and older who work full time, year-round, those with an associate's degree have median annual earnings that are roughly $9,000 higher than those whose highest level of education is a high school diploma or the equivalent (Figure 12.7). Single mothers with bachelor's degrees earn nearly twice as much as those with only a high school education ($48,000 compared with $26,000), on average. The extent to which women benefit economically from higher levels of education, however, varies across racial and ethnic groups. White and Asian/Pacific Islander women with bachelor's degrees, for example, earn considerably more than Hispanic women (median annual earnings of $40,000 compared with $32,000; IWPR, 2017b).

Poverty rates among single mothers who complete postsecondary education are considerably lower than among those with less education. Fourteen percent of single

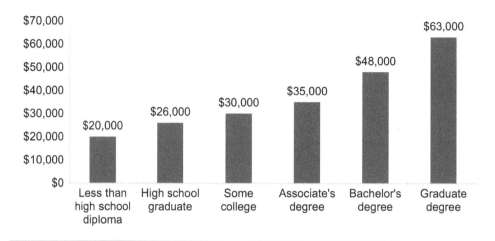

Figure 12.7 Median annual earnings among single mothers by highest level of education, 2015
Source: IWPR analysis of 2015 American Community Survey microdata (Integrated Public Use Microdata Series, Version 6.0).

mothers aged 25 and older with a bachelor's degree, and 26 percent with an associate degree, have family incomes below the federal poverty line. Among those whose highest level of education is a high school diploma or the equivalent, more than four in ten (44 percent) live in poverty (IWPR, 2017b).

BROADER EFFECTS OF INCREASING SINGLE MOTHERS' EDUCATIONAL ATTAINMENT

Research indicates that earning a postsecondary credential not only increases the earnings and economic stability of single-mother families, but also may contribute to better health and well-being; higher educational attainment is associated with better health outcomes (Cutler & Lleras-Muney, 2006) and college graduates have higher levels of civic participation (Bureau of Labor Statistics, 2016; Dee, 2004). In addition, research has found that mothers' postsecondary attainment has important benefits for their children's educational outcomes, including their vocabulary, reading and math scores, and college attendance (Attewell & Lavin, 2007), as well as their study habits and grades (Jones-DeWeever & Gault, 2006).

Increasing postsecondary attainment among single mothers also benefits the nation and society as a whole. Because college graduates have higher earnings, they contribute more in taxes than individuals with only a high school diploma (Baum, Ma, & Payea, 2013). This increase in taxes paid, in turn, means that the government has greater resources to fund public goods. While the transient nature of single motherhood makes accurately measuring the lifetime increase in taxes that result from single mothers' investments in college education difficult, IWPR estimates that in the year after completing an associate degree, a single mother would pay, on average, an additional $900 in both federal (Federal Insurance Contributions Act (FICA)) and state taxes. If these tax increases were added up overall for single mothers currently obtaining associate degrees, the increase in tax contributions would total approximately $121.7 million in just one year. Among single mothers earning bachelor's degrees, the increase would be even greater: $2,500 for a single mother in the year after obtaining her degree, with the total increase in taxes for single mothers equaling approximately $141.2 million in just one year (IRS, 2017; IWPR, 2017c; Social Security Administration, n.d.; Tax Form Calculator, n.d.; U.S. Tax Center, 2016).

Having a higher income also means that single mothers are less likely to receive public assistance from programs such as the Supplemental Nutrition Assistance Program (SNAP, formerly food stamps) and Medicaid (Ma, Pender, & Welch, 2016). According to the Census Bureau, among the 168,000 single mothers expected to graduate with an associate or bachelor's degree, an estimated 46,300 received public assistance over the past four years, resulting in a total value of $472.30 million spent on this assistance over the four-year period.[1] College education would reduce the number of single mothers receiving public assistance by approximately 24,300, the average number of months receiving public assistance to 3.6, and the average monthly benefit by $61. In total, these changes would reduce spending on public assistance by $309.10 million over a four-year period (Irving & Loveless, 2015; IWPR, 2016, 2017a).

Investing in single mothers' education would benefit the nation by developing a more skilled workforce that can meet the demand for jobs. Research suggests that by 2020, more than 6 in 10 jobs in the United States will require at least some college education, and the nation is predicted to fall short of being able to fill these jobs by 5 million college-educated workers (Carnevale, Smith, & Strohl, 2013).

Increasing single mothers' access to and success in postsecondary education is also critical to addressing racial inequities in educational access and employment opportunities. Because single mothers in college are disproportionately women of color, improving their graduation rates would have a disproportionate impact on families of color. Increasing supports for single mothers in college is a critical component of fostering racial equity in higher education and the U.S. labor market.

STRATEGIES FOR SUPPORTING SINGLE STUDENT MOTHERS' SUCCESS

Postsecondary institutions and policymakers can support single student mothers' access to and success in higher education in a variety of ways:

Expand Access to Supportive Services

Supportive services such as child care, housing assistance, and transportation assistance are essential to helping student parents in college persist to graduation. Research indicates that student parents face a range of support needs, yet the resources to meet them are often in short supply (Hess, Mayayeva, Reichlin, & Thakur, 2016). Some institutions have developed effective strategies to help meet these needs, such as establishing community-based partnerships to provide residential opportunities for single parents that include services such as family support services and an onsite child development center, setting up ride shares or other transportation programs, or providing campus-organized child care or assistance with finding child care in the community (Schumacher, 2015). For many student parents, such initiatives can make the difference between having to interrupt or drop out of school or persisting to graduation.

Given the multiple demands on their time, student parents often do not have the opportunity to build support networks on campus and may benefit from additional supports such as mentoring, coaching, and peer support. Institutions can connect student parents with counseling services or classes on topics such as child development, parenting education, life skills, and stress reduction. Los Angeles Valley Community College in California, for example, has created the Family Resource Center on its campus, where student parents can come to workshops, playgroups, exchange baby clothes and books, and obtain mentoring and advice (Los Angeles Valley College, n.d.).

Increase Access to Financial Assistance

Single student mothers often need a substantial amount of financial aid to complete college, given their low incomes and the high costs of raising children, including paying for child care. In the survey of women community college students in Mississippi mentioned above, 76 percent of single mothers said they found it somewhat or very difficult to pay for living expenses such as transportation, utilities, groceries, gas, and other bills, and 37 percent had difficulty covering the costs of books and school supplies (IWPR, 2014). Colleges can increase student parents' access to and success in higher education through targeted scholarships or emergency assistance to help cover these expenses. Colleges can also help single mothers by providing financial education that can help with budgeting and financial planning. For example, Porterville Community College in California provides financial education and resources to parents at their child development center as a part of their campus-wide student success initiative.

Protect, Preserve, and Expand the CCAMPIS Grant Program

Child Care Access Means Parents in School (CCAMPIS) is a federally funded competitive grant program, administered through the U.S. Department of Education, intended to support the participation of low-income parents in postsecondary education through the provision of campus-based child care services. CCAMPIS grants are awarded directly to higher education institutions and have been used by a number of colleges and universities to support and improve student parent success (Sykes, Reichlin, & Gault, 2016). The Madison Area Technical College Child and Family Center in Wisconsin, for example, uses funding from CCAMPIS and other sources to provide scholarships to qualified students (Schumacher, 2015). The Child Development Center at Pikes Peak Community College (PPCC) in Colorado Springs, CO, uses CCAMPIS funding to help students develop a degree plan, provide subsidized child care to student parents, and provide access to an onsite case manager (Sykes et al., 2016). Ensuring adequate funding for the CCAMPIS program is essential to provide student parents with the support they need to persist to graduation.

Improve Federal Financial Aid Policies to Meet the Needs of Student Parents

Federal financial aid policies often do not consider the unique circumstances and financial responsibilities that student parents face, making it difficult for these students to participate in scholarship or other financial aid programs. For example, many student parents rely on the federal Pell Grant program to help cover their postsecondary education and related living expenses, yet the maximum Pell Grant award for the 2017–2018 academic year is $5,920 (Federal Student Aid, 2016b), an amount that is, for many student parents, not enough to cover their full cost of attendance. The Pell Grant program is also not indexed to inflation, meaning its value over time has declined as inflation has risen (Alsalam, 2013); as of 2017, its ability to cover a meaningful share of college costs was at a 40-year low (TICAS, 2017). Increasing the maximum Pell award and pegging it to inflation would ensure greater financial security for low-income parents in college.

Student mothers would also benefit from an increase in the Income Protection Allowance (IPA), or the amount of income, meant to cover basic living expenses, that is excluded when calculating how much money students are expected to contribute out of pocket toward college costs. A student's IPA is determined by a number of factors, including dependency, marital status, and parent status, as well as family size (Federal Student Aid, 2016a). For many student parents, the IPA does not protect enough income to allow them to meet their basic needs. For the 2017–2018 academic year, single student-parent families with one dependent child can protect $25,280 (Federal Student Aid, 2016a). In comparison, IWPR's Basic Economic Security Tables (BEST) Index, which estimates the income level needed to achieve economic security in the United States by family type, indicates that the average single adult with one child needs to earn at least $49,080 to cover basic expenses and achieve financial self-sufficiency (IWPR, 2017d). Increasing the IPA to better account for student mothers' basic living costs would enable them to protect enough income to meet daily needs, without decreasing the level of financial aid for which they are eligible.

Improve Integration of the Early Childhood Education and Higher Education Systems

Improving coordination between the early childhood education and higher education systems could benefit student mothers by increasing their access to affordable, quality child care while they are pursuing postsecondary education and preparing their children for school. One way to strengthen linkages between these systems is by developing partnerships between Head Start programs and institutions of higher education. With grants from the U.S. Department of Health and Human Services, several college and universities have partnered with local Head Start or Early Head Start programs to offer high-quality early childhood development on their campuses (U.S. Department of Health and Human Services, n.d.). These partnerships are mutually beneficial: colleges can help improve the quality of Head Start programs, since colleges with early childhood development programs have the ability to train teachers and offer degree programs that could help Head Start teachers meet credential and professional development requirements. At the same time, Head Start programs have a strong focus on parental supports, which can help support success among low-income student parents, or parents who are interested in pursuing higher education, through referral services and counseling on college-related, child-related, financial, or personal issues.

Modernize Child Care Subsidy Eligibility Rules to Allow More Student Parents to Benefit

The Child Care and Development Block Grant (CCDBG), which provides child care assistance for low-income families needing child care to work or participate in education and training in addition to other activities related to child care quality and coordination (U.S. Department of Health and Human Services, 2012), also offers a source of funding to support low-income parents in higher education. To date, most states have allowed this funding to be used for parents in education, although resources are limited and many states place limitations on eligibility for parents receiving subsidies for time spent in education and training. For example, 11 states require parents pursuing higher education to also work a certain number of hours in order to be eligible to receive child care subsidies; seven states and the District of Columbia link subsidy eligibility to specific vocational degrees, limiting the level of education parents can pursue; and nine limit the amount of time parents can receive subsidies while pursuing education (Eckerson et al., 2016). Removing such requirements would help the nation meet its higher education goal of increasing the number of U.S. adults with postsecondary credentials.

QUESTIONS FOR DISCUSSION

1. What is needed to transform college campuses into environments that are welcoming and supportive of students with different backgrounds and family types?
2. How can campus staff and faculty better accommodate the unique circumstances experienced by single mothers in their day-to-day interactions with students? What other steps could be taken to adapt college campuses to the needs of students with caregiving responsibilities?

3. What changes to institutional, state, and federal policies would increase student parents' access to and success in college? What are the greatest challenges for implementing these changes, and potential strategies for addressing them?

NOTE

1 Public assistance here includes any means-tested programs: Medicaid, Supplemental Nutrition Assistance Program (SNAP), Housing Assistance, Supplemental Security Income (SSI), Temporary Assistance for Needy Families (TANF), and General Assistance (GA).

REFERENCES

Alsalam, N. (2013). *The federal Pell Grant program: Recent growth and policy options.* Washington, DC: Congressional Budget Office.

Attewell, P., & Lavin, D. (2007). *Passing the torch: Does higher education for the disadvantaged pay off across the generations?* New York, NY: Russell Sage Publishers. Retrieved from www.russellsage.org/publications/passing-torch.

Baum, S., Ma, J., & Payea, K. (2013). *Education pays: The benefits of higher education for individuals and society.* New York, NY: The College Board. Retrieved from http://trends.collegeboard.org/sites/default/files/education-pays-2013-full-report-022714.pdf.

Bureau of Labor Statistics. (2016). *Volunteering in the United States, 2015.* Retrieved from www.bls.gov/news.release/volun.nr0.htm.

Carnevale, A. P., Smith, N., & Strohl, J. (2013). *Recovery: Job growth and education requirements through 2020.* Washington, DC: Georgetown University, Center on Education and the Workforce. Retrieved from https://repository.library.georgetown.edu/bitstream/handle/10822/559311/Recovery2020.FR.Web.pdf?sequence=1&isAllowed=y.

CCSSE. (2016). *2016 Community College Survey of Student Engagement.* Austin, TX: Center for Community College Student Engagement, The University of Texas at Austin.

Child Care Aware of America. (2017a). *Parents and the high cost of child care: 2017 Appendices.* Arlington, VA. Retrieved from https://usa.childcareaware.org/wp-content/uploads/2018/01/2017_CCA_High_Cost_Appendices_FINAL_180112_small.pdf.

Child Care Aware of America. (2017b). *Parents and the high cost of child care: 2017.* Arlington, VA: Child Care Aware of America. Retrieved from https://usa.childcareaware.org/wp-content/uploads/2017/12/2017_CCA_High_Cost_Report_FINAL.pdf.

Cooper, D. H., & Wang, J. C. (2014). *Student loan debt and economic outcomes.* Boston, MA: Federal Reserve Bank of Boston. Retrieved from www.bostonfed.org/publications/current-policy-perspectives/2014/student-loan-debt-and-economic-outcomes.aspx.

Cottom, T. M. (2017). *Lower ed: The troubling rise of for-profit colleges in the New Economy.* New York, NY: The New Press.

Cutler, D. M., & Lleras-Muney, A. (2006). *Education and health: Evaluating theories and evidence.* Working Paper No. 12352. National Bureau of Economic Research. Retrieved from www.nber.org/papers/w12352.

Dee, T. S. (2004). Are there civic returns to education? *Journal of Public Economics, 88*(9–10), 1697–1720.

DeMario, M. A. M. (2017). *Outcomes of Monroe Community College student parents who used the campus child care center vs. those who didn't, Fall 2006 – Fall 2014.* Unpublished overview of research findings.

Deming, D. J., Goldin, C., & Katz, L. F. (2012). *The for-profit postsecondary school sector: Nimble critters or agile predators?* New York, NY: Center for Analysis of Postsecondary Education and Employment. Retrieved from www.capseecenter.org/wp-content/uploads/2016/07/ForProfit_Nimble-Critters_Feb-2012.pdf.

Eckerson, E., Talbourdet, L., Reichlin, L., Sykes, M., Noll, E., & Gault, B. (2016). *Child care for parents in college: A state-by-state assessment.* Briefing Paper, IWPR #C445. Washington, DC: Institute for Women's Policy Research. Retrieved from http://iwpr.org/publications/pubs/child-care-for-parents-in-college-a-state-by-state-assessment/.

Federal Student Aid. (2016a.). *The EFC formula, 2017–2018.* Washington, DC: U.S. Department of Education. Retrieved from http://ifap.ed.gov/efcformulaguide/attachments/071416EFCFormulaGuide1718.pdf.

Federal Student Aid. (2016b). *Federal student aid at a glance: 2017–18.* Washington, DC: Federal Student Aid, U.S. Department of Education. Retrieved from https://studentaid.ed.gov/sa/sites/default/files/aid-glance-2017–18.pdf.

Goldrick-Rab, S., Richardson, J., & Hernandez, A. (2017). *Hungry and homeless in college: Results from a national study of basic needs insecurity in higher education.* Madison, WI: Wisconsin HOPE Lab, University of Wisconsin-Madison. Retrieved from http://wihopelab.com/publications/hungry-and-homeless-in-college-report.pdf.

Hess, C., Krohn, S., Reichlin, L., Roman, S., & Gault, B. (2014). *Securing a better future: A portrait of female students in Mississippi's community colleges.* Report, IWPR #C417. Washington, DC: Institute for Women's Policy Research and the Women's Foundation of Mississippi. Retrieved from https://iwpr.org/wp-content/uploads/wpallimport/files/iwpr-export/publications/C417.pdf.

Hess, C., Mayayeva, Y., Reichlin, L., & Thakur, M. (2016). *Supportive services in job training and education: A research review* (IWPR #C434). Washington, DC: Institute for Women's Policy Research. Retrieved from https://iwpr.org/wp-content/uploads/wpallimport/files/iwpr-export/publications/C449-Supportive%20Services%20in%20Workforce%20Development%20Programs.pdf.

IRS. (2017). SOI tax stats – Individual statistical tables by filing status. Retrieved from www.irs.gov/statistics/soi-tax-stats-individual-statistical-tables-by-filing-status.

Irving, S. K., & Loveless, T. A. (2015). *Dynamics of economic well-being: Participation in government programs, 2009–2012: Who gets assistance?* Washington, DC: U.S. Department of Commerce, Economics and Statistics Administration. Retrieved from www.census.gov/content/dam/Census/library/publications/2015/demo/p70-141.pdf.

Institute for Women's Policy Research (IWPR). (2014). *IWPR survey of women in Mississippi's Community colleges: Data tables.* Retrieved from http://iwpr.org/wp-content/uploads/2018/02/IWPR-Survey-of-Women-in-Mississippi-Community-Colleges-Data-Tables.pdf.

Institute for Women's Policy Research (IWPR). (2016). Institute for Women's Policy Research (IWPR) analysis of data from the U.S. Department of Education, National Center for Education Statistics. Integrated Postsecondary Education Data Systems (IPEDS). 2015 Institutional Characteristics Component (2015 Preliminary Release).

Institute for Women's Policy Research (IWPR). (2017a). Institute for Women's Policy Research (IWPR) analysis of data from the U.S. Department of Education, National Center for Education Statistics, 2011–12 National Postsecondary Student Aid Study (NPSAS:12).

Institute for Women's Policy Research (IWPR). (2017b). IWPR analysis of data from the 2013–2015 American Community Survey, Integrated Public Use Microdata Series (Version 6.0).

Institute for Women's Policy Research (IWPR). (2017c). IWPR analysis of data from the 2015 American Community Survey, Integrated Public Use Microdata Series (Version 6.0).

Institute for Women's Policy Research (IWPR). (2017d). *Basic Economic Security Tables.* Retrieved from www.basiceconomicsecurity.org/.

Jones-DeWeever, A., & Gault, B. (2006). *Resilient and reaching for more: The challenges and benefits of college for welfare participants and their children.* Washington, DC: Institute for Women's Policy Research. Retrieved from https://iwpr.org/wp-content/uploads/wpallimport/files/iwpr-export/publications/D466.pdf.

King, J. E. (2002). *Crucial choices: How students' financial decisions affect their academic success.* Washington, DC: American Council on Education, Center for Policy Analysis.

Kruvelis, M., Reichlin Cruse, L., & Gault, B. (2017). *Single mothers in college: Growing enrollment, financial challenges, and the benefits of attainment.* Briefing Paper, IWPR #C460. Washington, DC: Institute for Women's Policy Research. Retrieved from https://iwpr.org/publications/single-mothers-college-growing-enrollment-financial-challenges-benefits-attainment/.

Kuh, G. D., Kinzie, J., Cruce, Ty, Shoup, R., & Gonyea, R. M. (2007). *Connecting the dots: Multi-faceted analyses of the relationships between student engagement results from the NSSE, and the institutional practices and conditions that foster student success.* Bloomington, IN: Center for Postsecondary Research. Retrieved from http://nsse.indiana.edu/pdf/Connecting_the_Dots_Report.pdf.

Los Angeles Valley College. n.d. *Family Resource Center: Los Angeles Valley College.* Retrieved from www.lavc.edu/family-resource-center/family-resource-center.aspx.

Ma, J., Pender, M., & Welch, M. (2016). *Education pays 2016* (Trends in Higher Education Series). New York, NY: College Board. Retrieved from https://trends.collegeboard.org/sites/default/files/education-pays-2016-full-report.pdf.

Miller, K. (2017). *Deeper in debt: Women and student loans.* Washington, DC: American Association of University Women. Retrieved from www.aauw.org/resource/deeper-in-debt/.

Miller, K., Gault, B., & Thorman, A. (2011). *Improving child care access to promote postsecondary success among low-income parents.* Report, IWPR #C378. Washington, DC: Institute for Women's Policy Research. Retrieved from https://iwpr.org/publications/improving-child-care-access-to-promote-postsecondary-success-among-low-income-parents/.

Schumacher, R. (2015). *Prepping colleges for parents: Strategies for supporting student parent success in postsecondary education.* Working Paper, IWPR #C406. Washington, DC: Institute for Women's Policy Research. Retrieved from www.iwpr.org/publications/pubs/prepping-colleges-for-parents-strategies-for-supporting-student-parent-success-in-postsecondary-education.

Social Security Administration. n.d. *Fact sheet social security: 2015 social security changes.* Woodlawn, MD: Social Security Administration. Retrieved from www.ssa.gov/news/press/factsheets/colafacts2015.pdf.

Sykes, M., Reichlin, L., & Gault, B. (2016). *The role of the federal Child Care Access Means Parents in School (CCAMPIS) program in supporting student parent success.* Fact sheet, IWPR #C436. Washington, DC: Institute for Women's Policy Research. Retrieved from https://iwpr.org/wp-content/uploads/wpallimport/files/iwpr-export/publications/C436-CCAMPIS.pdf.

Tax Form Calculator. n.d. *Tax form calculator.* Retrieved from www.taxformcalculator.com/.

The Institute for College Access and Success (TICAS). (2017). *Pell Grants help keep college affordable for millions of Americans.* Washington, DC: The Institute for College Access and Success (TICAS). Retrieved from http://ticas.org/sites/default/files/pub_files/overall_pell_one-pager.pdf.

U.S. Department of Health and Human Services. n.d. *Early Head Start-Child Care Partnership and Early Head Start Expansion Awards.* Early Childhood Development, ACF. Retrieved from www.acf.hhs.gov/ecd/early-learning/ehs-cc-partnerships/grant-awardees.

U.S. Department of Health and Human Services. (2012, December 6). *FY 2012 child care and related appropriations.* Retrieved from www.acf.hhs.gov/occ/resource/fy-2012-child-care-and-related-appropriations.

U.S. Tax Center. (2016). *2015 federal tax rates, personal exemptions, and standard deductions.* Retrieved from www.irs.com/articles/2015-federal-tax-rates-personal-exemptions-and-standard-deductions.

NOTES ON CONTRIBUTORS

Shafiqa Ahmadi

Shafiqa Ahmadi is an Associate Professor of Clinical Education and Co-Director for the Center for Education, Identity, and Social Justice at the University of Southern California (USC), Rossier School of Education (Rossier). Her research focuses on diversity and legal protection of underrepresented students, specifically Muslim students, bias and hate crimes, and sexual assault survivors. She has also taught at USC Gould School of Law and was a Visiting Researcher at the Center for Urban Education, at Rossier. Prior to joining the USC, she worked for the Hawaii Civil Rights Commission, where she investigated alleged violations of civil rights and discrimination in areas such as employment, housing, and access to state and state-funded services. She received her Doctor of Jurisprudence from Indiana University Maurer School of Law, at Bloomington, Indiana.

William Casey Boland

William Casey Boland is an Assistant Professor in the Austin W. Marxe School of Public and International Affairs at Baruch College – The City University of New York. His research explores the impact of state and federal public policies on minority-serving institutions (MSIs). This includes how state accountability policies affect MSIs, the relationship between federal policies and MSI student outcomes, and the role of politics in policymaking in majority–minority states.

Andrés Castro Samayoa

Andrés Castro Samayoa is an Assistant Professor in the Department of Educational Leadership & Higher Education in the Lynch School at Boston College. His work enhances experiences for students of color from under-resourced communities—specifically focusing on Hispanic-serving institutions. His expertise includes the social history of large-scale datasets in

212

postsecondary education; educational researchers' use of data to explore issues of diversity; and the institutionalization of services for lesbian, gay, bisexual, queer, and transgender students.

Children of the House of "Pay It No Mind"

Children of the House of "Pay It No Mind" is a collective *nom de plume* chosen to signify our indebtedness and to the legendary trans* lineage upon which we draw. This iteration of the collective consists of three trans* scholars in higher education and student affairs, in alpha order: Mx. Romeo Jackson (they/them/their), University of Nevada, Las Vegas; Dr. Z. Nicolazzo (she/her/hers, ze/hir), University of Arizona; and Dr. Dafina-Lazarus (D.-L.) Stewart (he/him/his, they/them/their), Colorado State University. The thinking and writing reflected in this chapter was shared equally across this collective.

Darnell Cole

Darnell Cole is an Associate Professor of Education with an emphasis in higher education and education psychology at the University of Southern California (USC), Rossier School of Education (Rossier). He also serves as Co-Director for the Center for Education, Identity and Social Justice at the USC Rossier School of Education. His areas of research include race/ethnicity, diversity, college student experiences, and learning. He serves on several review boards, including the *Journal of College Student Development*. He has published over 40 articles and book chapters and is featured in the major journals for higher education and other related fields including *The Journal of Higher Education*, *Journal of College Student Development*, *NASPA Journal*, *Journal of Classroom Behavior*, and *Journal of Creative Behavior*. His most recent article, "Examining a Comprehensive College Transition Program: An Account of Iterative Mixed Methods Longitudinal Survey Design," appears in *Research in Higher Education*.

Mary Ann DeMario

Mary Ann M. DeMario, Ph.D., holds a B.A. in Psychology from SUNY Potsdam, and an M.S. and Ph.D. in Human Development and Family Studies from the University of North Carolina at Greensboro. Currently, she is a Specialist in the Institutional Research Office at (SUNY) Monroe Community College (MCC) in Rochester, NY. She works to improve college-wide enrollment, retention, and graduation rates by providing strategic data-driven recommendations and key performance indicators to the college's administration. She also provides crucial visibility into the various experiences, opinions, and perspectives of faculty, staff, students, prospective students, and alumni by creating, administering, analyzing, and synthesizing surveys. She serves on multiple advisory boards including the Richard M. Guon Child Care Center at MCC, the Horizons at MCC program, and the Data Team and Data Sharing Task Force for ROC the Future, which is the local StriveTogether partnership.

Stella M. Flores

Stella M. Flores is the Associate Dean for Faculty Development and Diversity and Associate Professor of Higher Education at the Steinhardt School of Culture, Education, and Human

Development at New York University. She holds an EdD in administration, planning, and social policy from Harvard University, an EdM from Harvard University, an MPAff from The University of Texas at Austin, and a B.A. from Rice University. Her research examines the effects of state and federal policies on college access and completion outcomes for low-income and underrepresented populations. She has published widely on demographic changes in U.S. schools, minority-serving institutions, and immigrant and English learners.

Marybeth Gasman

Marybeth Gasman is the Judy & Howard Berkowitz Professor at the University of Pennsylvania. She also serves as the director of the Penn Center for Minority Serving Institutions. She is the author or editor of 25 books, including *Educating a Diverse Nation* (Harvard University Press, 2015 with Clif Conrad), *Envisioning Black Colleges* (Johns Hopkins University Press, 2007), and *Academics Going Public* (Routledge, 2016). She has written over 200 peer-reviewed articles, scholarly essays, and book chapters. She has penned over 350 opinion articles for the nation's newspapers and magazines and is ranked by *Education Week* as one of the 10 most influential education scholars in the nation. She has raised over $22 million in grant funding to support her research. She serves on the board of trustees of The College Board as well as Paul Quinn College, a small, urban, historically Black College in Dallas, Texas.

Barbara Gault

Barbara Gault is the Vice President and Executive Director of the Institute for Women's Policy Research, a non-partisan think tank based in Washington, DC. Her work focuses on policies to promote access to postsecondary education and early care and education, improved job quality for low-wage workers, and employment equity. She founded IWPR's Student Parent Success Initiative, which seeks to improve college access for low-income parents. Her recent publications include *Investing in Single Mothers' Higher Education: Costs and Benefits to Individuals, Families, and Society* (IWPR, 2018) and *Improving Child Care Access to Promote Postsecondary Success Among Low-Income Parents* (IWPR, 2011). She speaks regularly and is frequently quoted in media outlets such as *Forbes, The Atlantic, The New York Times, The Washington Post*, and *NPR*. She received her Ph.D. in Psychology from the University of Pennsylvania and her B.A. from the University of Michigan.

Manuel S. González Canché

Manuel S. González Canché holds a Ph.D. in Higher Education with cognates in Biostatistics and Economics. He joined the University of Pennsylvania's Higher Education division as an associate professor in 2017 and serves as affiliated faculty with the Human Development and Quantitative Methods division and the International Educational Development Program. His research follows two interconnected paths. The first concerns issues of access, persistence, and success, with an emphasis on institution effects such as two-year versus four-year college and distance from home on students' outcomes. The second focuses on higher education finance, with emphases on spatial modeling and competition based on spatial proximity and spillover effects. Methodologically, he employs econometric, quasi-experimental, spatial statistics, and visualization methods for big and geocoded data, including geographical information systems and network modeling. He is particularly interested in studying factors and policies that may enhance low-income, minoritized, and/or underserved students' opportunities for educational and occupational success.

Jarrett T. Gupton

Jarrett T. Gupton is an Assistant Professor of Higher Education at the University of Minnesota. His research agenda has two broad foci: equity and opportunity in higher education. Much of his work focuses on the experience of housing- and food-insecure students and issues of access, persistence, and completion in higher and postsecondary education. He has authored multiple publications on students experiencing homelessness, food insecurity, and foster care alumni in college. His scholarship highlights how social, cultural, and political structures constrain and enable educational equity and opportunity. His current research explores institutional capacity to support housing- and food-insecure students.

Yuri Hernández Osorio

Yuri Hernández Osorio is the Diversity and Inclusion Coordinator at the University of Portland. She earned her master's degree in Social Work at the University of Michigan, focusing her research on access to higher education for undocumented students. She was a graduate researcher for the National Forum on Higher Education for the Public Good where she co-authored *Call to Action: Ensuring Educational Opportunities for Undocumented and DACAmented Students in the United States* (2017, National Forum). Her work has earned her many recognitions including honors such as the Freedom Fighter Award, the Cesar Chávez Leadership Award, the Joseph Gallegos Leadership Award, the Martin Luther King Jr. Award, and the Phi Alpha National Social Work Honor Society Award.

Cynthia Hess

Cynthia Hess is the Associate Director of Research at the Institute for Women's Policy Research (IWPR) and Scholar in Residence at American University. She oversees IWPR research, including recent projects on workforce development and domestic violence. Under her tenure, IWPR expanded its Status of Women in States project and launched an accompanying website, statusofwomendata.org. She has directed several projects while at IWPR, including the Social Security Media Watching initiative, and has contributed to research on immigration, women's activism and leadership, and women in STEM. She is a sought-after expert and has been quoted in media outlets including *The Washington Post*, *Fortune*, *Governing* magazine, and *The Boston Globe*. Prior to IWPR, she taught at St. Mary's College of Maryland. Her scholarly work has focused on the intersection of feminist theory, theology, and peace studies. She received her Ph.D. from Yale University and her A.B. from Davidson College.

Nicholas Hillman

Nicholas Hillman is an Associate Professor of Educational Leadership and Policy Analysis at the University of Wisconsin-Madison. His research focuses on postsecondary finance and financial aid policy, where he has studied such topics as student loan debt, performance-based funding, and college affordability. This work also examines how policies reinforce and address educational inequality. He is also a faculty affiliate with the University of Wisconsin's La Follette School of Public Affairs and the Institute for Research on Poverty.

Frederick M. Lawrence

Frederick M. Lawrence is the 10th Secretary and CEO of the Phi Beta Kappa Society, the nation's first and most prestigious honor society, founded in 1776. Lawrence is a Distinguished Lecturer at the Georgetown Law Center, and has previously served as President of Brandeis University, Dean of the George Washington University Law School, and Visiting Professor and Senior Research Scholar at Yale Law School. He was elected to the American Philosophical Society in 2018 and the American Law Institute in 1999. One of the nation's leading experts on civil rights, free expression, and bias crimes, he is the author of *Punishing Hate: Bias Crimes Under American Law* (Harvard University Press, 1999), examining bias-motivated violence and the laws governing how such violence is punished in the United States. He has testified before Congress concerning free expression on campus and on federal hate crime legislation, and has lectured nationally and internationally.

Susan Marine

Susan Marine is Associate Professor and Program Director in the Higher Education Master's Program at Merrimack College. She has 25 years' experience leading in higher education with specific expertise in sexual violence prevention and response, feminist praxis, and advocacy for the LGBTQ community. She teaches courses in higher education history, theory, and practice, and her research interests include feminist praxis in higher education, trans* student inclusion and agency, and ending campus sexual violence. Seeing the classroom as a mutually trans-formative enterprise, she is deeply committed to preparing future leaders in higher education to transform campus cultures and to continually advance social justice in higher education. She has contributed to numerous scholarly journals and books, and is the author of *Stonewall's Legacy: Bisexual, Gay, Lesbian and Transgender Students in Higher Education*.

Debbie Mukamal

Debbie Mukamal is the Executive Director of the Stanford Criminal Justice Center at Stanford Law School. Her portfolio of work includes overseeing Project ReMADE, an entrepreneur-ship boot camp for formerly incarcerated people, and Renewing Communities, a statewide initiative to expand college opportunities for currently and formerly incarcerated students in California (in partnership with Rebecca Silbert at the Warren Institute at Berkeley Law). Along with Stanford Law School Professor David Sklansky, she is conducting research on the demo-graphics of prosecutors' offices. From 2005 to 2010, she served as the founding Director of the Prisoner Reentry Institute at John Jay College of Criminal Justice. She oversaw all of the Institute's projects, including the design and implementation of the NYC Justice Corps, an innovative neighborhood-based reentry service initiative, and the development of research in the areas of entrepreneurship, correctional education, long-term incarceration, and reentry from local jails. Before joining John Jay College, she served as the founding director of the National H.I.R.E. Network and a staff attorney at the Legal Action Center, where her work focused on the collateral consequences of criminal records.

Susana M. Muñoz

Susana M. Muñoz is an Assistant Professor of Higher Education and Co-Chair of the Higher Education Leadership (HEL) doctoral program in the School of Education at Colorado State University, Fort Collins. Her scholarly interests focus on issues of access, identity, and college persistence for undocumented Latina/o students, while employing perspectives such as Latino critical race theory, Chicana feminist epistemology, and college persistence theory to identify and deconstruct issues of power and inequities as experienced by these populations. She recently authored *Identity, Social Activism, and the Pursuit of Higher Education: The Journey Stories of Undocumented and Unafraid Community Activists* (2015, Peter Lang).

Monica Prado

Monica Prado Garcia is an Assistant Director of Academic Services at USC Viterbi School of Engineering and graduate student at USC Rossier School of Education in the Postsecondary Administration and Student Affairs program. Having served in admissions for six years, she has experience in enrollment services in graduate education, specifically law and engineering. In her current capacity, she works with first-year students as they transition into college. Her research interests include higher education access, persistence of underrepresented minorities in STEM, campus climate, and intersectionality.

Lindsey Reichlin Cruse

Lindsey Reichlin Cruse is a Senior Research Associate at the Institute for Women's Policy Research (IWPR). She manages IWPR's projects under the Student Parent Success Initiative, which raises awareness of and shares strategies to support the postsecondary success of college students who are parents. She also contributes to IWPR's research on workforce development, work–family supports, and global women's issues. Her recent publications include *Investing in Single Mothers' Higher Education: Costs and Benefits to Individuals, Families, and Society* (IWPR, 2018) and *Understanding the New College Majority: The Demographic and Financial Characteristics of Independent Students and their Postsecondary Outcomes* (IWPR, 2018). An expert on access to postsecondary education, she has been quoted in several outlets including *The Washington Post*, *Refinery29*, the *National Journal*, and *Market Watch*. Lindsey has a master's degree from Columbia University's School of International and Public Affairs and a bachelor's degree from the University of California, Los Angeles.

Maurice Shirley

Maurice Shirley is a Ph.D. candidate in Higher and Postsecondary Education at New York University. His research interests include college access and equity, college completion, and the student experience of underrepresented student populations. Prior to pursuing his doctorate, he worked in the postsecondary education sector primarily focusing on student engagement, leadership, diversity initiatives, academic advising, and admissions. He earned a master's in Higher Education and Student Personnel Administration from New York University and a bachelor's in English, Pre-Education from The Ohio State University.

Rebecca Silbert

Rebecca Silbert is a Senior Fellow at the Opportunity Institute in Berkeley and the Director of Renewing Communities, an independent statewide initiative to increase high-quality higher education for incarcerated and formerly incarcerated Californians. Renewing Communities is co-directed by the Stanford Criminal Justice Center and operates the Corrections to College California website. Previously, she was the Executive Director of the Chief Justice Earl Warren Institute on Law and Social Policy at UC Berkeley School of Law. Prior to her five years at the Warren Institute, she tried cases for nine years as an Assistant Federal Public Defender in the Northern District of California. She earlier worked as an associate at the law firm of Keker, VanNest & Peters LLP in San Francisco as well as with the Harvard Project on Schooling and Children. She has a J.D. from Harvard Law School and a B.A. from UC Berkeley.

Jason L. Taylor

Jason L. Taylor is an Assistant Professor in the Department of Educational Leadership and Policy at the University of Utah. He received his Ph.D. in Higher Education from the University of Illinois at Urbana-Champaign with a research specialization in evaluation methods and concentration in public policy. His broad research interests are at the intersection of community college and higher education policy and educational and social inequality. He has conducted and led several quantitative and mixed methods studies related to college readiness, developmental education, adult pathways to college, dual credit/enrollment and early college experiences, transfer policy and reverse transfer, free college programs, LGBTQ students, career and technical education, and educational access and equity. The goal of his research is to examine how public policies impact underserved students' access to, transition through, and success in community colleges and institutions of higher education to contribute to both theory and practice.

Jennifer Trost

Jennifer Trost teaches Sociology at Dougherty Family College, a two-year college within the University of St. Thomas that provides a cohort model and wrap-around services to first-generation, low-income, and/or students of color as they strive to meet their educational goals. She received her Ph.D. in Organizational Leadership, Policy and Development with a focus on Higher Education Policy and Administration. She conducts research on students experiencing homelessness, the supports available to these students, and how institutions support students with significant barriers to their educational dreams. Additionally, she studies the research opportunities for freshman and sophomores at two-year colleges and the influence of involvement with faculty on their educational pathway.

INDEX

Note: *italicised* page numbers denote illustrations and **bold** page numbers denote tables; the suffix 'n' indicates a note.